Praise for

TELL ME WHAT YOU WANT

"Weber's clear and engaging writing provides a pathway through complex concepts. Readers who enjoy pondering emotional intelligence and learning through storytelling will appreciate this book."

—*Booklist*

"*Tell Me What You Want* offers readers client-approved strategies to fathom, interrogate, and accept innermost wants and longings as a springboard for personal growth."

—*Shelf Awareness*

"Finely crafted, profound, and always generous, *Tell Me What You Want* is a very special book. Charlotte doesn't provide neat answers that promise to change your life. Instead she invites you to see the one you are living anew, in all its shining complexity. It made me feel excited to be alive."

—Natasha Lunn, author of *Conversations in Love*

"In *Tell Me What You Want* therapist Charlotte Fox Weber illustrates the powerful role that desire plays in human fulfillment. By bringing readers behind the scenes of her intimate therapy sessions, Weber makes a powerful case for articulating desire as a path toward greater mental health and self-actualization. This hopeful book demystifies the therapeutic alliance between counselor and patient and will surely convince even the most skeptical critic that effective counseling can truly transform lives. Most of all, this book provides a road map of how one might approach their own transformation by becoming willing to admit their deepest desires."

—Christie Tate, *New York Times* bestselling author of *Group*

TELL ME WHAT YOU WANT

*A Therapist and Her
Clients Explore Our
12 Deepest Desires*

Charlotte Fox Weber

ATRIA PAPERBACK

New York   London   Toronto   Sydney   New Delhi

To my family

It is a joy to be hidden but disaster not to be found.

D. W. WINNICOTT

CONTENTS

AUTHOR'S NOTE

The stories in this book are based on my work with real people. I have changed all identifying details in order to maintain confidentiality. I have learned and continue to learn from my clients. The people I have worked with have allowed me to discover so much about life and human experience.

My language is idiosyncratic at times, and hopefully sensitive. I do my best to use terms that aren't overly academic, and I've come up with some of my own. These expressions will appear in bold throughout the book, and the glossary in the back will explain their meaning in more detail.

INTRODUCTION

I spent years in therapy waiting for therapists to ask me about my big wants.* No one ever did. I distracted myself with small **desires** and big obstacles, pursuing some of what mattered to me while holding myself back in countless ways. I repeatedly got in my own way. I attached myself to burdens more than possibilities.

Ask me what I really want! What makes me come alive?

I sought permission. And shame and pride patrolled me. As expansive as I longed to be, a narrowness kept me from fully participating in my life.

Finally, tired of waiting and feeling stuck, I began to ask these questions when I became a psychotherapist. Working with thousands of people from all walks of life, I was struck by the electricity of exploring deep wants. However dark, whatever the circumstances, distilling what we want propels us forward and gives us a sense of possibility. Understanding our desires gives us back to ourselves and is a springboard for growth.

We all have wants, and we're all conflicted. We show some of our wants, but others we hide, even from our own awareness. Our deep

---

* For the sake of simplicity, I use the words "desires, " "wants," "longings," and "yearnings" interchangeably.

desires frighten us and excite us. We're afraid of failing and we're anxious about succeeding. Recognizing and understanding what we want helps us face ourselves without flinching and galvanizes us to live lives that are more fulfilling and joyful.

We are socialized to perform and conceal desires. We pretend to want the appropriate things, in the right way. We banish desires that we're not supposed to have. We put our secret wants into a kind of psychological storage facility—our **unlived lives**.

We keep secrets not just from others but from ourselves. It's a breakthrough when we can uncover and talk about banished longings. Confronting our secret desires is an important part of psychotherapy. We deal with painful regrets and unresolved fantasies. We face whatever is lingering from our past and messing with us now. Sometimes the secrets we reveal are issues we already know we're hiding: affairs, addictions, obsessions. But sometimes our secrets are untold stories we haven't even told ourselves.

Our secret desires mess with all the shoulds—what we should want or should be doing to get it. We get stuck because we're afraid of failing and we're conflicted about our wants. People-pleasing and perfectionism can pull us away from daring to have fresh experiences; we spin our wheels in avoidance. We anesthetize ourselves with drugs or alcohol. We put on a show, concealing parts of ourselves. We want what we feel we shouldn't want, and don't want things we think we should. We're often conflicted about our actual feelings and overdetermined to have life proceed according to a script. *Tell Me What You Want* encourages you to know and accept your desires. It provides an alternative to the sense of shame that patrols and silences our secret longings. The best way out of feeling stuck is to understand our desires, recognize what they mean, and clarify priorities.

In our fantasies we imagine how our lives could be. *One day* we will do what we really want to do. *If only* something had gone differently for us or we had made another choice, life would be what we want. But "One day . . ." and "If only . . ." jerk us around, tantalizing us with glimpses of the past and of an imagined future while obstructing our ability to make the most of all the possibilities in our present lives. The stories in this book are about people from different ages and stages of life, struggling with their underlying longings. By facing their desires and their own truths, they have begun the work towards resolution.

Tell Me What You Want will help you get in touch with your own depths, accept what you are hiding from others and from yourself, and, through awareness, get closer to finding your true desired path forward as you live your one precious life.

TELL
ME
WHAT
YOU
WANT

Chapter One

TO LOVE AND BE LOVED

We want to love and be loved. It can be simple and easy. It can be maddening and endlessly complicated. We search for love, grapple with fantasies, find it impossible, demand it, fear it, destroy it, push it away, yearn for it. We break hearts, including our own. Life can be heartbreaking. But love makes life beautiful.

We all have love stories. They are the stories you believe about love. You might not have voiced them directly, but they're internal scripts about love, often unfinished, that shape the love you want, the love you imagine, the love you give. You've learned about love from your experiences, from culture, from people who loved you, disappointed you, rejected you, educated you, cherished you. You're still learning. As long as you're alive, you can continue to learn. You learn about love from strangers, setbacks, books, movies, other people's stories, nature. Sometimes hell is loving other people, and sometimes love feels like salvation. You can love and hate the same person, and yourself.

It helps if we continually update our love stories. There's happenstance, character, mystery. The world changes and so do we, and an expansive mindset about love provides flexibility for the particulars. One of the biggest obstacles to finding real love can be hanging on to a rigid story about how it's supposed to be.

The stories we tell ourselves about love touch us to the core.

They shape our beliefs about human beings, about other people, about ourselves, about life itself. Our stories are usually both painful and pleasurable. What we believe about love can be life enhancing and it can be life diminishing. Therapy helps people voice stories, revise them, and understand the meaningful ones. Think of your experiences of love. Do you remember feeling unloved too? How did you come to know love and to feel it?

There are countless ways to love and be loved. Love can be promising and disappointing; we may trust it or doubt it. We can behave very badly towards people we love, and people who love us can hurt us. Love can feel safe and it can feel terrifying. We might shut the whole thing down or keep love at arm's length. We can sabotage love in a thousand ways. Denial is one way. Displacement is another.

We're often afraid to really love ourselves. We think it will make us egomaniacs, or we'll discover we're wrong to approve of ourselves and we'll feel foolish. We think we need proof of our lovableness from others before we can let ourselves love fully. One of the best things I can do as a psychotherapist is hold space for the ways we don't love ourselves. It's a problem to think we must be lovable all the time. We can also realize that we love people who have failed us, betrayed us, hurt us.

People talk to me about love all the time. They come to therapy wanting help with love. They feel frustrated by the ways they're loved or not loved, misunderstood, let down, scared. But a lot of time the desire for love is less direct. Issues of love come into therapy no matter what. Our anxieties, our fears, our losses, our enthusiasms—these fundamental feelings are about love in all its variations. Love is the plot and purpose of most stories. My work is about dealing with the complexities of relationships—the relationships we have with other people, with ourselves, and with the world. Self-love is one of those concepts we like in theory but, up close, is challenging. It may come easily for some people, but for many of us it can be our core struggle.

In therapy, some clients are reluctant to express their desire for love because they don't think love is likely. Part of what they learn in therapy is all the ways they need to unlearn their assumptions about love. We are often terrified of making mistakes, and the tyranny of perfectionism locks us into an anxious, frozen state that acts as an obstacle to any pursuit of relationships and experiences out in the world. We both want and fear love. The **curtain of rejection**—our fear of rejection—holds us back. When we recognize our basic desires, we can distill the myths from the facts, and the shape of love becomes real and possible. This might mean sitting with our own uncertainty or realizing what we already have.

In the words of George Bernard Shaw—someone I find more inspiring than many psychotherapy textbooks—"People become attached to their burdens sometimes more than the burdens are attached to them . . ." When it comes to our big wants, we find ways to talk ourselves out of thinking clearly about our true desires and needs. We get enmeshed with obstacles. Love is no exception to this. We describe the reasons we can't do something, the problems that hold us back. We can find it easier to say what we don't want than what we do want. Letting ourselves want love exposes us to our vulnerabilities and risks rejection and humiliation that we've experienced or we imagine. It takes great courage to express the desire for love.

Wanting to love and be loved is simple and primal. It can also feel hellish and hard. Saying goodbye to life, Tessa faced love. She told me her stories of loving and living.

WHAT TESSA KNEW

My first psychotherapy placement was in a busy London hospital. I was part of a team that did time-limited psychotherapy with acutely ill patients and relatives of patients. There was no real privacy and the setup was makeshift; we worked bedside, in utility closets, in hallways. I felt a kind of unwavering optimism that therapy could offer something, no matter what the conditions and circumstances. I still believe this. There are lots of ways we can improve our lives.

The first referral note was given to our team by one of the ward nurses. In old-fashioned penmanship that I struggled to decipher, a man had written that his wife, in her sixties and in the late stages of pancreatic cancer, would like to speak with someone. This should be arranged as soon as possible.

I arrived at the open ward feeling very grown-up, wearing my new ID badge on a cord around my neck, marking myself as a professional. I felt so proud of my ID—it was the first time I'd seen myself described as a psychotherapist—that I sometimes kept it on before and after work. The nurse led me into a room lined with patients, to the bedside of a noticeably elegant woman. Though Tessa was ill, she exuded a soft vitality and womanliness. Her hair looked done, she was wearing lipstick, and she was sitting up with the help of several cushions. She had the *Financial Times* on her bed and a stack of books and cards on the table beside her. The ward was full of sickness and chaos, yet around her was a small zone of thoughtful order. A distinguished man was seated beside her bed, and when he saw me, he immediately stood up and introduced himself to me as David, her husband. He graciously excused himself without any awkwardness and said he'd come back in an hour.

Tessa locked eyes with me. "Come closer," she said.

I seated myself in the chair beside her; it was still warm from her husband. Something quickened within me. I drew the curtain around us to create a sense of privacy, at least a symbolic therapeutic frame. I told her we'd have fifty minutes. I was trying to convey some kind of authority and professionalism. Up close, Tessa's hands were purple and bruised, and I could see the frailty she was doing her best to hide.

"I mustn't waste time. May I talk to you really?" She spoke with a kind of diction and clarity that gave me better posture. I said yes, of course: that was why I was there.

"I mean really talk. Honestly. No one will let me. I assume you're prepared. The nurses and doctors, my family, they try to distract me and make me comfortable. They fuss and change the subject if I dare mention what's happening. I don't want to change the subject. I want to face this."

"Tell me what you want to face," I said.

"My death. My life, I want to see it. I've avoided things my entire life, and this is my last chance to look properly."

I paid attention to every word she spoke and how she spoke it. The way people describe things in the initial encounter can be illuminating for years to come. I wrote down some of her statements with fervid intensity, preserving scraps, but I was adamant that we maintain eye contact as much as possible, that we experience the session together. Meeting her where she was, that was what I could offer, and so I kept returning to just being present with her.

"I feel myself fading each day. I want to get my house in order. To do that, I have two things I simply must discuss. Concision has always been a strength of mine. I've never before had therapy. It's essentially a conversation where I can speak freely, find some truth and maybe meaning, and see what's possible. Am I correct?"

"Yes, yes," I said, nodding agreeably. Concision indeed!

"But, please, let's agree on something first. I'm going with my immediate impression of you. It's not based on much, but I feel I can talk to you. So let's really do this, then. I don't want this to be a one-off. I'm not a one-night-stand gal. Let's agree that you'll come back, and you'll continue visiting me until I'm no longer able to talk with you."

"We can agree to have more sessions," I said.

"To clarify: you'll keep coming until I'm no longer able. If I'm going to speak my mind, I need to know that I can count on this, on you, with everything else happening, for however much time I've got. All right?"

"Yes, all right." The placement had a strict limit of twelve sessions, and I had no idea what Tessa's timeline would be, but how could I not agree? She'd taken charge, and, given her situation, this seemed fine. We had established a therapeutic alliance, based on safety, rapport, trust.

"Okay." She looked up into my face and leaned slightly forward as though she'd finally found her own space.

"I'm going to contradict myself. Don't stop me. Having said that concision is a strength of mine, I'd now like to say whatever I want, knowing we still have some time." Her voice had total authority. She also had a touch of mischief.

"Go ahead." Had she wanted prompting from me, I could have asked her questions and guided the discussion in a conventional first-session manner, but that wasn't what Tessa wanted, and it wasn't what she needed.

"My first 'issue,' as people in therapy say—in my day, issues were about publications, not emotions—is one of regret. I want to tell you about the regret but, please, Charlotte, do not talk me out of it. I just need to say it." I agreed.

"I wish I'd spent more time snuggling my boys. I have two sons, all grown up now. Stuck in this bed, it's what I long for more than anything. I don't miss that much about my life—the dinners, travel, clothes and shoes, jewelry. I can let all that stuff go. I like wearing lipstick and having beautiful things, but it doesn't feel important to me now. But I ache when I think of how I could have snuggled them so much more. I sent them both to boarding school. Young. Before they were ready. Especially our older son. He really didn't want to go. He begged me not to force him. At the time, sending them away seemed like the right thing to do, for all sorts of reasons. David and I were moving countries every few years. I won't bore you with the justifications. The point is, had I really listened, maybe we could have at least snuggled and been closer. Snuggling, cuddling, I can think of little else . . . I just want to hold the boys and be in our old house together, warm and close. You seem young, too young to have children. Do you have any?"

"No, not yet," I answered immediately, despite knowing my supervisor at the time would have disapproved of my unguarded disclosure.

"Well, you probably will, and when you do, snuggle them. Do the other stuff too, but snuggling is very important. That's the bit that's surprising to me . . . I spent my life not realizing its importance. 'Snuggling'—even the word sounds silly. But it's significant. It's what matters. I'm only learning this now."

I met her instructive eyes and felt a need to demonstrate that I was absorbing her life lessons. She spoke eloquently and began to recall some of the beautiful times she'd had in her life. I continued to listen as attentively as I ever have, wanting to really take in her voice, her messages, her story.

Her husband, David, was a career diplomat, with postings in Asia and Africa, and they'd lived in six different countries.

"As you can imagine, we got invited everywhere. Elegant residences. The most glamorous events and parties. We met fabulous people. Some fascinating characters. And some really deadly dull ones too." She described the dinner parties she gave, the shift dresses she wore, her cooking for intimate gatherings, which was "unexceptional but trusty, and always over-peppered. 'Too much pepper, Tessa!' Everyone said this, but I adore pepper, and I consider myself to be peppery, so I refused to stop. I feel no remorse over that. And, gosh, I miss my family teasing me with such affection. No one teases me now that I'm ill."

She told me how she loved lighting candles. "David used to laugh at me for all the candles. He'd say that I shouldn't bother to make such a fuss. He'd say it rather sweetly. 'Don't go to so much trouble, Tessa. No one even notices.' But it was good trouble, and you see, *I* noticed. Some fusses are worthwhile simply because we want to be charmed by ourselves. Yes, that's it, now that I say it: I charmed myself in those small pretty ways. I loved doing it. Charlotte, make a point of charming yourself. It's part of loving yourself. And loving life."

She would have liked to be an editor. "I adore finding little mistakes and seeing what can be improved. I would have been rather good. And I always grasp intention, however muddled the expression. Except perhaps my own." But she was fine with not having held a job. She'd moved around so much, she'd worked hard in other ways, and she'd enjoyed a great deal. She asked me to picture her at other moments from her life. "You're meeting me now, in this state, but imagine me with big hair. I've always loved big hair, no matter what the trend. You know, 1960s, Jackie O hair." She missed her body, her choices and ways of expressing herself when she was healthy.

When she recalled the socializing, the countless hours spent with friends, she wondered how they passed the time, what they did in each moment together. She supposed they drank, talked about books, people, theatre, film, travel, art, politics, all of it, but she couldn't really recall the details. But, actually, she was okay with the hazy blur of that aspect of her life, because she knew she'd had "a good old time." She'd needlessly worried about what people thought of her. "Come to think of it, the friends who liked me, I knew they liked me, and I liked them very much. And those connections added to life. But I fretted over people I didn't even care about. Simply a waste," she said. "A bit of squandered time is inevitable, but it's what it was instead of."

Tessa needed to say again how much she wished she'd spent more time snuggling her children. Trapped in this bed, the thoughts and feelings had found her and there was no escape. She finally had to accept that it was simply a deep regret. "The boys insist they're perfectly okay with how things turned out. They've never really complained. They're on their way to London now, actually. I'll see them tomorrow."

"Oh, that's so nice," I said. This prosaic remark was just about all I said, along with some encouraging murmurs and sounds to show that I was following every word. I was deeply engaged, and there wasn't much need to speak. I was there for her. She wanted me to listen.

"I'm just not that close with the boys. I do love them both, very much so, and they probably love me simply because I'm their mother, but I wish I'd let myself feel the love, show the love, *more*. You know, they're both married and in their thirties. No children of their own yet. Maybe one day. How funny that I still call them 'the boys.'" She let out a captivating little laugh. "I don't feel I know them all that well. There's a distance. Maybe there wouldn't be if I hadn't sent them to boarding school. And if I'd spent more time snuggling them and telling them I loved them." Her laughter stopped and turned to a face of haunting sorrow. The transformation was rapid. Her eyes—wide-open—suddenly looked like those of a terrified child.

"Can you express any of this when you see them tomorrow?" I asked. I couldn't help myself. My question nudged her back into conversational mode. I realized even then that, as honest and willing to face everything as I thought I was, I was avoidant in my way, unable to just sit with sadness at times without trying to intervene supportively. It's hard to witness pain and do nothing.

"Perhaps, but somehow doubtful. Maybe. We'll see. But this leads me to the second thing I must discuss."

"Go ahead."

"I know that my husband has a secret child in Brazil, with a woman he had an affair with years ago. A daughter. She must be around twenty. David doesn't think I know, but I do. He's felt so guilty and ashamed all these years. I can tell. He's made several bank transfers to the woman, from an account he didn't think I knew about, and that's how I found out. Being a career diplomat, David's probably petrified of scandal, and he's fairly nimble and stealthy, but I'm clever too."

I asked her how she felt about it all.

"You may struggle to believe me, but the truth is, I don't know. I've never asked myself how I feel about it. . . ."

I did believe her.

"You know, he's probably treated me better because of what he did. And maybe I didn't confront him because it's suited me. . . . He's been on his best behavior with me all these years. . . ."

She said David would be deeply saddened to know he'd hurt her, and the boys too. "It would be too much." I sensed that the details of the secret, the logistics of her concern for family dynamics, her desire to keep anyone from being hurt, were ways she stayed busy and avoided having her own feelings about his secret child. I asked how it felt to tell me.

"I needed to tell someone. It's just somehow very important. Honesty, at least with oneself, it matters. I couldn't end my life without saying it aloud. So now you know, and telling you, it's released something for me. This would be even better if we were in nature. I don't like being here, in this place. I miss the feeling of mud, of soggy grass. Let's imagine that's where we are, on a grassy, muddy hill, getting our bums wet, breathing in fresh, cold air. That's my one escape, the one thing I'll pretend. The rest I'll face honestly."

Her longing to escape and imagine herself in nature felt honest too.

When I left the ward that day, I passed her husband at the nursing station. He was trying to arrange a private room for Tessa. I could hear him politely persuading the nurse in charge, and he interrupted his discussion to stop me on my way out. He seemed nervous.

"Before you go, I won't pry, I want to respect the privacy of how this works, but just tell me, Tessa spoke with you? She's needed to talk. I'm grateful she could."

"Yes," I said, feeling overwhelmed by the nebulous boundaries. I didn't want to offend him, nor did I want to engage with him. I felt the enormity of the secret she'd trusted me to carry, and even my "Yes" felt like too much.

The following week, I showed up at our agreed time. I looked for her the way I'd scan a restaurant if I were meeting someone formidable. She made me want to be my very best, whatever that meant. One of the nurses on the ward told me Tessa had moved upstairs to a private room. Hooray! Helpful for therapy, among other things. Up I went, and David was there, but he gave us space and left promptly. She had an assortment of magazines fanned out on the bedside table, and cosmetics, and I spotted her embroidered velvet bed slippers; everything around her was a personal, elegant choice of creature comfort.

"I still feel such regret, Charlotte," she said, her eyes landing on me. In the days since we had first met, she had become severely jaundiced, and her sunken eyes had a kind of piercing blue quality that came through intensely.

"Tell me about the regret," I said.

"It's what I told you before. Snuggling my boys. Closer love. It's all I want."

I found it very hard to hear about her regret—the unfulfilled longing, which was so truthful and moving—I didn't know what to do. I felt a kind of desperation to fix things, to soothe her, especially knowing she was terminally ill. Though she'd instructed me not to talk her out of her regret, I went against her orders. She'd forgiven other people for their mistakes. Couldn't she forgive herself? I asked her again if she could express any of this to her sons. Looking back, I see the hubris in my thinking that I could get her what she so badly wanted.

"Yes, I suppose. But you must understand something. I don't regret the regret. It gives me hope for a fuller life. It may not be *my* life, but it shows what's possible. I had so much love. I still do. It's not that I don't have enough love. It's really not that. Everyone thought I was cold. My sons. Even my friends. Friendly and social but cold. But I'm not. I acted cold to cover up the warm. A baked Alaska, David once called me. See, he loved me and got me exactly right in those ways. He knew my secret warmth. I just couldn't stand the depth of my emotions."

Her words stayed with me, even though I struggled to grasp the full meaning. She may have given me more than I gave her. For the rest of the session, she slipped in and out of making a great deal of sense, sometimes with flashes of total presence, but at other moments she reverted to garbled sentences, fragments of thoughts, word salad.

We met at the same time each week, and there was a sense of progress in our relationship and in clarifying certain issues. A major feature of our connection was the fact that I acknowledged the difficulty of her situation and she found this helpful and, in her words, "soothingly realistic."

As our therapeutic relationship developed, her physical state deteriorated, and—much to my shock and disappointment—I arrived for our fifth session and discovered that she was going into organ failure. Barely able to speak, she managed to say the words "More time." These poignant words continue to haunt me.

The following week, I arrived in her room and there was a terrible smell. Tessa was distressed and kept pressing the buzzer for the nurses. She'd lost bowel control, and I could see what had happened and she knew I could see. Comportment and containment were fixtures of her character, and this breakdown of her bodily boundaries felt like a betrayal of her privacy, of her control, of her dignity. She was just lying in her filth, and it felt unbearable and ridiculous for me to sit there doing nothing. I offered to fetch someone who could help and soon returned with a nurse. Tessa had a slightly haughty manner with her. "This really isn't acceptable," she said. True in so many ways.

None of this matched my training. This was not how I imagined psychotherapy worked—the "talking cure." There was no cure for this.

I excused myself for a few minutes, and when I stepped back into her room, Tessa was clean and in a freshly made-up bed, and she was in the mood to talk again. Really talk. She was having a lucid afternoon. She told me she'd hugged her sons and it didn't feel comfortable because it wasn't. "It's not just because I'm so physically weak that it felt strange," she said. "It felt strange because it wasn't natural for us, and we all knew it. 'Natural' . . . such a strange word. Things that are supposedly natural have never come easily to me . . . breastfeeding . . . hugging . . . the natural feels unnatural to me . . ."

I asked about her experiences of affection growing up. Her parents had been aloof and not the snuggly kind. She recalled her mother slapping her on a few occasions, but she really didn't have memories of physical tenderness. Her father was "rather po-faced and formal with everyone, even himself. Born with a hat on." Occasionally they had awkward and perfunctory hugs. Her parents were crisp thinkers, but they struggled with feelings. There was love, she suspects, but they didn't show it easily.

"My parents, and David too, we're all a bit odd about the L-word. We've sometimes said 'Lots of love' at the end of calls. And in cards especially. Even 'All my love.' David signs his letters with that. What rubbish. When is it ever true that you're giving *all* your love? But nor is it true that there's no love if you don't say the words . . . It's easier in some ways with dogs. Dogs give us permission to express unfettered affection, and they don't demand words."

She said she could accept her life, she could accept her husband's secret child, she could accept it all. "The compression of my illness, it's simplified and cleared out a great deal. Already, vast portions of my life are gone, and I don't mind. I'm letting go. I've got these few final bits to bring together . . . I've thought about the question you asked me recently, about how I feel about David's secret child. I feel okay with it, oddly. As I've just said of my parents, closeness is so hard for some of us. Even with those we love and know best—actually, more so. I know he loves me. He doesn't only love me, and he may have even loved this other woman, but he loves me dearly. Always has. I don't doubt that. I do wish he'd found a way to tell me the trouble he'd got himself into, because it must have come at a terrific cost to him emotionally. And to me. I could have been there for him. He couldn't face the hurt, but if he'd been able to, perhaps we'd have been closer. And he deprived me of a chance to be noble in my handling. And I feel bad for the girl. I told you, Charlotte, I would have been a good editor: if I could edit this tale, I would clean it up and polish David's rough and tangled mess, welcoming in the daughter, getting furious at David, forgiving him, turning the whole thing into an elegant story. He didn't let me have that glory!"

"There's glory in your story now," I said.

She ignored my comment. Perhaps it embarrassed her, or maybe it was unconvincing. And it was also my wish for glory. She returned to her regret. "Telling you about my regret, it helps, and it's changed how I feel about it all. I still regret not snuggling the boys more. Not showing them love more openly. But I understand it now. It's my upbringing, the world I'm from in some ways, but also I didn't particularly feel like touching them and holding them, and it didn't seem important. Telling them I loved them, directly, I felt it went without saying, but maybe what goes without saying goes even better said . . . I kept thinking, throughout my life, that one day life would be what we wanted. David and I had big plans for his retirement, when we'd finally spend some of the money we'd stashed away. I was certain it would be marvelous one day. It turns out that one day happened every day for all those years I've been alive."

I found her acuity and understanding astonishing. And completely at odds with the chaos and disintegration of her body.

"I can accept that this has been my life. I have no choice now but to accept. But I'm still holding on to the regret. It means I can hope that you'll appreciate snuggling. It's letting yourself love and connect fully. Give in. You'll still think about the next thing, whether it's your plans for that day or whatever is on your mind. That's inevitable. We can't be satisfied for too long. But I beg you to take note: Do not believe that meaning will arrive one day, later on in life. It will come then too, but it's already happening. It happens just about every day throughout your life, if you pay attention."

She let out a light whimper and I could see her contorting her body in pain. She rarely talked about her physical discomfort. My heart set into a trot as I sat there, watching her suffer. She was shipwrecked.

"Give in," she said again. "I had more love to give but I didn't let myself feel it for most of my life. I mean, *really* feel it. It's so clear and obvious now, even as I'm chasing clouds. What matters, and all the ways I held back. My love was never total. I always had reservations. I'm not holding back, letting myself admit my regret. I'm finally honest, admitting this to you."

"Your honesty is admirable," I said. "Though I don't think love is ever total. There are always complications."

"Complications, perhaps, but it can also be simple. I might tell my sons that I wish I'd snuggled them more. But before you even think it, hear me when I say it won't suddenly make us close. It might give them a sense of the love I couldn't show. I don't know. Figure out how to live fully now. Don't wait. If you wait to find life's richness, you're left with ashes."

Everything she said made sense to me. I still hoped she'd tell her sons how she really felt. Our time was up.

"Charlotte?" she called after me. I went back. "I want you to know that I forgive David for his other child. And hopefully my boys can forgive me for my shortcomings too. We all want to love and be loved. It's just about everything, and it's so damned hard."

The following week, I arrived at her room, and a nurse said she'd been moved to the liver ward. I went to that floor, where there was a permeating terrible smell. I couldn't find her, and one of the nurses pointed to a bed. I looked around and couldn't see her. I felt impatient with the nurse; she didn't seem to understand me. I enunciated Tessa's name in a condescending way, spelling her surname loudly.

"Yes, miss, she's right there," she said, gesturing back to the bed I had walked past before. I returned to the bed. This wasn't Tessa. This was someone else. Where was Tessa? I couldn't see her husband either. I went back to the nurse again.

"That's not my patient," I said, pointing to the bed. I used the word "patient" in an imperious way.

"Yes, Tessa is right over there," she said.

I returned to the bed and looked at the details on the chart at the foot of the bed. This was Tessa. Completely distended and swollen, transformed beyond all recognition. I couldn't accept that this was the same woman from just a week earlier. It was the most confusing and shocking transformation, and it didn't make sense. She looked at me, her face bulging and contorted, her lips parted, and I saw her blue eyes, now glassy and faded. Nothing belonged or felt familiar. I hoped she hadn't tracked my not recognizing her.

"Hello."

I pulled up a chair, drew the curtains around us, and prepared to spend fifty minutes with her. It was very different from our previous encounters. She spoke in a faint and vague whisper, and it was a struggle for her to express herself. Her breathing was labored and came in ragged, shallow gasps. "Thank you, darling," she said at one point, after several minutes of silence. "Love you."

No "I," and I have no idea if she meant it, if she was delirious, and who exactly she was saying it to. I didn't say it back. It wouldn't have felt right to say "I love you" to her. Or even "Love you." In all the years since that moment, I have never said these words to someone in therapy with me. I've felt plenty of love. I've talked about love, allowing for love in therapy, but I haven't said the words "I love you" in therapy. It feels too naked and intimate. Perhaps imposing.

The nurses interrupted us to do something with a tube, to remove and replace something. I was upset that they were intruding on our private space. I longed to make Tessa feel connected, contained, not alone. I couldn't work out who she was, how this had happened, and I felt a longing to stick to our plan to have ongoing sessions. We'd made a commitment! We were still developing her story. This was my fantasy of glory, that I could help make the end of her life beautiful. She faded in and out, and I don't know what she got from my being there, but I stayed for the full fifty minutes, trying to join her, wherever she was. When I got up to leave, I looked into her eyes and told her how much I valued our conversations, how I would never forget all that she'd told me. She curled her mouth slightly, and I couldn't tell if she followed my words. I told her I looked forward to our next session. "I'll see you next week" were my last words to her.

"Goodbye," she said clearly.

When I discussed Tessa tearfully in supervision, my supervisor thought I should have said this was our ending; I'd avoided reality by pretending that Tessa and I would meet again. But even if she was obviously about to die, how could I say that out loud to her?

"We discuss difficult truths," my supervisor maintained. Had I acknowledged to Tessa that she was clearly about to die, I could have said goodbye—after all, she said goodbye to me—and we could have come together for the ending. I'd become like the other people in her life, acting, distancing myself from what was happening.

Maybe she'll still be here next week, and I'll say goodbye to her then, I thought. Tessa died before our next session. When I found out, I went outside, looked up at the clouds, and let myself sob. I phoned my mother and told her I loved her. I let myself feel it all, however irrational in some ways. I didn't know Tessa very well, or for that long, so why did I feel heartbroken? A colleague in the department saw me crying. "I'm sorry for your loss," she said. It *was* a loss. But I felt it was unjustified for me to claim it. Had I crossed a line, letting her matter so much to me?

The end of Tessa's life marked the beginning of my work as a psychotherapist. I was so fresh and professionally inexperienced, and the brevity and circumstances of our connection protected the romantic sheen. I had held back from challenging her and saying things I might have said if she had life ahead. There was only so much we could do in the very short amount of time we had together, but we still did something. I cherish that sense of possibility.

She gave me more than I was able to give her. In the years since, I've been struck by the enjoyment that comes with generosity. It's almost glaringly obvious, but still easily overlooked, how life is richer when we give to others. It's not about depleting ourselves and giving more than we have; it's that giving is part of having. The author Natasha Lunn once spoke with me about the joy of giving love, not just having love. "We get so much from loving and seeing ourselves. Giving love is as rewarding," she said.

Tessa was a gracious giftee. She let me give to her. And she knew how to say goodbye, even if I didn't. She taught me something about the courage to face the truth, the significance of telling and adjusting our stories, holding secrets, letting go, acknowledging regrets and the privilege of bearing witness. And how hard these things can be for us.

I'm reminded of the psychotherapist and poetic writer Irvin Yalom's idea of rippling, where small encounters can have lasting influence in surprising ways. *We all want to love and be loved, and it's so damned hard* comes to mind countless times when I'm hearing about distressed relationships, frayed familial dynamics, the challenges of work, internal conflict. And, of course, I've thought of Tessa's longing to snuggle her children.

We appreciate what we have when we know it's about to be gone. Facing the edges of existence, Tessa knew what she wanted and what was possible, and she figured out certain things before it was too late. Endings can feel abrupt and messy, even when we know they're coming. We make mistakes with people we love. The lessons continue. Don't wait for life's richness.

The fact that Tessa had therapy for the first time on her deathbed showed a capacity to learn and have new experiences all the way throughout life. She embraced the freshness of lived experience. I was emboldened by how quick and alive she was in her openness as she lay dying. The act of telling a story can shift something until the last breath.

WHAT LOVE MEANS

We love and we lose. We might hold back from letting ourselves love too closely, too intensely, because of the painful threat of loss and rejection. We might cling to love, grabbing it where we can. Either way, we get it right and wrong when it comes to matters of the heart. And in the words of the playwright Arthur Miller: "Maybe all one can do is hope to end up with the right regrets."

What do you do with regret? We think that what's done is done. And yet, regret is part of the human condition, however uncomfortable. The biggest problem with regret is that we haven't been taught how to deal with it. It gets rerouted into blame, shame, defensiveness, righteousness, rage, displaced guilt, and, perhaps most of all, fantasy. Undealt-with regret is fodder for fantasies about the lives we could have lived, the love we'd have, the versions of ourselves we're now deprived of. Unprocessed regret can be a catastrophic trouble-maker. Acknowledging regret is a courageous and loving thing to do. It's an act of love for yourself to recognize that you'd like to have done something differently.

Loving and being loved gets expressed through desire, care, re-sponsibility, respect, closeness, differentiation, ideas, generosity. It can be abstract and it can be concrete. It can be the act of snuggling. Saying the words "I love you." Not saying the words but knowing they're felt. Showing up. Comforting. Helping people. Allowing for help. Accepting. Love is the most universal but personal thing for each one of us, and it's both the big things—the love we value, which feels substantial—and the specifics—the small, charming details, like Tessa lighting candles—that seem to matter. Allow for some enchantment and fondness. What's small and inessential can still matter.

We all want love, but even when we have loving relationships, we can lose touch with the everyday-ness. We get so familiar, we forget to notice it. The eye cannot see its own eyelashes. Love can see itself better from a distance. Sometimes the distance is the flash of per-ception when we are saying goodbye—just a momentary reminder of separation, a glimpse of **defamiliarization**—that reunites us with our appreciation.

Chapter Two

DESIRE

The conflict of desire plays out in relationships, bringing people together and breaking them apart. In Chapter 11, I talk specifically about how we want what we shouldn't. We also want what we're supposed to want. We are constantly negotiating the rules of desire. We follow the rules, we bend the rules. For every desire that feels acceptable, there's often another one lurking that could pull us in a different direction. We sift through an assortment of desires throughout our lives, and even without awareness we're often selecting and choosing which ones to prioritize at any given moment. Desire is more than a basic instinct, and it's full of polarities. Desire is motivating and distracting, bolstering and paralyzing, novel and familiar, social and natural, pleasurable and painful, enhancing and diminishing, healthy and harmful. What's particularly rattling is how desire and fear are closely related. Look at the sins of Adam and Eve, banished from Eden because they gave in to temptation. Desire both defines us and gets us into trouble. It's the story of our survival—the procreative drive and the wish to leave our mark. But it's also the story of all the ways we misstep. Four of the deadly sins—envy, gluttony, greed, and lust—have to do with desire. We can be torn between temptation and terror when it comes to aggression and sexuality. Shame and pride do a lot of patrolling to shut up whatever feels taboo.

We're socialized to consume and have. But having is not enough: we often struggle to want what we have, and we want more of what we don't necessarily value, so satisfaction is fleeting. Denying is not enough: we're haunted by the strong desires we've pushed away, and we either act out or shut down. We **musturbate** about how life is supposed to be, expecting relationships to follow rigid scripts. This never works, and our demands leave us profoundly exasperated and often alienated from others. We only begin to grasp what "enough" means when we understand our desires.

When we're scornful or rigid about our desires, we can find ourselves sleepwalking through areas of life. What used to excite us no longer wakes us up. We don't desire much of anything. We've stopped wanting sex. Excessive consumption can consume and preoccupy us but leave us feeling empty and unfulfilled. Severe boredom can present itself this way. It can seem passive and deathly. In the words of author Leo Tolstoy: "Boredom: the desire for desires." Even if we struggle with it, we still want desire. Desire wakes us up. Looking at what we want can engage and revive our curiosity and thirst for life. During a recent therapy session, a man said to me, "I want to want something. I want to feel desire. To know I'm alive."

Our erotic longings are often layered and shadowy. Our libido can be at odds with our values. Our childhood impressions of desire and sexuality can play out in surprising ways throughout life, and our deepest desires often scare us. What we desire passionately we fear we won't get, or shouldn't get, or we fear we'll lose it when we do get it. In the words of Arthur Shannon, a character in the play *Spring Storm* by playwright Tennessee Williams, "I want what I'm afraid of and I'm afraid of what I want so that I'm like a storm inside that can't break loose!" When our desires feel unacceptable, even to ourselves, we might conceal, displace, and act out mixed feelings. Even in healthy relationships, we can feel love and hate for the same person, and abusive, traumatic relationships can leave us with unresolved ambivalence and conflicted yearnings. Fear and desire can be hard to distinguish. We can fixate, disavow, repeat, defend something, all in a bid to protect ourselves from acknowledging the underlying desire. A sense of deprivation and disappointment is a clue to a deep desire.

We struggle to admit some of our desires partly because it's horribly unsettling to want something too much. Anyone who has longed to conceive and has been told to stop thinking about it understands the discomfort of desire. Desperation feels unbearable, and we're repeatedly told that it's unsightly and will work against us. Acting too keen is mortifying. In this way, sexual desire can be terrifying as well as titillating. There's intense vulnerability and possible rejection and shame that comes with the exposure. And we might feel superstitious about really wanting something, as though admitting our desire, even internally, will stop us from getting what we want.

When we're frustrated, we often compensate with getting and spending, consumption, satisfying other more accessible desires rather than admitting our darkest longings. As sophisticated as we are as a species, we still struggle to make sense of sexual desire. Sexual fantasies are pervasive and ordinary. Justin Lehmiller's extensive research on sexual fantasies shows the pervasiveness of fantasy—97 percent of people surveyed fantasize regularly—but we are so easily embarrassed and ashamed of our unspoken desires. (*You can't fire me: I quit!*) If we obey our impulses, we may get into trouble and still not be satisfied. And if we ignore them, we're turning away from some inner part of ourselves. We might keep our desires secret or hate something instead.

As a therapist, I'm continuously listening closely to complaints and fantasies, which very often contain concealed desires. My first clue to a hidden wish often comes from a story of disavowal or protest of some sort. And the obstacles. Obstacles make it safe for us, in case what we want is unattainable.

It's easy to be critical about what's available. It's also a way of externalizing our inner conflict, grafting the issues onto another. That's true generally, and specifically in our sex lives. We can grow bored with what is utterly, comfortably familiar, and there's truth in the painful cliché: familiarity breeds contempt. When we yearn for something fresh in a sexual partner, we are also externalizing our inner conflict, yearning for something in our sense of self. We may have grown tired of sleeping with our own familiar, worn-out selves.

The role and aim of desire can be nebulous and sneaky. We feel a desire for something or someone, but this object of our desire seems to stand in for something else that's missing in our lives. Desire can come from a sense of lack. We can form desires to compensate for deprivation, loss, emotional pain. Desires can come in costume. A central mission of therapy is to uncover the hidden longings, the cloak-and-dagger feelings, the stories of desire we imagine for our unlived lives.

This mission has been central to my work with Jack, a man in his late fifties who came to therapy to figure out whether he should stay in his marriage of nearly four decades.

JACK'S CHOICES

"I see Helen's blond moustache gleaming in the sunlight and it disgusts me," Jack says to me as he closes and opens his fists.

He has a pleasant demeanor, quick eyes, and he enunciates his words with precision and weight.

"That sounds difficult for you," I say.

"Well, that helps."

I can't tell if he's joking. As though he can read my insecurity at that moment, he jumps in.

"No, really, it actually does help. At least you accept me. And you get me."

"You talk about your disgust, and I wonder what it's really about," I say, feeling a vague obligation to push him further at this moment.

"I just can't believe that this is it, this is marriage. I want more," he says.

"More of what? What is it that you want?" I ask.

"I want Helen to be sexy. I want her to desire me the way she did when we first got together and we had sex three times a day. I'm angry that she doesn't want me anymore. We used to fuck standing up. On the stairs because we couldn't wait to get to the bedroom. Outside. In toilets at clubs. Now there's just nothing. What the fuck? How many times can I say 'fuck'? I'm fucking furious."

"I hear that." I can see it too. He's squinting his eyes and wrinkling his nose as though he's detected a vile smell.

"Where are you right now?" I ask. I feel he's wandered off in a cloud of contempt, but I don't want to make assumptions. It's grounding and clarifying when he locates himself.

"She ripped me off," he says. He says he was sold a bullshit story of love and marriage. His discontent became unbearable for him shortly after their son, their only child, left for university (college, as he puts it, since he's American). He hadn't expected to feel the empty nest, but his son was his best friend in some ways, and the loss and separation felt excruciating. He feels alienated from his wife, and deeply rejected.

He wants to desire her.

He wants her to desire him.

He wants to feel desire again.

We laugh about how many times we are now using that word. We gaze at each other fleetingly. The energy is not exactly erotic with Jack. There's rapport, there's projection, there's fantasy, but it doesn't feel sexual to me. I'm more of an idealized mother to him, even though he's decades older than I am. We work remotely, and in the virtual realm we are truly connected without being in the same physical space, so any threat of transgression feels different. He lives in California and works in food retail, and I live in London, so we are collaborating in this deep connection from afar, which suits someone who wants and resists closeness.

Jack idealizes his own mother, even though she neglected him. He's both revealed and protected her in his portrayal. But his poor wife has never really stood a chance. Meanwhile, Jack's responses to me feel like a repetition of his maternal love in certain ways. Even when I try, I can do little wrong. I feel his belief in me, his trust that I understand him, that I get him. Even when I get stuff wrong or don't understand something about him, he overlooks my failures. His emotional frugality towards his wife is a sharp contrast to his generosity with me. Gloom-tinted glasses for the moustached wife, while I'm held in a glowing light. The clearly defined limitations of our dynamic safeguard the idealization.

"Our conversations help me, but this isn't enough," he says, wagging his finger. "I need sex. It's nonnegotiable. That's why I sleep with sirens, you know." He insists on calling paid escorts "sirens."

"I know; that's what you've said many times."

"Well, what the fuck does she expect? I can't spend the rest of my life fuckless. The women enjoy it too. It's not just the money they're getting."

I'm doubtful about that, but I choose to let this one go by. I find it highly unlikely that paid escorts enjoy sex with him the way he claims. He often looks at me for cues, and as if he can read the doubts flickering across my face, he elaborates.

"This last girl, she orgasmed so hard. I'm telling you." Did she? Why does he need to believe that? I'm struck by his need to feel wanted.

"Jack, let's get back to what this does for you. There's a lot to these physical encounters, they mean so much to you, they keep you going, as you say. You also insist that they protect your marriage. Do you think there's something about breaking the rules that gives you a sense of freedom and authority as well—the idea that your wife isn't entirely in charge of you?"

"That was a leading question," he says with a mischievous grin. "Maybe you think that, but it's not the illicitness that makes it meaningful. Coming here is meaningful to me, and this isn't about breaking rules. And my wife knows I see you."

I nod. In the silence that follows, I feel the full force of what he's said. I cringe at comparisons between therapists and paid escorts, but I get his point. He pays for transactional connections and finds them meaningful and personal.

Even in the virtual realm, the pronounced silence between us feels uncomfortably close. I think of the jazz adage that it's the notes we don't play that make the music. Holding space and not saying anything, just for a moment, says more than words. "I feel you enjoy working with me for the most part," he says.

"I do."

"I pay for time with you," he says.

"Yes, you do."

"If you're wondering about the sirens and how you come in, you see where I'm going with this."

"Yes, but with sirens, you act out certain fantasies, whereas therapy is a space for considering what they're about." I hear myself saying "Yes, but . . ." too often with him.

"Good point."

After a few months as Jack's therapist, I find myself entering this circular kind of discussion with him again and again. We make progress and reach great insights, we make links, connections, and understandings, and still the behavior doesn't change. I call this **insight as a defense**, and it's something I've done in my personal life, and I wish some of my therapists had confronted me on it. We reach profound, pithy insights about ourselves, making all sorts of links and connections and understandings, and nothing outside of therapy actually shifts. In Jack's case, he claims his behavior isn't problematic. The only intervention I can offer that pushes him to delve further is when I question what he wants—what he *really* wants.

"I want to be wanted," he finally says in the following session, when we again take up the question. Helen does, with her moustache and all, actually love him. It's not sexual, but it's tender and genuine. And she makes him laugh. And he makes her laugh. There isn't much laughter or mirth with the paid escorts. But the loss of sexual desire in his relationship with Helen pains him. And maybe it's more than that: being loved by Helen may not feel like enough for him, no matter how much love she has for him, because she's his wife.

And what about me? Yes, he employs me by the hour. But as my supervisor points out, he pays for everything but my care. And I do care about him, and even have loving feelings for him, insofar as he is my client. Accepting the affection in our therapeutic relationship prompts him to realize something about himself.

Freud famously wrote of some patients: "Where they love, they have no desire, and where they desire, they cannot love." I wonder if this is the case for Jack and Helen. And maybe I'm the reparative mother he can idealize without having sexual intimacy, and the paid escorts are for sex but not real emotional intimacy.

"But, actually, I just want to be desired," he says. "I want to feel appealing." The love he feels from Helen doesn't make him feel desirable. He insists that sleeping with paid escorts makes him feel appealing and wanted. Even when we get past the shame, and the pride, and the explanation, and the insight, what he needs is to feel wanted—deeply wanted.

In our next session, I ask him about his longing to feel wanted. This is clearly a huge artifact of his childhood deprivation, and we trace his feelings of rejection. He's moved by this and sheds a few tears. Once he starts to cry, his face seems to open itself to a deluge. He removes his glasses and lets the tears fall. This has happened a handful of times over the course of our work together, and it feels like a breakthrough each time. His tears feel authentic and whole-hearted, as though he's giving himself entirely to the process, and I feel close to his pain and suffering. The tears are for the little boy who was abused and neglected by his mother, even if he now elevates her in his mind. And for the boy whose father abandoned him and his mother without explanation, replacing them with a new family. The tears are for the adolescent pimply boy who soiled himself at school and felt humiliated. And for missing his son who is no longer a child. And for missing his own youth, and his grandmother who died thirty years ago. Jack cries with gladness that he can safely explore these painful stories he's carrying around. He thanks me for caring so much about his life story.

"I very much care," I confirm. As the words leave my mouth, I realize how often I'm reinforcing my enthusiasm for him. I hear myself soothing him repeatedly and telling him in different ways that I want to work with him.

"I like that you care about me. I know you do. And you're busy and could choose not to see me, but you make time for me," he says. He feels prioritized. Never did he feel this way with his mother. "I was an accident. Mom was young; Dad drank too much. Nothing about me was chosen. And when I did come, she didn't really look at me." He longs to be held in the gaze. He wants to be the object of desire, not just the desiring subject.

He recalls the early days of his relationship with his wife. "I mean, she had this come-hither look, this come-and-get-me-if-you-can quality that made me want more. But the best part was the way she looked at me. The tenderness. I could cry just thinking about it."

Jack misses the **limerence**, the expansive exhilaration of infatuation. It just doesn't last in a relationship over time. I'm somewhat surprised that he's reached his fifties and insists on certain expectations. Is he willfully naïve or is he oblivious that he's holding on to a fantasy?

"For the first year or so, we were constantly discovering life's offerings in some way, and we went on endless adventures in the early days. Together, we conquered and explored. We were allowed to be exactly who we were, and it was all . . . unfolding in some way. 'The best was yet to be, grow old with me' . . . but Helen doesn't look at me that way anymore . . .'"

"Do you look at her that way?" I ask.

"Not really. I don't see Helen as sexual anymore, and I don't find her attractive. She's become masculine, in a way that bothers me. But I do love her," he says. "And she actually does love me. She's a fat pain in the ass but she makes me laugh and we have fun eating roast chicken together and drinking red wine." He sheds another tear for the Helen who made him feel desired when he was in his twenties. "I think I've resented her for sticking by me all this time. What's wrong with her for choosing me?" We want to feel wanted and we wince at people who are fully available and truly want us.

We look at his Groucho Marx struggle to enjoy membership in a club that would accept him. We map his varying levels of self-loathing over the years. His wife's value is reduced because she's a loser for being married to him, he says. But at other moments he thinks he could have aimed higher, and she's beneath him. If only he could be young again and have it all to do over, better. He would like to have liked himself more, and not to have suffered just so much, for so long. He would like to live a lot of his life differently. Of course, these things aren't possible for any of us. The most useful therapeutic work from here for Jack will be recognizing the painful regret about the impossibility of a return to his youth while working on what is possible, working with the givens—both the particulars of his circumstances and the universal dilemmas of being human.

Jack can only live his life forward from the present moment. What can he change? What can't he change? What can he accept? What can he celebrate?

In the next session, Jack says something utterly remarkable.

"I like that I'm married to Helen, but in my next life I would like to settle down later and be with someone entirely different. I'd also like to be an artist and have many more children. Not in this life, though." He's half kidding as he says this. He doesn't believe in an afterlife. He's a staunch atheist, with a pragmatic approach to death and finitude. And yet, underlying so many of his behaviors and his beliefs is a misguided and subtly confusing fantasy that he can live many lives. We distill this belief and he's astonished by the discovery.

"I mean, I thought I knew that this is it. Really and truly. But I don't think I've actually accepted that up until now. As crazy as this sounds, I'm pretty sure I've thought I'd get loads of chances to live many lives, and this is just one of many. I haven't really accepted this path. This one wild and precious life of mine. Helen is that reality tollbooth for me that I have to face each and every day, a painful reminder of what it means to live just one life. Does that make sense?" he asks me. To me, it makes complete sense. I value these "aha" moments in therapy when we can acknowledge reality and look at what's possible and what's impossible. Clarity is kindness.

I realize that I've held back from asking for details about his sexual desire for paid escorts. What does he desire in them, and how does he feel when he's with them? What's his sense of self in those encounters? I finally ask him, and I discover how much I've assumed and avoided without fully understanding.

"Well . . ." He shifts in his seat. "I dress up as a woman when I'm with them," he tells me.

I did not anticipate this plot twist. He hasn't ever talked about dressing up as a woman or fantasizing about playing with gender.

He gets aroused at the thought or image of himself as a woman. The desire, he explains, is for himself in this way, and it doesn't feel possible to show this side of himself to anyone but paid escorts. I ask him why he hasn't mentioned this until now.

"You never asked," he says. And what about Helen? Does she know about this fantasy?

"No way. Look at how hard it was for me to tell you. I waited for you to ask. Maybe I'm doing the same with Helen, and she's yet to ask. I doubt she ever will. We're liberal, but also judgmental in some ways. This part of me . . . it's embarrassing."

I ask him about who he becomes in his fantasy. "When I dress up as a woman, I don't feel that I'm my true self," he says. "It's not that I want to become a woman. I have no interest in transitioning. What I want is to admire myself as a beautiful woman just occasionally." He's had this secret side since dressing up in his mother's clothes as a young boy. He's always loved costumes.

"Halloween," he says. "Best day. Every year I found a way to dress up as a woman, and most women dressed up as prostitutes. Maybe not literally, but on some level, that's how I saw a lot of the costumes, throughout my teenage years. It's this pretend-scary day where we eat lots of candy and wear objectifying outfits. Don't we *all* long to desire ourselves in some way? This is *my* way."

We look at what desire means to him: "It makes me feel alive," he says. "I guess I'm grieving for the aliveness Helen and I used to have together; that's just gone." We briefly consider why Helen stopped desiring sex, but he doesn't know, and I try not to speculate. They've discussed her menopause and had clipped, careful discussions about her hormones, but they haven't really acknowledged the sexless state of their relationship.

"Is there a term for this?" he asks. "The loss of sexual desire?"

"'Aphanisis,'" I say. "Not sure how helpful that is, but it's the psychoanalytic term and actually comes from the disappearance of a star, astronomically."

"I like that. It's a good term, I'm writing that down. Because that's exactly what it's like for me. It feels like a vanished star. The light just switched off. And now I pretend. There's so much pretending. I can see your face when I tell you about the sirens orgasming. They're probably pretending to orgasm, and I'm pretending to be a woman. And you're pretending not to doubt my telling you that the sirens orgasm. It works. Even if it's not entirely real."

He has a point. I have my concerns. I know the statistics about paid escorts, and I feel for his wife, and I want him to have real intimacy. But this seems to be my desire more than his.

"Thinking it through, I can see that I made a solid choice in deciding to marry Helen, and in choosing to stay married to her," Jack says. It turns out that this is what he needs: to accept his own choices. And I need to accept his choices too.

I think about Jack dressing up as a woman occasionally and what this fantasy might mean for him. "Did you ever imagine life as a girl and how your father might have related to you?" I ask.

"His next family gave him girls," Jack says, gazing into a far-off corner I can't see. "When I think about it, it's about both my parents. My mom used to say that having a son was especially hard for my dad, and she imagined that if only she'd had a daughter instead, he might have stayed. He wanted a girl. That's what she told me over and over."

The fantasy makes sense. It's a way of partially identifying with his father, who had multiple families and relationships. He can play the part of the imaginary wanted daughter. The beautiful woman everyone desires. He doesn't consciously want to repeat his father's pattern of abandonment and rejection. He's proud of committing to his family, and especially his son. He would never leave his son the way he had been left. But dressing up as a woman, and being with paid escorts, gives him a kind of space for fantasizing about other versions of life, even if it's just for an hour or two. "I always come home," he says.

His fantasy is also about his wish to feel desired by his mother. If he were a girl, maybe she would have loved him more and treated him better. And maybe his father would have stayed if only he'd been a girl. Life could have been so much better. He realizes, saying it aloud, that his mother's treatment of him and her explanation for his father's inexplicable abandonment was about her wounded story, not his actual worth. But he still struggles to believe that he's enough, as he is, in this one life. He feels the ache of his father's being left behind and realizes that he's protected his mother in his mind. Admitting her rejection and blame of him has felt too painful. But the pain has found him. And maybe his son leaving home reactivated the trauma of abandonment, being left, even though he's also glad that his son is growing up and becoming independent.

"We all have so many different sides and so many different parts to play. I won't skip town like my dad did, but I do like dressing up. I need fantasy to accept my reality."

Jack and I continue to work hard to figure out what desire means for him. "In the words of Robert Frost," he says one day, "the irresistible desire to be irresistibly desired." He likes being clever. He lets out a sigh. He's never felt irresistibly desired by anyone, starting with his parents.

What I can do is make him aware of his choices, the impact, the context, the significance. His hostility towards Helen seems to be the outgrowth, in large part, of his displaced desire to feel wanted by his parents. Not literally. Not sexually. But on some level, what he's wanted is to feel desired by his mother and father, and he never fully had that experience. He has to grieve that deprivation. It's not Helen's fault—or his. For Jack, issues of desire hover around affirmation. The affirmation he didn't get from his parents he gives to his son but withholds from his wife. Going both ways, there are echoes of rejection and deprivation in his marriage, but Jack and Helen are still together, and there's still love.

During one of our sessions, Jack's laptop battery is about to run out and his charger is in another room. He carries me with him as he walks through his house, and he comes across Helen. He greets her and introduces her to me. She looks up and smiles. I smile back and I'm astonished by her sanguine pleasantness. No sign of a moustache—from this angle, anyway. Her face is so inviting, so human. I realize that I've absorbed a projected, deformed picture of her. He's cast her in such an undesirable light, in his fury at her for not desiring him the way he wants.

He doesn't plan on dressing up as a woman in front of her, or telling her about this fantasy, but he can forgive her for not wanting to have sex with him. He continues to wish she wanted him sexually the way she used to, but he tempers his expectations and forgives her for failing to compensate for all the rejection he's felt his whole life.

Jack stops hating her, and maybe he stops hating himself too, when he realizes all the ways he's wanted to feel wanted.

DESIRE AND YOU

We all struggle at times to respect and own and accept our choices. Desire usually leans towards fantasy, whereas choice leans towards reality.

There's a saying that emotion plus reason equals wisdom. We can apply this to how we make decisions: choices fueled entirely by desire, or choices devoid of desire, often land us in a space of disappointment. Where possible, think about the underlying desires when you're making a choice and what part may be fantasy and what's realistic. Desire exaggerates and minimizes. Notice the ways you've embellished something you want or distorted your perception when you've felt unwanted. Looking at the choices you've made, consider the factors.

If you hadn't chosen to marry your life partner, you would be able to act on your desire now for this other person who has come along. If you hadn't committed yourself to law school, you could have lived the peripatetic life of a free-spirited novelist. If only you'd chosen to take that trip, how different things would be. If you hadn't chosen to settle down in the suburbs and have children, you could have lived a wild and adventurous life working to better human-kind. Whatever the fantasy may be, very often we get caught up with issues around desire because we feel hampered by our choices. And what we really desire may be something that we simply cannot choose. Jack didn't choose his parents.

It turns out our choices aren't usually all that appalling, but what's unforgivable and impossible to accept is that this is our one and only life. There's a lot that doesn't go our way. Desire pushes us to stretch ourselves and celebrate existence, but it can also enslave us when we don't understand what it's about. When you feel stultified or impeded from getting what you think you desire, consider what you feel you're essentially lacking.

Ignoring desires comes at a cost. We tend to protest, resent, dis-place, or punish others or ourselves. In the words of Socrates: "From the deepest desires often come the deadliest hate." Rather than dis-avow a desire, identify it and allow yourself the chance to see it for what it is, even if you don't act on it. You can also consider whether there's desire underneath something you hate.

Love and desire are not always aligned. Have you ever felt pas-sionate attraction towards someone and mistaken it for love? Have you ever loved someone deeply and not felt passionate attraction? Desire can drop at different times over the course of a loving rela-tionship. It's sometimes in sync with the love we feel but it can be at odds. We can feel burning desire for people we don't necessarily love, and we can deeply love people we don't necessarily desire.

Our sense of self comes into desire. When we feel attractive, or successful, we might feel more desire—and not necessarily for our loved ones. "I'm in the best shape of my life," a man told me re-cently. "And I suddenly see beautiful women everywhere. They may have always existed, but I didn't even allow myself to see them when I felt so unattractive. Now I see them, and I want them." When we feel low and dispirited, some people feel a surge of desire as a kind of life force, whereas others lose desire and find that activities that once were pleasurable don't feel enjoyable anymore. "It's not that I find my boyfriend unattractive," a woman in her early twenties told me, "but I don't like my body right now, and it's killed my horniness." Your sense of self influences your desires at different moments in time.

Why, I once asked the Yale brain research scientist Amy Arnsten, do human beings want to feel desire so much in the first place?

"I think this is a very primitive circuitry that allows an organism to thrive—pleasure in eating, drinking, sex, and being in the right temperature all allow us to be in the correct physiological conditions," she said, "and to continue our species."

Without desire, why would anyone do anything? What would it mean to be human?

Desire is possibility. Energy. Motivation. Desires are the backdrop for action. With the exception of occasional blissful moments of contentment when we want for nothing, we feel listless and directionless without desire. Desires light up pathways for us, shape our experiences, and move us forward.

Chapter Three

UNDERSTANDING

We see a photograph from fifteen years ago and feel shocked by the unfamiliarity. But then we see a baby photo of ourselves and think, *There I am. That's me.* Recognizing patterns helps us make sense of experiences and find paths forward. We keep getting drawn into unhealthy friendships. When we talk about this new one at first, we explain all the ways our connection is circumstantial and different from the others. But as we describe the constant paying (*Why did I insist? Why did she not then try to insist on at least splitting one of the bills?*), the harsh remarks, and our simmering resentment, we get it. When we understand something emotionally, there's a thread of continuity that brings experiences together in an organizing way. We breathe a different kind of air when we have this sense of order and clarity.

Therapy seeks understanding. It's a collaborative process and might include working through misunderstandings. When we process and make sense of our experiences, we can make a coherent narrative of our lives. We can understand how we hold ourselves back, how we take responsibility for other people but avoid seeing how we're responsible for what we do in life. We discover possibilities.

We are constantly trying to make sense of how the world sees us and what we see. We exist in the context of relationships, and our inner worlds are populated with memories, social messages, embedded beliefs from past relationships. Cultivating a healthy sense of self requires constant fine-tuning and updating. Some of us have an overworked people-pleaser inside us—possibly just a person-pleaser (and not a person we consciously seek approval from). When our people-pleaser gives too much and overspends (often the case), our resentment debt grows. The people-pleaser can be wildly accommodating and sacrificial, so we find ourselves squashed and pressured.

The people-pleaser poses a few problems for how to live. Only interested in serving and being liked, the people-pleaser isn't even aware of having desires. The people-pleaser tricks us by claiming selflessness. We like the idea of being good. At least somewhat. So we think that the people-pleaser's devoted acts of selflessness make us better people, better friends, employees. Up against the people-pleaser is the selfish seeker, resentful and determined to sort this out. The conflict between the polarities of selflessness and selfishness comes up all the time in therapy.

When people's opinions of us clash with how we want to be known, we feel alienated, isolated, at the mercy of injustice. We bounce from approval to rejection. We find ourselves speculating and agonizing about what people think.

It's easier to judge than to sit with uncertainty. It can be a breakthrough to rework an experience and discover that we do not actually understand something we thought we did. We judged, we assumed.

Let's keep trying to understand. Clarifying, revising, and updating our understanding is how we learn. Understanding is a continual work in progress.

Our quest to be understood can be compulsive and frustrating. We don't necessarily communicate effectively, sometimes especially with people close to us. We might hope we'll be magically understood without having to spell things out directly. Sometimes we want people to read our minds and understand our inner worlds even if we haven't expressed ourselves. It's liberating to recognize and work through self-deceptions.

We need help understanding ourselves. Beyond literal comprehension, feeling emotionally understood, by at least someone—a teacher, friend, therapist, partner, sibling, sometimes a stranger (it can feel easier and less consequential to confide in people outside of our daily lives)—is valuable and gives us a sense of relief and even joy. *Finally, someone gets me!* We feel less alone, less strange and unacceptable.

Truly understanding who we are, even if we don't like everything (and how could we?), makes the experience of being in our own skin more comfortable. When we comprehend our true motivations and can sort through our mixed feelings, we can accept and acknowledge contradictions and inconsistencies, both in ourselves and in others. We can make choices that feel right for us.

We need space for flexibility and change. Change puts enormous pressure on relationships of all kinds. This is true for most recovering addicts, couples over time, friendships, workplace dynamics, our relationship with ourselves. Change threatens our sense of understanding, and we're ambivalent. We seek growth and yearn for novelty and surprise, then revert to familiarity. We're comfortable with what we know. Learning something new demands effort and challenges our sense of mastery.

How do you talk to yourself? You may be selling yourself short in various ways, sometimes over many years. It may not be an accurate story, but it's a familiar story, and what is familiar feels true.

It's challenging work understanding ourselves. It can be a hall of mirrors, imagining how others see us, seeing ourselves through all those other eyes, perhaps going all the way back to childhood. We may summon flattering portraits some of the time, but we can also be haunted by deeply unflattering ones.

For everyone there are inevitably stressful moments in life when we may feel alienated, lost, estranged from how others see us and how we experience ourselves. Contradictions and paradoxes occur all the time, in a very ordinary way for most of us, but identity problems can feel like a psychological civil war, where different factions begin fighting each other. We can begin to disintegrate (literally, to dis-integrate), crack, splinter. Understanding ourselves, including our own inconsistencies, can be salvation. Therapy explores the external and internal, excavating deeply buried parts of the self.

Sometimes we come to therapy thinking we want to be understood, when actually we want sympathy and reinforcement. We might call it support, but we really want agreement. We want to be told we're right. We're blameless! This was my experience with Sying, a woman who came to see me because of an **identity crisis**.

WHAT'S IN A NAME? THE SONGS OF SYING

Sying is obsessed with her work. Or is it her boss? She didn't start out believing their relationship was unhealthy. People rarely do at first. It creeps in. And in her case, after nearly fifteen years of working for Victor Hill Architect, Ltd., she tells me that their relationship is a source of tremendous significance and meaning for her. She's here because of the ridiculous pressures she feels as a mother, the maternal guilt society still imposes on women who work. She feels judged by other mothers, by her in-laws. And she and her husband have begun to clash over attitudes towards work and family.

I recognize his name before I even know how to pronounce hers. When I'm not sure, I always ask.

"Oh, it's pronounced 'Sing,' as in 'Let's sing a song,' " she says. "But you can say it however you want, really. I don't mind."

But I mind. How could she not have a preference?

"I'm used to everyone mispronouncing it," she says. "It's Chinese, but, growing up in the UK, no one ever knew how to say it correctly. Maybe that's why my husband and I named our daughter Katie. It's easy to understand and pronounce. Anyway, I want to tell you more about myself. I love my work, but I'm not supposed to care so much now that I'm a mother. Isn't that ridiculous? I feel like no one in my life gets me."

She seems determined to get me on her side. But being on her side is going to mean challenging her, not just agreeing and nodding automatically.

When I ask about friendships, she looks embarrassed and frustrated. She's in touch with a few old friends but she often feels restless and disappointed when they meet. "Maybe I'm judgmental and critical," she says, "but actually *they* judge *me*." She'd like to have more friends but isn't sure how to make it happen. She wonders if she's on the spectrum.

"But work is going well," she says, and refers again to Victor Hill.

Work is where she comes alive. "It's not about the money: I'm not that well paid, though I do like the income. But it's more than that: it's kind of who I am."

She admires her lion of a boss deeply, and she's grateful for the opportunities he's given her. With a flush of pride, she calls herself a lion tamer. "My grandfather was tricky and demanding, and quite exceptional, and I know how to deal with the type well. I keep talking about Victor Hill and assuming you know who he is, right?"

Therapy is full of cultural references: words, places, news headlines, world issues, TV shows, books, come in and out of focus. If it's relevant and helpful to discuss this together, I'll admit what's familiar to me and what I have no idea about. What might feel like a detour can be a way of learning about someone's world.

I'm familiar with a few of Victor Hill's buildings. I have read profiles and articles about him. I have a vague impression of his "starchitect" public identity, his dapper style and notoriously outré social comments. I tell Sying I know of him but obviously I have no idea what he's really like. Sying values their private connection, she tells me. I notice that she says his full name each time she mentions him—Victor Hill—even though there are no other Victors in her life. In fact, no one else she describes gets a full name. Her references to other people are usually in relation to herself: "my husband," "my daughter."

Sying gesticulates widely and rarely sits still, while her animated stories shoot off in multiple directions. She's striking in appearance. Her hair is the color of "brandy in warm sunlight," a description I remember reading in one of Lee Radziwill's obituaries. I'm not sure why this detail comes to mind, but maybe it's something to do with Sying's effervescent, romantically dainty quality. For quite some time, when I gather my thoughts about her, she feels more like a charming character than a real person. She's an intriguing blend of flight and substance. She whirls around and doesn't quite land.

She returns to Victor obsessively. She respects his work, his aesthetic courage, his sheer efficacy and unwavering determination to do everything possible in architecture. "And it doesn't stop there: he does what's impossible too." Her admiration for doing the impossible grabs me. Does she believe that he's the path to her aspirational self?

"I'm obviously nothing like him," she continues. "I'm much more agreeable. He's demanding and temperamental, but never with me. I know how to navigate him. I think I bring out his best."

I ask what he brings out in her. Her best too. I ask her why she's so focused on him, and she says he's a big part of her life and I need to know this to understand her. He hired her when she was just twenty-five years old, green and inexperienced. His expectations of her show his esteem and faith in her, giving her so many opportunities—and she likes working hard. It's part of her character. "But don't worry, I know him far too well to ever be sycophantic. Not like his fawning superfans."

Her telling me not to worry doesn't make me unworried. Her sense of specialness depends on her rapport with him, and she describes their enmeshment in a protective way. She seems to want to persuade me, and maybe herself, that she's got this part of her life figured out.

"I'm a strong woman," she says, "but the nursery school mums, and my husband, don't make it easy for me." I can imagine! Does she want me to make it easy for her?

She's lucky to find her work meaningful, she tells me, especially when she thinks of all the unfulfilled people she knows. Her husband, for instance, is an example of someone who only works to live; she lives to work. She likes this about herself.

"I don't want to be one of those boring women who stops having any kind of identity outside of motherhood once she has a baby," she says. "Motherhood is so demanding."

The same word she's just used to describe Victor and her grandfather. But the demands of motherhood aren't rewarding for her.

"It's too late for me to be diagnosed as having postpartum depression," she says. "I mean, Katie just had her one-year checkup. The doctor didn't even ask me how I am. No one asks me how it is to be a mother at this stage."

"How is it for you to be a mother?" She keeps bringing it up yet dismissing it; actually, it's not too late to consider postpartum depression, or anxiety.

"It's overwhelming. I still don't feel myself. Except at work. But everyone apart from Victor Hill criticizes me for caring too much about my job."

I wonder what it is she really cares about.

When I ask her about motherhood, she describes Katie's beauty, her cuteness, and she shows me a picture. This moment feels slightly contrived, and I wonder if she feels forced to perform. The shift into motherhood—**matrescence**—is an identity challenge that can be easily minimized. The existential ripple effects of becoming a mother play out in myriad ways for years after giving birth. For a lifetime.

"But I'm not exactly depressed," she says.

So far, she seems clearer about the definitions that don't fit her.

"I feel energetic at work," she says. Her aspirational self lives through the prism of Victor. Sying's descriptions of their dynamic strike clear notes of idealization, the sense she has of herself as the golden girl, what it means for her to be a woman held in his adoring gaze. Her eyes brighten when she mentions him. Telling me about his affection for her brings out a kind of euphoria that feels extreme. She works tirelessly, diligently, pleasingly, as though her survival requires her to give every part of herself to him. Not just to her job, but to him. The pressure to perform and please sounds compulsive, urgent, not up for debate.

Why are you selling so hard? I want to ask, but I refrain. I need to let things unfold. The psychologist Alice Miller writes: "All the feelings the patient arouses in her therapist are part of her unconscious attempt to tell the therapist her story and at the same time hide it."

Sying continually posits theories about why others misunderstand her and object to her dedication to Victor, even though he's been good to her. I feel myself objecting—not to him per se, but her compulsive need to identify herself through him. He may be fascinating, but so is she. Does she realize this? She seeks sympathy from me but not necessarily real understanding.

A few weeks later, Sying arrives for a session frazzled and breathless.

"I ran to get here," she says. She collapses in the armchair opposite me, throwing her coat and bag to one side. "Ooh, is this water for me? Thank you." She gulps down the entire glass of water without stopping. As soon as she's put the glass down, she checks her phone, apologizing as she does it.

She's unsettled. Her appearance is charming and chaotic. She's whimsically dressed, with various textures and arrangements and patterns strewn together, yet somehow she usually makes it work. I can't quite make sense of her outfit today: Is she wearing a dress or a skirt and a shawl, and is that a scarf or a blanket? She's hot and cold over the course of the session, taking layers off, putting them back on.

Sying's British accent with its faint Chinese inflection lilts softly, and she's expressive and detailed at moments, though she often trails off in vague ponderings, leaving me looking for the link, wanting to finish her sentences. She leaves wisps of thoughts and feelings floating in the air. I find myself trying to gather, fill in, organize, bring together the various bits. I sometimes ask her to return to a point, to elaborate or clarify. Is there a thread? I wonder if this is part of her process, like an orchestra warming up.

"I don't know where to begin. There's too much. I'm bursting," she says.

"Let yourself just be here. It will come together," I say.

"There's so much. It's all so messy. I crave order. Look at the inside of my bag. Crap everywhere. Melted chewing gum and coins stuck to the bottom, and probably five lip glosses I really like but can't find. And I get so upset, not knowing where things are. Not knowing what I have. I want calm, clean lines." She gestures over my shoulder. "I wish my mind were more like the squares in that print behind you. My mind is more like a Jackson Pollock. That's my problem. Chaos. Splatters everywhere. Pissing this way and that way."

"What a vivid image," I say.

"I'm babbling . . ." She giggles. As insightful and aware as she can be, she lacks a kind of authority. She'll say something deeply smart and then add a self-effacing comment in a girlish tone. She needs approval and permission in some way. Her mistrust of her own voice, but her urge to express herself, come into the here and now.

"Start with the headlines, and we'll take it from there."

She tells me that, for the first time, her name will appear in the *Architectural Review*.

"Don't congratulate me," she says. "Victor Hill isn't happy about the news."

She needs his blessing.

"I didn't expect that I'd be given this opportunity," she says. "It just came about." A client found out that she was the designer of some of the most appealing aspects of Victor's last three award-winning houses. So hers will be the lead name for Wyatt House, a project that sounds exciting. At least, it did. Now she's wary. She assumed Victor would be proud of her, and pleased, but he isn't. Her desperation for his approval, her panic that he's displeased, is palpable.

"You seem ravenous in your hunger for his endorsement. What do you want from him?" I ask.

"I'm not sure . . . but what do you think he thinks of me now? Do you think I've ruined our relationship?"

She's more interested in being a detective about his personality than in making sense of her own motivations and longings. (This is a common pattern in therapy.) I don't see him or hear his side, but I picture him sulking, his ego injured. Therapists cannot help but be biased when it comes to perspectives. Yes, we try to keep the multiplicity of viewpoints in mind, and we know we get skewed versions of events, and people embellish and omit and select topics and keep us from knowing the whole truth even if they ostensibly try hard to convey things honestly. Such partiality, in our sense of ourselves and others, is simply an inevitable aspect of being human. As a therapist, the best I can do is maintain this awareness.

She's surprised that she really doesn't understand him, having thought she did. She justifies her consistency and feels he's the one who has stepped out of line. "I've worked so hard for him and am more dedicated to him now than ever. . . . How can he not appreciate my unwavering loyalty to him? How can he not be supportive?"

She's incredulous. Was she naïve? Surely this project is good for the office and his reputation, given that he's guided her, and she's served him all these years.

"I'm nearly forty. He must want me to succeed professionally, just out of respect for me," she says. She assumed he'd be caring, given how much she's sacrificed and cared about him and their work.

We unpack her fantasy and deconstruct her sense of being a little girl, along with her deep and constant yearning for approval, and his perfunctory, miserly response to her news, and how threatened he may be by her talent, by the attention given to her.

"You've kept him on a pedestal for a long time," I say, stating the very obvious. Her lion king was supposed to be the almighty father who adored and protected her. And cared about her! She saw and imagined and assumed all sorts of things about him.

"I thought I was savvy. I was onto him and could manage his tricky ego." She looks baffled.

In her perfectionist fantasy self-construction, she's always believed she could master this impossible man, charm him, bring out his best, most reasonable, loving, and lovable side. She was proud of her skilled connection with him. The lion tamer! But now she can see that she hasn't managed to do any of these things. She's fallen horribly short in her ideal sense of self. We explore some of the beliefs and worldviews held by this fantasy self. She wants to play the part of the powerful woman, she says, working and achieving, but her definitions are narrow and outdated, based on the classic story of a powerful older man and a younger woman whose purpose is to please him. It's not sexual, despite her husband's suspicions at moments, but it's certainly got complex overtones.

The dynamics between Sying and her famous boss have germs in her childhood. The reason to revisit and uncover the past is not so we will dwell there but rather so we can figure out together how she's gotten to where she is now and how she can shift something and free herself from falling into the grooves of old and problematic patterns going forward.

Her own father is passive, unexceptional, incredibly weak in her eyes, in her mother's eyes. "He's kind of a buffoon. He never came close to filling his father's shoes. My grandfather skipped past him and put all his hopes and dreams onto me."

"Do something you love," her grandfather told her shortly before he died. She was the only grandchild and knew she was his favorite, his golden girl. He gave her a sense that she was destined for glory, unlike her father. Unlike so many people around her.

Sying found something she loved—architecture—and she became an architect. Victor Hill Architect gave her space for expression, for activating certain yearnings. *This is who I am,* she thought. Victor provided Sying with a riveting reward system—his approval, his picking her as his favorite. She found in him someone she could endlessly idealize and dedicate herself to.

Meeting Victor gave her a sense of potential glory. She thought it was empowering, but what she gets—what she's gotten—is his approval for what she gives him. To be held in his gaze—is this her entire aim?

"When you say it back to me like that, I can hear what's off. Serving a man is really not what I want my life to be about."

This jolt of deprivation alerts her to an underlying problem. There's a sudden sense of clarity that cuts through the hazy mist of idealization she's had all these years.

But what happens next? Sying's **sufferiority** is fierce. She struggles to voice her deep yearning to be a formidable architect with a name of her own. It feels egomaniacal to her, grandiose and unrealistic. Even in therapy, with me. Serving a legend suits the tension within her that's both ambitious and self-marginalizing. The proximity to greatness. But doing something on her own, having her name out there, is exposing, uncertain, and she's embarrassed by her ego in wanting her name to be known.

Having **ego strength** is perfectly healthy, but, for Sying, the people-pleaser part of her overshadows ego. *I only want to serve Victor Hill* is the message the people-pleaser gives. But the ego, however covert, still sneaks in an agenda: getting her name on Wyatt House. The result is self-loathing and shame. Disappointing Victor and revealing her ego feels like a double fail.

Following the news of Wyatt House, at a staff meeting, Victor has made aggressive remarks to Sying about his friends who are on the editorial staff at the *Architectural Review* who might decide not to run the story once they realize that it isn't an entirely Victor Hill– designed house. She shouldn't count her chickens before they've hatched. Is he going to get the story killed? Will he somehow make her disappear professionally? Has she overstepped? Has she ruptured the hierarchy, dishonored the implicit system in a clumsy way?

In most work environments, power dynamics play out. This is partly why Sying has been willing to see her design work attributed to Victor, over and over. Nobody else in the office gets credit, though he employs a team of talented young architects. Everyone knows that Victor doesn't single-handedly do all the design work, including the editors at the *Architectural Review*. Sying has worked hard for all these years, and it's now a reasonable next step for her to have her own voice, her own identity. I've encouraged her in our sessions to think about what she wants for herself, professionally and personally. And now here we are. The imminent success and recognition for Sying turns out to be deeply unsettling for Victor, and so it is for her too.

She describes Victor looking at her with beady, squinted eyes. The fond gaze has vanished. She's turned into the bad object for him, a displeasing threat. And it's not just what he is in his response to her. It's also all that he isn't, and all that she's hoped for. It feels emotionally catastrophic.

Over the following weeks, things turn nastier at the office. Victor makes bizarre demands and instructions. He seems brutally jealous, controlling, transparently threatened by his protégée becoming known in her own right. His usual stream of compliments for her work has dried up.

Sying is quiet and anxious to avoid mention of the planned publication of the article in the *Architectural Review*, but word gets out. He tries to block any office discussion of her project and makes it difficult for her to get the final finishing details executed. He has a tantrum in a staff meeting and tells her she's given him health problems with all the stress she's causing. He screeches at her over the phone about a missed deadline caused by the office turbulence, and then he sulks and ignores her.

She feels diminished and out of sorts in the place where she had felt most herself for so many years. Some of her colleagues are sympathetic, and they reach out to her privately to see if she's okay. She isn't okay, but she tells them she's fine, and though a few of them are intrigued and curious about the apparent rupture, she feels they're too scared to rock the boat. Everyone continues to tiptoe around the famous boss.

We discuss what's happened—what's happening—repeatedly. It's a difficult life moment for Sying precisely because it's transformative. Growing pains of the most acute nature.

I reiterate and clarify. "I think that for so many years, you have, for reasons we've talked about, inflated and flattered Victor's already swollen sense of self. You were possibly a kind of extension to him, so he didn't need to see you as a separate individual, and it worked well for his ego. You were part of his process, his accomplishments, keeping him in supply. And it suited your wish to serve and please. But now you're emerging as an individual in your own right, and that's hugely threatening to someone as fragile as he seems to be."

I wonder if she's paying attention. She looks like she's on a **conversation vacation**. Though she goes through the motions of presence, she's elsewhere.

"I love that! God, you're good." She says it a little too emphatically, and I assume she also wants to put me at ease. She's like this. Attuned and longing to please, she rescues those around her, including her therapist. No wonder Victor liked having her at his beck and call.

"I was the golden child," she says with a sigh.

"Yes," I say. "Notice that you've said 'child.' And now you're becoming a grown-up. You're no longer the twenty-five-year-old newbie barely qualified architect."

We consider the meaning of growing up. It's a complex thing for all of us. In the safe space of therapy, where regression and childish feelings get explored, people can begin to really grow up. The best therapy I've ever had helped me grow up by letting me acknowledge my own childishness.

"Growing up hurts," she says. "Is it worth it?"

She didn't get to fully be a child during her childhood, which is part of her wish to play the child now. In her childhood, Sying's parents acted more like jealous children, and Sying took pride in being conscientious and responsible, revering her grandfather and earning his praise without feeling she could be messy or imposing. The **role suction** of motherhood feels unbearable at times. Her baby reminds her of her own unmet needs. She feels like a wounded child, but she's also a capable adult.

Between sessions, Sying is on my mind. I think of her at an event where I'm described as my child's mother, and although that's a part of my life I cherish deeply, it's not the entirety of my identity. The split between a working mother's professional self and maternal self is still hard. Some of us are in search of glory, however misguided.

In Sying's case, the glory comes from work, and the split has pushed her to burrow deeper in her professional identity. She's felt safer and stronger and better there than in her mother mode. And the split is further pressured by her mother-in-law, who strongly believes that mothers should stay at home and not pay for help. Her husband has pulled away, defending his mother's views. Sying feels judged. Her husband does too. Sying's work as an architect is her affair, the lover who gets the best of her, and it's where she feels most successful. Being held in the Victor Hill gaze felt fabulous. Now she's struggling to hang on to her place there. Letting go of this familiar dynamic could feel like a staggering loss.

"I looked up the name Sying," I say in our next session. "How interesting that it means star. Whatever you do, I want you to know that I think you've got a rich mind and your voice matters." This seems to reach her. As obvious as these words seem to me as I say them, she's never heard them before.

Our work stays focused on this topic for quite some time. Not just during this session, but over several weeks. The meaning of having her own voice, growing up, who she is, what parts of her identity can endure over time, and the core bits of her that will survive all the changes. We talk about how changing and growing means letting go.

She needs to lose something if she's going to make changes. If she wants her name on Wyatt House, she is probably at the end of her stage in life as Victor's protégée. It's a coming-of-age disaster of sorts, and a breakthrough.

"I want to understand myself, who I really am," Sying declares at the start of a session. "But it's so uncomfortable. Will I feel this lost forever?"

I could withhold reassurance. A psychoanalytic lecturer once insisted during my training that reassurance is never reassuring. Oh, but it can be, and now might be one of those moments. "You won't feel this way forever," I say. "But tell me about it."

"I feel . . . nervous . . . and stressed. I feel it physically right now. I'm . . . overwhelmed . . . My heart is racing, like I'm about to get into big trouble."

"In trouble for what?"

"For getting ahead of myself, being too cocky, too daring. Who do I think I am? What if I'm like Icarus, flying too high, and I'm about to get scorched?" she says. Her eyes dart around the room.

We look at the origin of her self-diminishment, how taking her work seriously somehow horrifies her. She's ashamed of her ambition, and we retrace her embarrassment for desiring a life and identity of her own. She feels unsettled. Now that she's finally putting herself out there in the world of architecture, she's found herself in an unprecedented and unexpected professional crisis.

"Wanting more, admitting that I want something . . . is exposing. And now that I've said it, if I fail, I have more to lose," she says.

"Yes. Consider what it is you want. You can choose to pursue things you might not get. It's reality that you might not get what you want." I'm suddenly conscious that I've nudged Sying to go further in her development. Will she feel judged by me if she doesn't leave this architecture practice? I say this to her, and we talk about how I don't make decisions for her. I feel an odd rush of joy not telling her what to do.

We look at what it would be like to leave this architecture practice, with its big, fancy name and her famous boss.

"I hate endings so much," Sying says, crinkling her face as though she's preparing to look at an unpleasant sight. "I just can't picture myself anywhere else. What would my week look like? Who would I be?"

We explore this struggle together.

"I'm so adolescent, asking what it means to be me," she says.

"Adolescents aren't the only ones who can ask that question," I say. As painful as identity crises may be, stagnation can be quietly dreadful.

"I've given my blood, sweat, and tears to this place," she says. "I'm not one of those people who just tick boxes. I go above and beyond. For Victor Hill. For every project I have ever worked on."

"I know," I say. "'Compulsively conscientious' is how you described yourself."

"Yes! It's been one of my humblebrags," she says.

We talk about what it's really for, why she does it. At first, she doesn't understand. She knows she can't pour from an empty cup, but she keeps trying to expand herself, adamant that she has endless capacity—an echo of her admiration that Victor "does the impossible"? She's increasingly frustrated, resentful, and overwrought.

"I think about the fretful nights when I've just been so . . . so preoccupied. I'll tuck Katie into bed, and I'll clutch my phone under the covers, and I'll sneak a peek, while she's still stirring, just to check one more email, read one more thing, add something or another to my endless to-do list . . . And my life is passing by. I'm missing time with my child, with my husband, all for what? Not for the money. We know I get paid crumbs and deserve more. Why on earth do I do it? Not just work, but work so bloody hard for this man?"

"You tell me," I say. "Is it the positive reinforcement? How much do you really need that from him?"

"It's even more than positive reinforcement . . . I think I've secretly hoped that, by giving him admiration, I'll be as big as him one day. It makes no sense saying it aloud," she says.

All the more reason to say it aloud and make sense of it. Obsession always has a secret plan. The plan isn't strategic, but we can understand it and figure out the direction of travel. She's secretly driven to be a huge architect. Endless admiration isn't the solution, but we can work with the material.

"When he's praised me, even if it's a one-line email, it feels like heaven," Sying says, her voice breathy. That's the drug that's hooked her all these years.

"I just crave knowing I'm good enough," she continues.

"I get that. What's it going to take for you to know it in a real, lasting way?"

"Everything. I'm joking. But not really."

"Well, let's explore that part of you that's not joking. Your contradictory demands and expectations send you on maddening and endless self-esteem errands. No amount of praise and validation gives you adequate evidence of your worth. Here you are, a fantastically bright and accomplished forty-year-old. Can you understand that you're good enough already?"

"Maybe. I like the idea, even though I feel awkward admitting it," she says.

"Let's assume you're good enough. Then what?" I ask.

"I don't know . . . I can't picture anything past wanting validation. Maybe I want something, but I haven't let myself think that far ahead . . . Maybe it's the bamboo ceiling . . . I'm not sure," Sying says.

"We've talked about your wanting to be bigger, and then you hold yourself back from imagining what that would actually look like. It's worth understanding what you really want—from Victor Hill, professionally, your personal life."

"As hard as I've worked, I haven't really thought about what it's for . . ." She's emotionally threadbare at these moments. Her embedded beliefs and Victor's hold have kept her ego disguised until this crisis.

"What's hard to think about can be the most important thing to face. I think you avoid this question by feeling that you should be small again."

"Victor just doesn't seem to recognize all that I do or who I am. And I don't either."

"You finally called him Victor. Not Victor Hill," I say. We think this through together, looking at the myths, his fame, the projections, her past and present feelings of inadequacy.

"I've been so deferential for such a long time," Sying says. "I think, in some ways, I thought that endless devotion, doing excellent work without genuine recognition, would somehow elevate me, and one day I'd arrive at some kind of secure heavenly place."

At this moment, we both see the fantasy of what she's longed for.

"Did you know that Victor still says my name incorrectly?" Sying tells me in our next session. "He pronounces it like 'sighing.' How could he do that?"

"I've got to challenge you on that one," I say. "When we first met, I asked you how to pronounce your name, and you said you didn't mind how it was pronounced. Did you ever tell him how to say your name correctly?"

"I don't remember. Possibly not. I think I thought he'd ask. And he didn't."

We spend time looking at this dynamic. Sying hasn't wanted

to make a fuss when her name is mispronounced, which is part of her wish to fit in and not highlight her otherness. She thinks she's amenable and accommodating, but she sets traps for herself and for others—little tests that people fail, and she stews in the salty broth of disappointment.

We explore her professional development alongside her journey into motherhood. We look at her name, first and surname. Why did Sying never tell people how to pronounce her name correctly? Did she really not care? And why did she change her surname when she got married, even though she loved and preferred her birth name? And why was she so tolerant of not having her name appear anywhere in her work for all these years? She's been complicit in some of the erasure. No one is forcing her to erase herself. She's often minimized the impact of having a child, clinging to a kind of professional pride, which has meant depriving herself of fully embracing this huge change in her life. She's been so adamant about not being tied down by the identity of motherhood, she's denied its reality, escaping into her professional mode. Dismantling the fantasy of her work role, she starts to let in other parts of her life she's pushed away.

Her ambivalence about whether to stay with Victor Hill or exit the firm plays out for a few months. The tension quiets, but the fond gaze doesn't return. Her wholehearted devotion to Victor has faded, along with her motivation to serve him.

We look at what it would mean to be her own person, to make mistakes, to have a sense of her worth that isn't entirely contingent on feedback from others. Naturally, she wants love and respect and support from people, but it's the proportions. She feels a kind of disintegration when people let her down, or she lets them down, and it's emotionally taxing.

Who is she without Victor? A mother? An architect? A wife? A sibling? A friend? A daughter? Yes, of course, she's all these things, and so much more. She begins to gather her strength over time. It's not always easy, and she misses the support of what seemed to be a simple system and team that could hold and carry her, but she's finding her way and she's clearer about the direction of travel. It's a process.

"The intensity of your need for approval makes it hard for you to see what you're stepping into," I say. "You've been so desperate to push forward and design spectacular buildings with Victor, or rather for Victor, you spent years being inattentive to your own structural well-being. You pay attention to the structure of what you build, and now you're building yourself." We talk about how she's been willing to overlook some of Victor's glaring negatives because it felt safer to idealize him. In search of reflected glory. And the loss of that ideal hurts. We talk about the pain of seeing the truth in him and seeing the truth in herself.

"It reminds me of how I felt when I first wore glasses. I remember feeling so upset when I put them on and suddenly saw dirt and grime so clearly. It had been a blur before. I didn't like the clarity. I guess I liked being the golden girl. It kept me from speaking my mind to him," she acknowledges. "I said yes to most things, and told him what he wanted to hear, and did what he wanted me to do. Until I didn't. I'm the one who shifted the dynamic." She takes responsibility for her choices without blaming herself or holding herself responsible for Victor's character.

The feature about Wyatt House does not, in the end, get published. Victor has used his power and influence and connections to kill the piece. Sying learns this from one of the editors, who mumbled that there was nothing he could do. While infuriating, this development is the **decisive moment** for her. She knows she needs to exit now.

"He's trying to erase me," she says through tearful fury. "I know this isn't violence. I know I can't feel sorry for myself, given the brutality that happens to people in the world every day. But I'm raging."

"Erasure is brutal."

"My work is basically who I am. And yet for so long, even though I worked tirelessly, I didn't feel that I was allowed to want my own name as an architect. I thought wanting visibility would seem narcissistic. How did I diminish my worth for so long?" Her distress and sudden horror at what she's put herself through spark a realization that her identity had been in a precariously diminished state.

Over the course of our work together, Sying's motivation shifts from pleasing Victor to making her project happen on her own. "I didn't grow up religious," she says, "so I put my faith into people. I had faith in Victor." But no longer. She wants to have faith in herself now, which is challenging.

When people ask her about her work, she will have to find a new answer. "I can no longer hide behind his impressive name. He used me, but I used him too. I wasn't entirely pure." Her revelations are part of her individuation. It's her professional adolescence—the time of great ambivalence and negotiation around authority.

The harsh snap of disempowerment jostles something within her, an emerging, felt sense of self. Sying wants to scream in Victor's face, find some way to hurt him, punish him, but she recognizes the need for restraint and diplomacy, and she sends him a thoughtful and reserved resignation letter, giving notice.

Sying isn't sure where she'll go next. She has reason to trust that she'll have options and possibilities, even if she doesn't know what or when. In the words of Tennessee Williams in *Camino Real*: "There is a time for departure, even when there's no certain place to go!" She knows it's time for her to exit the limited world of Victor Hill Architect, Ltd. She's relieved by her clarity. It's the culmination of an identity crisis.

There are moments of doubt and second-guessing, unsurprisingly. "In some ways, I feel like no one believes me," she says in the following session.

"No one believes you about what?"

"About Victor Hill, and his ego, and his rivalry with me."

"I think this is about authority, and you're developing your own sense of authority, about your worth, about your experiences. Most people hearing the story would believe you," I say. "And it's up to you how much of the story you choose to say, to whom. There will be superfans who struggle to accept that an architectural elder statesman like Victor Hill is actually a petty egomaniac—but it's still true. And plenty of people know this story in variations. The person who struggles to believe this story is you, Sying."

"True," she says. "And maybe Victor too."

"Victor has been a huge authority figure for you, so it's particularly confusing to see him in a new light, and to see yourself in a new way too, without getting his validation, and that's our work," I say.

Again and again, we tell the story of what's happened and what's happening. And finally, over time, after many narrations and discussions and retellings, like a bedtime story, its familiarity makes it utterly accepted and undeniable. And even a little less obsessive over time. The repetition required for understanding reminds me of French class, where we would write out sentences again and again, all the way down to the bottom of the page. Learning new material requires practice and repetition. And then there's the next page.

"I understand the real story, and feel a bit safer," Sying says. "Not just of Victor, who gave me something, in his greedy way, but also the story of myself: I'm beginning to understand myself. And my worth. I'm more than a server." She will need reminders of this along the way, no doubt. We still have a distance to go. But she's building something of her own now. Not entirely alone. She's recruited a few supporters and advocates, and I'm glad to champion her. But it's her project.

In the countdown days to her departure from Victor Hill Architect, Ltd., she's offered a role at a prominent architecture firm, and she accepts it, promising herself she won't obsess and please in the same way. I don't think she will. There's a sense of potential space and discovery in her emerging identity: she's finding and building a room of her own where she can accommodate and assimilate and organize who she is. We are in an emotional sense packing her up and gathering her belongings from the fifteen years she's been at Victor Hill Architect.

Sying's still furious at Victor and wants to say something to him, even if it isn't a full confrontation, or total justice. She wants to be able to remind herself that she did speak up.

On her last day, she says to him, in front of others, "Victor. Thank you for these past fifteen years, for letting me serve you and work on such exciting projects. Your ideas about identifying the essence of a building—it applies to people too."

He looks flummoxed, and a little vulpine. It doesn't matter. She's said something, and in a way that feels reasonable.

Sying tells me about Frank Lloyd Wright's red square signature. No matter how varied his buildings, he always placed a square red tile somewhere to show that it was his. "He completely erased some of the women who created his buildings, so he's no example for correctness," she says. "But that signature, I want that for myself. No matter how varied the context, how drastically different each project of my life may be, there's something core. I can change, in part because I can hold on to that sense. When I'm picking Katie up from school, designing a sunroom, dealing with my in-laws, talking with a friend, I may show different sides, but I'm Sying wherever I go. I want that signature, not just for what I show the world, but for what I remind myself, for what it means to be me."

This is post-traumatic growth. When we can make meaning in the wake of loss and crisis. The pain of Victor Hill subsides over time. It's a story Sying knows and understands. It's a story about power dynamics and authority, self-worth and competing voices. It's about the inner conflict between the people-pleaser and the ego, and the desire to be known. She's finding out who she is and what she really wants for herself.

Sying knows the themes, the issues. It's a story she can pick up and put down again, like an old book on the shelf. She can locate the story when she wants to, but it doesn't grab her or consume her entire world. Sying has made space for herself, for a larger, more elaborative existence, with various facts and parts and features and roles in the composition of all that she is and could become. Her voice is shaky at moments, uncertain, questioning, little-girlish, and sometimes she's grown-up and confident and in charge.

Motherhood continues to be a struggle for her, but she also has moments of tenderness and pleasure. Perhaps most of all, she loves being an architect. She recognizes some of her inconsistencies, her true motivations and fears. She was surprised that she didn't actually know the real Victor Hill she thought she understood so well and could tame. Nor did she understand herself. But she's clearer now.

UNDERSTANDING WHO YOU ARE

Parts of our personality are formed and fixed, while other parts are mutable, more malleable. When we recognize, identify, and understand the varied nature of our layers, we can build a stable emotional identity and develop a richer sense of what it means to be us. With that, we can face reality with a greater sense of confidence. We can feel more comfortable about the private corners of our minds, our different personas, what it means to be authentic, when we need to wear a mask. Being authentic doesn't mean telling everyone everything. It can mean knowing that you're holding back, recognizing the difference between the public and the private spheres.

Even when we try to show our true selves, we are misunderstood and defined inaccurately so much of the time. Other people don't necessarily know us all that well. How we behave can be quite different from how we feel. One big example of this split is self-confidence versus self-esteem. You might appear to be confident while feeling insecure. You might be depressed and appear to be cheerful. Sometimes these masks are helpful for functioning, but your internal world needs space for care. Once you explore and uncover some of your embedded beliefs and inner conflicts, you are rewarded with a clarity and insight that will help you to navigate life with more ease and strength.

There's a medieval philosophical term "haecceity" that means "thisness"; it's the essence that makes a person singular, like no other person. We can't necessarily explain our thisness or fully capture it in words, but it serves us well for each of us to grasp and hold on to a sense of our own thisness. We are all inimitable and unique. Who we are isn't set in stone, and we all have the capacity to change to a greater or lesser degree, but we can have a kind of internal anchor that keeps us grounded and true (in the sense of both truth and alignment) while other parts of us expand, change, and evolve.

Philosophers and psychologists have long debated whether or not identity changes over time. Are you the same person you were when you were ten years old? Will you be the same person when you're ninety? What's the connecting thread linking the different life stages? The ship of Theseus is a famous philosophical question about the metaphysics of identity. Is an object (the ship) that has had, over time, its components replaced, still fundamentally the same object, the same ship? It's a useful illustration of the idea that there can be a persistent and enduring identity even as there is growth and loss and change and permutation over time. Ideally, we can accept this continuous flow and the way that aspects of our identities are a perpetual work in progress.

Growing and evolving can both threaten and bolster your sense of self. Think of who you were, who you are now, and who you want to become. So it matters enormously to think about who we are, who we were, and who we want to become. Self-knowledge is a continual work in progress, and it's illuminating and expansive when we allow ourselves to be surprised, to change our mind, or to revise our judgment. When you understand yourself well enough, you can recast the roles you play. You can be much more flexible when it comes to embracing change.

While allowing for change and variety and development, think of your signature, the mark that makes you who you are, both internally and what you show the world, no matter how varied the context. Wherever you go, whatever you do, there's a thread of continuity. It's a profound core sense of who you are throughout life, something enduring that connects the different ages and parts and gives you a sense of being uniquely you.

Never stop thinking about what it means to be you. It's a lifelong pursuit.

Chapter Four

POWER

Wanting power feels bald and bold. Like most desires, we receive mixed messages about its acceptability. Power is a central focus in so many cultures. Given that it means influence and authority over others, the blatant pursuit of power often makes us uncomfortable. We talk ourselves out of understanding ourselves when we judge our desire for power, and fear that we'll be judged by others as foolish and greedy, even corrupt. And power can be all of these things. When we consider what it's really about, we can make our own choices.

Some of us are conditioned to undercut ourselves. Or at least we might pretend that's what we're doing. Personal empowerment sounds kinder and more modest; it's power's slightly softer, more demure sister. Empowerment is about seeking personal responsibility and reclaiming confidence to live one's own life. So that ambition seems less intimidating. When someone says she wants to feel empowered, we tend to find it impressive, inspiring. Especially if she's survived something tough, more power to her! But when it comes to wanting power, we tend to wince if the pursuit is too direct.

Our false self does a patchy job managing the PR around wanting power, even inwardly. We cover up our wish for power in one area of life, and then we act like dictators about something else. Or we deny our own possible power and instead attach ourselves to other people's power. We work against ourselves when we're convinced by our show of false modesty. We avoid or pass up opportunities, sacrifice and serve, and give up on pursuing something we've never admitted we wanted. Our desire for power can stay at fantasy level and go into storage for our unlived lives. We can find ourselves enraged and despondent when we feel powerless and we don't understand how this happened.

Starting in childhood, when we feel small and vulnerable, we fantasize about omnipotence. We struggle with dependence. We wish for magical powers that will instantly make us larger-than-life. We often continue to harbor secret longings for power. Although the scenarios change over time, there are power grabs at every stage of life—in babies, toddlers, children, adolescents, adults, well into old age. We see it in the workplace, where petty tyrants try to grab power over the tiniest of issues in order to dominate others. At moments of fragility, people of genuine gravitas still struggle to trust their own power.

We can bend ourselves into pretzels around the ways we do and don't desire power over others. Especially in romantic relationships. People who are initially attracted to power and want powerful partners can still minimize and undermine another person's power in insidious ways. Equality may be the agreed ideal, but power struggles can still threaten relationships.

And the loss of power in a partner is a serious problem too. There's often a wish for partners to show real vulnerability, but then when it happens, it can be a turn-off. It's uncomfortable to admit our real feelings about power, even in a relationship. We often project and deny power in each other as a way of negotiating our own ambivalence.

Power is about being in charge, having influence and authority. It's also about proving significance in the world. Power and control can seem like variations of the same thing, but there are considerable distinctions. There are so many powerful people who are out of control. Controlled and controlling people often don't actually have a huge amount of power. Self-control, and restraint, are in many ways the ability to marshal private power over oneself. To pause instinct and conditioning in order to reflect. But compulsive control, over oneself or over others, is actually at odds with power. It suggests a kind of distrust, an unease in letting go. We can think of powerful leaders who inspire and empower, and we can think of controlling managers who stifle and intimidate. The same applies to how we govern ourselves emotionally. When we trust our power, we can let go of needing to be in absolute control of everything.

Awe for someone else's power can be our way of compensating for the awe we dare not admit we crave for ourselves. It might be a friend, or a crush, or a lover. The loss of these relationships can be quietly devastating. The shame of secret grief is marginalizing and enfeebling. We mourn an affair, a severed friendship, a relationship no one knows about, and we feel alone with the pain and bewilderment. We are suddenly aware of a deep deprivation. We yearn for power and possibility, a sense of glory we tasted.

For Elliot, hidden loss illuminates buried desires for power. But wanting power feels deeply unacceptable. He's strenuously avoided confronting his true wants his whole life. We begin to piece together the motivations that operate in his life, the secrets he's kept from others and the fictions he's believed. When he begins therapy, he feels diminished and invisible. Will therapy empower him?

THE UNTOLD STORY OF ELLIOT

"No one can even know I'm upset," Elliot says. "I haven't even told anyone I'm here, meeting you." A clandestine start, and I'm already part of something secret.

It's our first session, and we've just begun. I ask him what brings him to therapy now, at this moment in his life.

"I'm grieving, but for something, or rather someone, I haven't been able to tell anyone about," he says. "I'm a very private person. I've always kept things to myself. But since this person's death, not talking about this is suddenly killing me." He asks if he can say the name of this someone, as though he needs my consent, and I say yes. He says the name carefully, nervously, and I feel his hot eyes on me to see my reaction.

"Do you know who he is?" he asks.

"I don't recognize the name," I say. "Who is he?"

"Oh, he's a famous actor. Quite well-known in some circles. His death has been on the news. I thought you might have glimpsed the headlines or read some of the obituaries." Elliot looks disappointed.

"I haven't read anything about him. Who was he to you?" I ask.

"Tom? Oh. Who was Tom to me? Who was Tom . . . who was Tom to me . . . ? What a question. He wasn't the Tom I keep reading about in the papers, the great legendary actor. But I don't know who he was, in truth, and I'm not sure who he was to me. I have a better picture of who I was to him, but that's not what you asked. Thank you, by the way, for asking. I've been dying for someone to ask me this sort of question, not that anyone would have reason to. But finally."

His emphasis on particular words gives his sentences a passionate, pressing shape. He sounds Irish. I want to ask, but it can be a mistake to throw out clever guesses. And there's a delicacy. It feels as though he's arrived with suitcases packed full of fragile secrets. He looks contemplative about whatever he's holding. I don't need to pinpoint anything about his life story yet. It will emerge, the facts, the history. He needs space.

Elliot is incredibly tidy and compact in presentation. Clean-cut, with a certain schoolboy charm, he's in his early forties but he could be in his twenties. His jumper looks soft, and his fuchsia socks seem carefully selected. It's a form of self-expression that feels important; these small daily acts of saying who we are can matter.

Elliot has a kind of meditative, sculpted face that is interesting and inviting. Something about him commands me to want to learn more and understand him. In fact, I notice myself sitting on the edge of my seat. But I also feel like I could overwhelm him if I'm too reactive.

He begins to tell the story, and I put my pen down.

"I've been in love with Tom for nearly fifteen years," he says. "Fifteen years. That's a long time. Far too long." He says this in a slightly hesitant, whispery way. He raises his right eyebrow. I'm intrigued and drawn to each word he says. It feels significant to be the sole audience for someone's untold secret story. I value the power of focus.

"The whole time, he's been married to a woman, and they have two grown children who are close in age to me. No one knew about our relationship. Ever. He was petrified of being found out, as was I. And unless I tell the story, no one will ever know about it. It's as if it never happened. I feel like I'm making it up. Did I imagine this whole thing? I know I didn't. It did definitely happen, but it's just vanished. Dust in the air." He draws an upwards sweep with his hands.

"What's your sense of self in all of this?" I ask.

"Well, that's the thing. I have no idea. For so long, I've kept this part of myself hidden, denying its very existence. And it's as if this whole thing, this secret relationship I've kept so separate and out of sight, this was actually me—the real me—the most alive me—and if Tom is dead, all that went with it is gone too. I know I'm still here, but I don't really feel alive right now. I don't want you to think I'm severely mentally ill saying this. Do I sound nuts?"

"You sound incredibly cognizant of what's happening," I say. "Hidden loss is particularly difficult."

"Hidden loss. Yes. The loss is hidden, and I'm hidden. I'm invisible."

"How do you feel invisible?"

"People don't see my pain, my loss. I'm not in Tom's story. His family is. And if Tom can't see me, I'm not sure who I am. Maybe I'm not anyone without him."

"How deeply painful," I say, "to have that sense of yourself in all of this, that you need Tom's perception of you to know you exist."

"Yes, it's as though the best of me died with him, and no one can even be sad about it because it was unknown to everyone but Tom. And Tom is gone. I think I'm still in shock that he's gone. He's really gone. I will never see him again. Everything's changed. It's all gone. The untold story. By an unknown. Jesus. The world thinks I'm the same person I've always been, nothing's changed. Not that the world even gives a shit about me or knows me from Tom, Dick, or Harry."

"I didn't know who Tom was until you told me," I say.

Elliot smiles and his eyes look deeply sad.

We acknowledge the sheer enormity of this loss, holding space for what's never been spoken about. The invisible mourner is visible here.

"You're the first person I've ever told any of this to—my involvement with Tom," Elliot says. "Just as this whole thing ends."

"Carrying this secret around for fifteen years—what a heavy load you have borne. I'm glad you're telling me," I say. The story feels intensely close.

"I actually liked carrying this secret around in a lot of ways. First of all, my girlfriend would probably find me disgusting and leave me. Second of all, my family in Ireland and my friends, the idea of them knowing I've been, you know, with a man—any man—no way; I don't want that known. But also, I've felt proud. When I see his name in the news or watch him on telly, which I once did in Dublin with my gran and loads of relatives, I knew I had a special secret. I knew stuff about him that no one else on the planet knew. I liked keeping it secret. But it's different now that he's dead, just entirely different. That's the bit that's surprised me so much. His death was sudden, so maybe that's part of the shock. . . . It's this secret part of my life that's just vanished. For all my mixed feelings of shame and pride, now there's nothing left of it. . . . It's all gone. . . . Not a single token, no whiff of scandal, no acknowledgment. I guess this is what it must be like to get away with a crime." He looks like he's groping for something, a grain of insight, a foothold to find his bearings.

"Am I sexually attracted to men?" he asks.

This is a question he asks me repeatedly in our session. And he adds this as a reason he's come to therapy: to find out if he's gay.

He's been living with his girlfriend for ten years, and he's fond of her, and bored sexually, and what if it turns out he's gay and was meant to live an entirely different life?

He was ambivalent about sex with Tom. He would have been a top if it were up to him, but Tom was always the top and so he was the bottom, and that was nonnegotiable. He never told Tom he would have liked to try a different position. Always wanting to accommodate and prioritize Tom's pleasure over his own, he enjoyed serving and gratifying Tom's longings. This felt more important than anything he might have personally desired. In fact, he felt important by pleasing him. "Knowing I was giving him what he wanted, sexually, that thrilled me erotically too. That mattered most to me. Gosh, thinking about that makes me tear up. Sex with Tom surpassed any other experience I've ever had. I was so powerful with him."

I feel he's swapped roles not just in top and bottom but in his sense of power. Tom was clearly powerful to him. And Elliot's power came from having power over this powerful man.

"Tom fancied me," he says. "He'd go weak in the knees looking at me. He once said to me when he undressed me, 'Look at you.' Those three words."

Elliot's awe, his desire to be seen, is for himself, but it's netted in Tom's desire. His sense of self seems to have been rooted as the object of desire, and what a powerful feeling, in the moment. Lots of moments. But it's a risky game to be the secret object of desire with someone who is powerful, impressive, mercurial, intimidating.

"It was the heightened consciousness I felt with him," he says. "I just felt so entirely alive. So observed. So wanted, even in a deranged way. I liked that." He suddenly looks stricken. "Oh God, what if Tom was the love of my life, and now he's dead? Am I completely screwed and hopeless?"

Elliot came of age at just the wrong moment, he feels. He grew up in a Catholic family in Ireland and was a teenager in the nineties, when homosexuality and sexual experimentation were still frowned upon deeply. The ferocity of his homophobia is clear, and I point this out to him again and again. He says it's true, he dislikes the idea of gayness, but he's also outraged and bothered by homophobes, especially people he grew up with.

Imagine his life had he been born ten years later. He might have had the chance to experiment with other men and discover his real sexual preferences, his real identity. He'd have had the freedom to taste different things. If he wanted to be gay, he could have been gay. And for all he knows, he might have discovered that, in fact, he isn't attracted to men after all. He might have been more at ease with his attraction to being the object of Tom's desire without that threatening his very existence.

If only Elliot had been born thirty years earlier; then he and Tom could have lived together, would have made it as a couple. Or would they? He pictures them living in Provence, sipping rosé and discussing film. Is this pure fantasy? Even if it is, he's still convinced by its lure. Scrap the life with Tom, he says, interrupting his own reverie. Imagine if he was attracted only to women. He'd have a wife and maybe some kids by now, and he wouldn't feel tormented by this conflict. Fiercely envious of these fantasy alternate lives, alternative-self versions, he struggles to accept his life as it is. And he struggles to accept himself.

"Do you think I'm gay?" he reverts to asking me repeatedly.

I still can't answer that question, not for him and not for anyone. I talk to him about how sexuality is different from sexual orientation. He says he fantasizes about some men but certainly not all. Sex with his girlfriend is extremely dull and feels like a chore, but doesn't this happen over time with all relationships? he asks.

"I'm stultified," he says one afternoon near the end of a session. He looks dazed. Great word. "Stultified" sums it up. "Not just in my love life, but at work too. It's not going anywhere, my role. When I'm not obsessing over Tom, how much time do I spend complaining about how Joanne treats me?"

"Quite a bit," I say. Joanne is his line manager at work. He often starts sessions with a list of slights from Joanne and speculations about what she really thinks of him and theories about why she's such a bitch. He seems chronically annoyed by the situation, but we are yet to reach any sense of what resolution or progress would even look like. He seems disaffected and somewhat resigned.

"You must be so bored hearing about her. She blocks me in so many ways. I'm beyond frustrated," he says, looking dejected.

"Beyond frustrated," I repeat back to him. "Let's go further. If you weren't consumed with frustration, then what?"

"No bloody idea," Elliot says.

We pause and sit in silence for a few moments.

Elliot admits that he resents how much time he spends talking about others in this space that's meant to be entirely his own. I wonder if I can galvanize him to own his space, to put him in charge of his life. I feel a déjà vu from my work with other clients. Themes and issues overlap, but I also contribute to the shape of this work. I suddenly feel the responsibility of having power in this way.

"Elliot, I feel like you give other people prime real estate in your mind, and you push yourself into a tiny corner. Where are you in all of this?" I ask.

"Not a clue," he says. "A speck in the margin. Can you locate me?"

"This needs to come from you. You cannot google who you are. Yes, the world and fresh experience and other people come into your life story, but there's a lot to be said for cultivating an inner sense of what it is to be you. I want to know more about you."

"That's it," he says. "I want it to be up to me. I don't even care about what exactly; I just want to be in charge. But I don't know how. At work, forget it. I'll never have the power I want. Sitting here, right now, I feel a surge of something. But is there any point in going further with it?"

"Tell me more," I say.

"I have to admit, I kind of want power," he says, in a way I can only describe as coy.

"That's interesting. I'm glad you can recognize it and say it aloud. Can you say it again?"

"I want power. That sounds absurd," he says. "Power."

This time he says the word "power" precisely, specifically, his eyes widening. He winces, as though startled by the discovery of scandal.

"Am I allowed to want that?" his voice has returned to the usual more reticent tone.

"Of course you are," I say. "It's entirely human, and understandable. How interesting that you think you need my permission. I'm also struck that you said you can't be in charge at work. I've never heard you say you want that—to be in charge professionally and have more power. I wonder if that's part of the underlying tension between you and Joanne."

"Joanne and me? Oh my goodness, I've never even thought of that possibility. Do you think I might want her job? Gosh . . . I suppose I wouldn't mind. I'd do it better, that's for sure. Jesus, no wonder she's seen me as a thorn in her side. Here I am, believing in my own innocence, but fair play to her sniffing me out."

Elliot's face flushes and he looks shocked by these discoveries. He thought his outrage was about Joanne's way of treating him, but it's also about his desire to have her job. His desires have been under-ground or kept secret. No wonder he's felt stultified.

"Can I have any power now?" he asks. He misses the power he felt with Tom initially. The power of feeling so wanted. And seen. And alive. And the power of being connected, even if secretly, to this formidable famous man. "Having Tom inside my body, it's like he injected me with significance."

His girlfriend, and his sense of self with her, represent nothing but ordinary dullness.

"It used to be a bit exciting. We were curious about each other. I know we were, but that's faded," he says.

Their dynamic has gone from nose-to-nose adoration to side-by-side complacency. They spend tons of time together, but they don't really engage with one another. They're on their phones; they're watching TV; they're in their own worlds, coexisting inside their cramped flat. They're autopilot flatmates more than lovers.

"We have this dreary beige carpet, full of stains. We can't be bothered to change it. We don't take our shoes off, and we bring in more muck. We hoover. We spill wine on it and we clean it up. Some of the stains come out, but even then, it's just an old beige carpet. We barely notice it, but it adds no joy."

Elliot's **found object**—the beige carpet—becomes pivotal in the tapestry of his life story. He trusts himself enough to sift through and select the details that shape him. We need to assemble the de-tails that texture our lives to make sense of who we are and what we want.

He and his girlfriend have never been particularly passionate, "but we got on with each other. In a pleasant, warm-bath kind of way," he says. How did they get together? It was all so circumstan-tial. Through friends. Respectable, lovely friends. Much about his life has felt circumstantial, comme il faut, decided by what's accept-able. This is why he's middle management in advertising instead of being an artist, he explains. It was the sensible path with his skills.

"I think I suffer from the disease of conformity," he says, looking almost despondent. "I didn't dare rock the boat. I just admired the boat rockers from the sidelines." He and Tom met at a glamorous party, a rarity for Elliot, an everyday occurrence for Tom. Elliot was shocked when Tom asked for his number. They had secret phone calls for weeks, and they plotted and imagined how they'd meet again. Terrified and excited, Elliot gave in, breaking all his rules, choosing something reckless and unusual for the first time in his life. Their passion for each other seems both true and made-up the way passionate stories often do. Like most affairs: part reality, part fantasy.

Was the affair with the famous actor the most exciting, most adventurous thing Elliot's ever done? I ask this at a moment when he is pouring out his unbearable pain, and I regret my timing. Strike when the iron is cold in therapy, not burning hot.

"Yes. And what if that's it?" he asks with a look of anguish. "What if he's the great adventure, the big story of my life, and there's nothing ahead?"

I suggest that this is just part of his story. Not his entire life, but part of the rich tapestry of his existence. "Tom and the beige carpet—that's the whole arc of my story," Elliot says. Of course, it's painful that Elliot's life with Tom is over, and what was an exciting secret is now an invisible, voiceless, vanished piece of the past, scrubbed. Like debris on the beige carpet. He reverts to feeling his own weightless insignificance.

"I don't matter," he says. "My voice, whoever I am. I'm nobody."

"You're here, telling me this story," I say. I think of Rebecca Solnit's wisdom at the end of her essay about powerful men and sexual inequality: "Nobody is nobody." I think of this line constantly. Someone powerful like Tom may have exploited Elliot precisely because he felt that Elliot would never use his voice, have power, or tell the story.

Part of the confusion for Elliot is his continued vacillation between feeling diminished and feeling enhanced by the whole thing. "I haven't felt significant outside of my relationship with Tom, maybe ever." And then in a softer voice: "I would like to."

Admitting that he'd like to feel significant in his own right is a revelation. We continue to look at his embarrassment and fear about thinking too highly of himself. His father mocked him for being soft as a child, and his mother instructed him to be stronger than he felt.

"I don't want to overestimate myself and be one of those fools. You know, with notions. My family would laugh at me if they heard any of this," he says.

We explore the cultural norms of his family of origin that demanded avoidance of boasting at all costs, required that he self-deprecate regularly, that characterized anything remotely like showing off as vulgar and uncouth.

Tom, a huge show-off and performer himself, wanted Elliot to enjoy being himself, be flamboyant, make droll quips, feel impressive. Elliot was enthralled by this power, even if it took place secretly. They were both enthralled by each other, at least for a time.

"He was a great raconteur," Elliot says. He starts to tell me some of the stories. I urge him to tell me more of his own, rather than trying to impress me with Tom's big life. He squashes himself down in size in these rhapsodic, nostalgic recollections. While Tom is magnified, Elliot reduces himself to being the awestruck observer.

Seeking reflected glory, Elliot sails close to the wind of his secretly grandiose fantasies, claiming significance by proxy through this legendary, powerful man. The world lionizes Tom (though perhaps not as much as Elliot thinks), which adds to Elliot's sense of being unknown. But the link to this great actor also gives Elliot a strong feeling of specialness.

"I feel like Tom is my lifeline for mattering in any way. What happens now? What can I do with the story?" he asks. It's his story. He needs me to hear his story so he will know he has told it fully to someone. Or as fully as possible. There's always more. But I know the details, the events, the diverse feelings. My bearing witness consoles him and fills in that part of him longing desperately for acknowledgment and recognition. I hold space. His story moves me too, and not just for its beauty but also for its horror. The toxicity of the entanglement, the cruelty, the deceit, the requisite phoniness in pulling off their long, intermittent affair—it's quite brutal at moments. It's the powerful truth that our desires can be painful and destructive.

I convey my distress and retrospective concern for Elliot as he lived through it, as well as my empathy for how he got himself so enmeshed and overwhelmed and seduced.

"Where am I?" Elliot asks, returning to feeling bereft and devastated. "And who am I outside of this story?"

We consider the Pygmalion aspects of their dynamic, how he feels like a piece of shapeless clay without the sculptor, Tom, helping him become something. Tom's sculpting was quite self-serving, without any evident intention to help Elliot to a better life. Elliot continues to feel painfully excluded, not just by this man but by the whole world, in so many ways.

"Tom has only just died," Elliot says, "but I was grieving him throughout. He'd love me so passionately, and it was the best thing on the planet, but then he'd vanish, and he'd look elsewhere, or he'd retreat, back to his life, away from me. I spent years chasing that feeling of power I'd had with him, again and again and again. I'd do just about anything to get it back each time. I was constantly yearning and grieving the loss of that high, and then I would have him again for a while. The secrecy was part of the high, and maybe the scarcity too, as much as it tormented me. I always knew it wouldn't last forever."

He's grieving what he never had enough of. There's a sense of deprivation in Elliot's life, not just in this experience. What's obvious but still revelatory for me is how isolated we feel when we're in the throes of these tumultuous moments. Enthralling entanglements can feel sharp and original, and our experiences feel special and disconnecting from everyone else.

"I get it," I say. "Of course this is hard for you. What you're describing is as addictive as crack in some ways. And the fact that it was with this famous man gave you so much shame, and also so much pride, as you say. And a deep and continued attachment—even to something and someone that's a source of misery."

"Is there a term for what's happening to me? Why am I holding on to this connection?" he asks, looking hungry for an explanation.

"**Trauma bonding**," I say instantly. "We can get incredibly attached to the sources of our pain, and it's hard to let go, even when we desperately want to move on. The person who hurt you is the person who can restore your sense of self. This is the fantasy that keeps you hooked."

"That's it. It's the fantasy version of myself that I miss so much. He would look at me with such desire," Elliot says. "He wanted to consume me. And then he would ignore me. And now dying on me, and leaving me out of his story—it's the ultimate rejection."

"You're hurting and rejecting yourself too," I say, "leaving yourself out of your own story and making him the prime subject." It's a struggle, but finding his voice, telling the story, can give him authority.

In the following session, he's read up on trauma bonding and it's resonated.

"I still want his approval, because he's the one who hurt me, so he's the one who can make me feel better. I don't want to link this too closely to my parents, because they weren't abusive, but there were some elements of this. The depriver has such power. And now, realizing all of this, looking back, I'm just so sad," he says. "I'm sad for the young me. As cocky as it sounds, the beautiful me. I'm feeling so much right now."

"Wow. I get it, and you're describing the tricky issues of consent and power dynamics. I have to say, you keep talking about the power you felt when he wanted you, but what you've just described—your obeying his impulses, aiming to make yourself and keep yourself the object of his desire—that's not real power."

"I guess not. I guess it made me the object of his desire, which I enjoyed and suffered from."

After a brief pause, he continues: "I never confronted him. I never told him I loved him and he hurt me. Why didn't I confront him? I'm so angry at myself for never standing up to him."

"Though you may have felt powerful at moments, as we've just discussed, those moments were fleeting, moment by moment. He held sway. You were so deeply impressed. That makes confrontation pretty overwhelming. Confronting someone powerful, and famous, who has traumatized you in some ways is unbelievably hard," I say. "Stop beating yourself up for thinking it should have been easy and you could have managed it."

"I'm so mad at myself for not being braver."

We look at how he continues to beat himself up, and in this way he holds on to the pain Tom caused him. Elliot discovers, in this moment, some of the reasons he avoided confrontation. He didn't think confronting Tom would help. He didn't want him to know the depths of torment he caused. He was intimidated. He was afraid Tom might respond in a way that could hurt him further. Whatever the reasons, on some level, it felt like self-preservation not to confront him. He begins to let go of some of the self-flagellations.

"I feel myself forgiving myself, which is pretty empowering. There's something to be said for facing this stuff."

"You're confronting yourself, which takes courage. Confronting yourself, as opposed to attacking yourself or avoiding parts of yourself, might feel a little bit new?"

"Yes. I've avoided confronting myself my whole life, in some ways. Maybe I can thank him for that. There's still so much material here, so much that I never got to say to him."

"And? What would you say to him?"

"Let me go . . . want me. Let me matter to you as much as you matter to me." Elliot lowers his head. "He got me. Is this where the story ends?"

"It's your story. You tell me," I say.

"Everything feels so mundane after Tom. Airports. Cafés. People on the street. Online food shopping. It's all so unexceptional. Things felt exceptional with Tom."

"And you feel unexceptional without him?"

"Yes, I do. They say never to meet your heroes. He wasn't exactly my hero when I met him, but he became one. And my villain. And the main plot."

"He doesn't have to be the main plot for the rest of your life. You're still here, and this is your life, not his. Keep going."

"But it's nothing exciting, my life," he says.

"Not at this moment. I love a line quoted by Freud: 'What we cannot reach flying, we must reach limping.' Allow yourself to limp along for now. You can't instantly substitute something for the thrill of Tom, but you can limp along and open yourself to possibilities. There's so much more for you."

"Possibilities . . . I'm struggling to consider anything beyond him. Right now, it feels tragic and final, the story of Tom and Elliot," he says, suddenly fighting tears.

"Elliot, I think by insisting that this is a tragedy, you're still elevating it to something; you're making it more powerful than you. If it isn't tragic, maybe the story also feels less exceptional. It's as if in your bid to feel exceptional, you have to at least be part of a grand tragedy, not just a tale."

"Yes, better to live tragically than be boring and insignificant."

"I get that. But in your tragic version, you're still not casting yourself fairly," I say.

"I feel so small. And he looms so large. Tom was my star." Elliot says these words and looks sad. "And now I'm just in the gutter, looking up at the stars. Oscar Wilde."

"There's a reason the mystery is part of that enchantment. There's space for longing, for fantasy, for endless imagination. The fact that you and Tom never lived a normal beige-carpet existence is part of what keeps the sheen on this story. You never slipped into the side-by-side ordinary life that happens with true commitment and long-term love at different times. So it's got the elixir of absence, of scarcity, of fantasy, and now, with his death, the deprivation and space is even greater, the longing even fiercer. The sense of what's **unpotentiated** has expanded. Of course everything else feels dull by comparison."

"Yes. Everything else is so beige. The mystery is so binding, so mesmerizing, not just for how I saw him, but for how he saw me. The physical attraction. It was out of this world. And I still try to impress him sometimes. Even though he's dead. The other day, I tried on a Sunspel jumper and wondered if he'd fancy me in it."

"Many of us try to impress dead or absent people at moments. You're still grieving and trying to hold on to his elevated perception of you. Be kind to yourself."

"I know I'm asking again, but is this where my story ends? Back to dreary shops, back to Starbucks mutterings, boring sex, decent conversations with mates, surface-level conversations with cousins in Ireland each summer, unexciting work meetings, the odd meal out, customer-service-life admin, frustrating emails with Joanne?"

"You keep asking me about your story's ending. First of all, I'm not writing it for you, and nor is Tom, or some predetermined tragic fate. I want more for you, I must admit. Ordinary days, certainly, because that's part of any steady life. But there's still room for the extraordinary even in daily existence. This is where your story begins, in some ways," I say.

"I want to believe you," he says. "But I still worry Tom is the most fascinating thing about me."

"I can't dissuade you at this moment," I say. "But let's just consider this: there's what you're born with, there's what happens to you, and there's what you make of it. This is the part that's up to you. That's where you have power. He's a footnote in your story, and you'll never have not known him and had this intense experience. But a footnote isn't the whole thing. It's a detail, and maybe a formative one. But it's still your story. You're reclaiming your power, or even discovering your power, in telling me, and yourself, this story. Your voice is your authority, not Tom. You can now have a different kind of power. Tom elevated you, degraded you, ignored you. And occasionally elevated you again. It's the addictive cycle of **intermittent reinforcement**. It's like playing against the house and hoping you'll win each time. It's a powerful cycle, but it's not real power."

"The power he gave me was fleeting at best. True. Real power . . . What does that even mean for me? I must confess that sometimes I wonder if I'm actually afraid of being too powerful. Of letting myself shine."

"Tell me more."

"I'm pretty self-sabotaging in certain ways. Maybe this is my moment to shine quietly. Not onstage. Not in the press. Not via Tom. But in facing myself and being in cahoots with myself. That's it: I want to be in cahoots with myself."

"What an interesting kind of power," I say. "In cahoots with yourself—I love that."

So what happened next in Elliot's life story? He didn't suddenly and dramatically quit his job. It turned out he didn't need or want to. But he became more assertive, and less snarky, in his communications with Joanne. He applied for a promotion he wasn't particularly excited about, but he still applied. He understood that he wanted more professional power, and even if it made him squeamish, he could know it for himself.

The big choice he made was to tell his girlfriend about Tom and about his occasional attraction to men. She was distraught, but he was glad he'd been honest. He suspected they'd split up, but at least she knew him now, and he could be himself for the first time.

Having felt powerless about his sexuality for so long, Elliot began to accept that it was his life to live. What had been a source of shame was no longer something that reduced the size of his own worth. He felt strong enough to acknowledge and embrace the range of his sexual preferences, a power he had longed for and feared most of his life. He was curious to have new sexual experiences. He wanted to be a top as well as a bottom. He didn't want his role to be fixed. His willingness to finally express his different desires said a lot about his relationship with power; he began to let his own longings and preferences matter. His purpose was about more than pleasing and obeying someone else. He no longer felt like the beige worn-out carpet.

Part of his life experience had been this long and complicated affair with this older famous actor. He didn't have to tell the story to the world. But he knew the story for himself, and he'd told me, and his girlfriend. And maybe he would tell a few others if he wanted to. It was his story to tell. Or not tell. Up to him.

WHAT POWER MEANS

The philosopher Bertrand Russell argued that the desire for power is universal and insatiable: "To those who have but little of power and glory, it may seem that a little more would satisfy them, but in this they are mistaken: these desires are insatiable and infinite . . ." How untrue this felt for Elliot. Sometimes the power we think we want isn't actually desirable up close. It takes a mature and confident person to see this and change the direction of travel.

Power can corrupt and destroy our sense of self and how we treat others. We know its dangers, and its cruelties. We know about Machiavellian leaders and demonic and ruthless power moves. We know about the horror of power dynamics in abuse scenarios, and we also know about the quieter but still damaging power manipulations that play out in **frenemyships**, in rivalries, in financial feuds, in family dynamics.

The psychologist Dacher Keltner studied the relationship between empathy and power and discovered that the very qualities that helped people gain power—empathy, fairness, sharing—began to fade once these people became powerful. Powerful people can become oblivious and insensitive to the experience of others. This is always worth thinking about, for anyone who gains power or is drawn to charismatic, powerful people.

Rebecca Solnit warns us: "Overreach is perilous . . . enough is enough," she says. "And too much is nothing." Grasping for power leaves us with deformed reflections of ourselves. Equality gives us honest mirroring. For Elliot, his appetite for power comes from starvation. He's felt deeply inadequate and insubstantial, not just going back to his relationship with Tom, but starting in his childhood. Desperation can drive us to have ravenous desires. Once Elliot had a sense of **enoughness**, he didn't need as much.

There are times when the desire for power is beautiful and life enhancing. But when our longing for power is an attempted compensation for a lifelong deficit, we often zigzag between swelling visions of glory and crashing despair. Embrace flexibility and moderation.

Power can be about authenticity and authority. It can be our way of claiming adulthood, recognizing our responsibility for living our lives.

When you think of the personal power of your voice, consider some of the messages and attitudes you've absorbed. There may have been times when you felt encouraged or discouraged to trust the power of your own voice. Consider how you can have healthy power as an individual, where you can make your own choices and have internal authority. You may be handing over power, or seizing it, in how you scale and size yourself and others in your mind. Consider some of the ways you reduce and magnify your sense of self and others. All too often, we want to feel big and claim space and then we worry that we'll be rejected for it: we fear that we'll be "too much" for other people.

Agency, authority, and responsibility come into personal empowerment and power. We can have enough awareness to make choices that align with our values. It's up to us to prioritize and sift through the knots so that we have agency and **congruence**.

Chapter Five

ATTENTION

In my work, I observe, notice, bear witness, and make sense of what's happening. Curiosity is key. A therapist with zero curiosity is an insult. Curiosity is our way in and it's what directs and guides attention. The shared curiosity of a great therapy session can be the key that turns in the lock and opens the door to new insights.

Wanting attention is utterly human but it's still stigmatized. "That's so attention-seeking" is a common line dispirited adults say when people act out. It gets said of the addict, the anorexic, the self-harmer, the exhibitionist, the drama queen. We often describe people as attention-seeking as a way of justifying our frustration. Underneath attention-seeking behavior lies a plea to be witnessed, however disguised and painful.

Let's consider the urge for attention. We see it in the playground when small children want their parents to see them climb high. ("Watch me! Watch me!") We see it in insistent anecdotage: we all know the ageing raconteur who requires a perpetual audience and needs applause from young acolytes and sycophants. We are less forgiving of grown-ups who crave attention: attention seeking is the birthright of babies and children. But the desire doesn't necessarily expire. We just try to banish it. "Take a picture of me before I vanish into a handful of dust," a man I knew would ask me. This went on for years, and he is now a handful of dust. But his requests to be noticed and savored were honest and sympathetic. Our desire for attention tends to be extremely exaggerated, or minimized, and often disavowed. We struggle to be direct and undramatic about this desire. It's vulnerable to ask for proof that we're noticed and cared for.

We're socialized to pretend not to need much attention. We're supposed to outgrow the desperate need to show off, so we try to show off discreetly instead. We act gracious and faux-modest to make ourselves more bearable. Our **bootleg desires** set up covert attention bids, fussing over others, hiding our true intentions behind someone else's needs—caring for others and voicing our concerns about them, in order to be seen ourselves in turn. Pride and shame are viciously effective in convoluting our desire for attention. We want people to witness our existence. Who are we if no one knows what's going on in our lives? Even the most private types among us, those who may not want to live out loud on social media, still want to be noticed or acknowledged by someone. Over here! Ignore me! Never mind!

But the terror of vanishing into the dark night, the horror of being forgotten, unwitnessed, or replaced, stirs people to behave appallingly. Beneath the staggering theatrics and absurd behaviors, characters such as King Lear and the wicked stepmother in *Snow White*, with her mirror, are desperate not to lose their place. Having had lots of attention, they want reassurance about their visibility and status. They behave like spiteful horrors. But their wants are understandable, just vainly concealed.

The desire to be noticed has always been an essential part of the human condition. But the need to be witnessed can never be fulfilling when it's compulsive, dependent, and based on exaggerated ego ideals. What is enough? People who aren't getting enough attention often struggle to pay attention. And paying attention can diminish the need for attention. When we find a way to give full focus to a conversation, a book, or a project, the need for others to pay attention to us can recede and feel less desperate.

Noticing and giving attention is both crucial and challenging. Consider the language we use. Paying attention. Giving attention. What does it cost us to pay and give these things? Children are pushed to pay attention, often to things that don't interest them. Being interested and having the ability to focus are essentials for learning and developing. It's how we learn to discern, to be observant.

We express love and care through attention. Paying attention to one another is how we connect, engage, grow. "We have an innate survival instinct, a drive to be aware and alert to our environment," the psychiatrist Gurmeet Kanwal said to me in conversation. "It's a core part of being human, noticing what's going on. Attention organizes our experiences."

How do we get attention? Sometimes we shake our fist in the air; we scream, we shout, we fire missiles. Even forms of panic and severe anxiety can be considered roundabout ways of soliciting attention. Our bodies might express what we struggle to say. Sometimes we sulk and retreat, hoping, on some level, that making ourselves scarce and withdrawing our attention will get us the attention we deserve.

Life is dynamic; we move on to new contexts, new things happen to and around us. We crave attention at some moments more than others. As with food, our appetites vary, and we need refills and top-ups and repeated helpings.

This comes into therapy in so many ways, and crucially, for the therapist too. "Feeling unnoticed by clients is just about the worst feeling," a very pale, very timid colleague once said to me. He'd had an operation and had missed a week of sessions and, having told his clients why he needed to take those days off work, not one of them asked him how he was upon his return.

"I didn't want them to ask me how the op went. I'd been dreading dealing with their questions. But then not a single person even enquired or acknowledged that anything had been going on for me," he said. We were on the Tube, rocketing through a tunnel, and he spoke so softly I could hardly make out his words, but what he said has stayed with me. This quiet man, who would awkwardly apologize to furniture he bumped into, wanted to be thought about by his clients.

Watch me! Watch me! This song continues for so many of us throughout life. Do we ever feel sufficiently witnessed? Do we ever get enough applause? When we are alone, with no one to bear witness, to keep applauding, what happens? It depends on how we keep ourselves company. Can we be curious about ourselves? Can we pay ourselves attention? I remember thinking that attention deficit disorder (ADD) was about not getting enough attention.

There are times when there's a link between struggling to pay attention and struggling to get it. When we encounter people who seem desperate for attention, just ravenous, they are often the same people who can't listen, who have difficulty granting attention to others, as if there is a shortage, not enough attention to go around. When we don't feel attended to, we are less likely to want to pay full attention.

Conversely, paying attention is also part of the cure.

"I haven't looked into my children's eyes for a very, very long time," a client of mine confided to me at a moment of deep discovery. "I've been so angry at my husband and at my life, I forgot to notice these beautiful creatures we created." She began noticing. More and more. And noticing her children helped her feel less wounded. Attending to them in a deep, attuned way healed something for her. By really seeing, she felt less deprived.

It's not one or the other, of course. Think of the early days of a love romance, when lovers marvel and gaze, and see and feel seen, in a kind of mutual rhapsodic dance. The symmetry is magnificent. But when we are feeling deeply unseen, we often react by withdrawing our own attention, by refusing to see, disengaging in subtle and not-so-subtle ways. The willingness to open our eyes and observe takes courage and can be reparative. We can feel less needy when we see what's outside of ourselves.

Let's be honest about our wish for attention. For adults, it's oddly taboo. My seven-year-old son recently said he wishes he were a baby so he could get lots of attention. And yet he feels easily smothered if I offer him too much focus. Who in the world hasn't felt this way at some point? When we say "Go away! Leave me alone!" we may not think we want attention, but we may still long for someone to see us, even when we hide.

CHLOE'S DRAMA

"I had everything ahead of me," Chloe says, her skin dry, her eyes bulging, her hair uncombed and wild. She is spectacularly beautiful still, but she's aging, and right now she's a hot mess. Chloe is close to fifty-five, and the gods have been generous to her in some ways and harsh in others. She's a fiercely bright human rights lawyer, with a beautiful face and figure, so by some accounts she's lucky. But the aging process might be kinder if she weren't drinking so voraciously, bingeing, and purging compulsively—which she might do less if life felt more merciful to her. But the combination of misery, bitterness, seething resentment, disordered eating, and severe alcoholism hasn't helped her face. I feel guilty for noticing this and judging her appearance, but it's also a significant part of her story.

Chloe's beauty is something that has helped and hindered her. It's opened countless doors and given her instant access to entire worlds. When I say she's beautiful, it's hard to explain. I try to describe her when I meet with my supervisor, and I try to describe her to myself while I'm sitting across from her, because her looks are distracting, consuming, such a part of what it means to be in a room with her. Her features are sparkly and inviting and yet she looks drawn. When she tilts her head in moments of sorrow, I'm sometimes struck by her exquisite profile.

Chloe is French, but she grew up in a variety of cities around the world, and she speaks English with an urbane, internationally educated accent, saying "No?" at the end of most sentences. There's a false and provocative innocence in her face, combined with something hyperfeminine. Even in her depleted state, her looks distract me, and I'm certain other mental health professionals have been bamboozled by her appearance. She's seductive, she's mesmerizing, she's charismatic. These are distractions when someone is in desperate need of help and challenging support.

Her biggest struggle is her resistance and her defensiveness. She is insistent that her ex-husband, Graham, is the villain of her life story. It's very hard to get her to even consider self-authorship as a concept. The need for exceptionalism—special treatment—plays out in our work together. She's exceptional for how I think of her, and despite many personality traits that could put her into categories such as borderline personality disorder, she cannot simply be defined by a set of standard criteria and slotted into a diagnostic category. She's not exactly a type. Not a typical personality disorder, not a typical addict. But she's also not above the normal rules and impulses and pitfalls of ordinary mortals. This is the thing about addicts: being special doesn't mitigate the tragedy.

"I had everything ahead of me," she says again, "and Graham came along, and he destroyed me. He talked me into making a life with him, and he misled me. He lied to me. He robbed me!"

"How did he rob you?" I ask.

"All my beauty, my skills, my vast potential. He took it all. Everyone wanted to marry me. Do you know how many people were obsessed with me? In love with me?"

"Many," I say, because she's told me several times. And I can imagine.

"I had so many options. And countless more men could have given me a better life had he not taken me away. He robbed me of the life I was meant to have," Chloe says, looking anguished and angular. She seems adamant that her trajectory be tragic in some way. I'm often aware of the language she uses—"the life I have" rather than "the life I live." On another occasion I ask about the things she could have done, and she responds with a litany of all the things she could have had.

It's hard to respond to these statements after so many months of patient (I feel) listening. I feel restless and concerned by her fossilized narrative. I want to tell her she's acting like a victim, but I know that if I name this, I will be cast as the cruel villain. I'm also pregnant while working with her, which adds, possibly, to my own ambivalence about giving so much to her.

"Chloe," I say, sometimes hoping that, by saying her name, it will help her realize the force of my wish to get through to her. "I hear everything you're saying. But I also want to say that you still have a big life ahead of you. Your work as a human rights lawyer is meaningful. Your children and friends care about you. You have siblings who have tried repeatedly to get you help. And you're coming here, week after week, ostensibly wanting help. Let me help you."

"Charlotte, no one listens to me. Graham is so horrible to me. The kids take his side. My friends take his side. Even my parents and brothers take his side. Why are *you* taking his side?"

"I'm not taking his side," I say. "But I want you to recognize that you can have authority over your own life. He is not in charge of your entire life story."

"He's the father of my children, though. It's hard to ignore him."

"I'm not suggesting you ignore him. I'm wondering if we can think about who you are in all of this, your sense of self, your voice." I'm repeating myself, and I've said this in variations countless times. In the words of John Updike, I'm trying to "transform[ing] pain into honey," and this is a failed part I play over and over. Repetition is the theme of our work, for both of us. Chloe is, in many ways, entrapped by repetition compulsions all over the place: her drinking rituals, her bingeing and purging cycles, her circular fights with her ex-husband, and her parents, and her siblings. And our sessions are full of repetition and circularity. Something isn't holding. Repetition compulsion is essentially about resistance. Chloe repeats what she resists remembering. The resistance is to this process—to therapy together.

I feel stuck with her, resentful of our appointments, angry when I have to chase payments, screwed over by her when she fails to show up for appointments we've scheduled, so that I sit waiting for her, without a call or message of explanation, leaving me feeling undervalued.

And even when Chloe is sitting across from me, we are like Saul Steinberg cartoons, talking right past each other, meeting but really not engaging in a meaningful, changing way. For all the repetitive talk that occurs between us, very little is actually said or heard. I offer interpretations and she doesn't hold on to them, which feels analogous to her bingeing and purging: for all the filling, very little gets retained. The nurture, the nourishment—where is it going? I feel wasted.

My supervisor has challenged my continued work with her. Chloe is still drinking, which is enough for some therapists to terminate the work. But not for me. I vacillate between feeling heroic and virtuous, the only person who can help her and save her, to feeling frustrated and persecutory when she inevitably fails to let me help her. I also feel like the victim. It feels futile to work with an addict who is using and repeating and forgetting a great deal. But I'm locked in the dynamic too—a little enmeshed, a little dangerously hopeful that I can rescue her.

By day, Chloe's work as a human rights lawyer is when she feels strongest in some ways—when she's helping true victims. A feisty advocate for disadvantaged people, she commands respect and admiration for all she does. And she's formidable and competent professionally. But her role as a wounded healer—the term for those who are inspired to treat others because of our own wounds—drives her work energy.

In supervision and daydreams, I consider the importance of differentiation. Chloe frustrates me, as though I'm responsible for her.

I go back to the maxim that we are responsible *to* people, not *for* people. I'm often saying this to people, but I'm struggling to apply it myself. Why do I feel so responsible for her, and pissed off at her, so much of the time? Chloe is the squeaky wheel of my caseload; I discuss her in supervision more than any other client. And I resent her for taking up so much space. Especially when she constantly suggests that she doesn't get enough space.

When she and Graham reach a new financial settlement, and one of her children goes to a new expensive private school, she asks if we can reduce my fee, and I agree. She asks if we can increase the frequency of our sessions, and I agree. Part of this may be because of my impending deadline of maternity leave, still many months away, but there's a pattern where I keep agreeing to things that should help feed her, yet she's never satisfied, her need is never satiated. Our dynamic neither seems to help her nor feels fair to me. For all I'm offering her, I feel we are getting nowhere. I give and give, and I still can't fully gratify her. There's a sense of constant loss in our exchanges. It's like trying to fill a bucket with a hole. Whatever I give, however much she takes in, it doesn't hold, and I feel depleted from giving. For all the pouring and filling and emptying. Her bulimia is symbolic in this way.

"How can I help you?" I hear myself asking Chloe, moments after she's accused me yet again that I'm taking her ex-husband's side. I sound like a waitress, or someone in customer service, with a script. I'm asking her because I want her to at least have enough agency to construct what help would look like.

"Why are you on Graham's side?" she asks.

"I'm not on Graham's side," I say. "I want to know what I can do to help you," I say again, my exasperation coming through. I feel as though we are at the beginning again. In fact, many sessions feel like we are starting from the beginning.

And then Chloe says, at a moment of clarity and honesty, "You can give me back my youth." This is a good moment for us. It's a moment of insight and realization. And relief. The absurdity of her request illustrates the force of her fantasies, her ego ideals, her longing to return to the past. We can now drop anchor and look at what's real and possible.

"I can't do that, of course," I say. "But I want to tell you that, in our work together, I often feel we are at the beginning. It can frustrate me, because I want to help you, and I want you to progress, but maybe there's something about your wish to return, to turn back the clock to your youth, that's vitally important here. The circularity of our discussions, the return to the beginning, it plays out in our work and in your fantasy too—that you can go back."

"I would like to go back."

"I understand. What did your youth contain that you so desperately long for now?"

"That's a really hard question to answer," Chloe says, suddenly looking flushed.

"Try to sit with it for a moment," I say.

"I was so damned hot," she says after a pause. "I mean, I was just unbelievable. I lit up any room I walked into. It was pretty glorious to be me in some ways. My face. My body. I was incredible. I sometimes imagine what it must have been like to fuck young me. Unbelievable."

"That's really powerful," I say, imagining her feeling so beautiful and feeling so utterly seen and noticed. "As you say, in some ways it was glorious. And in other ways?"

"In other ways it was hard. My dad's alcoholism, and my mother's enabling. Their codependency. The instability. The constant moving. Every couple of years a new school, a new place. It was exciting, but so unsteady. The attention I got from men—men who weren't my dad, men who weren't safe. It was pretty terrifying at times. And exciting. So much dancing. So much sex. So much drinking.

So much fun. All the parties. I felt so flooded and crowded but also lonely. Anyway, when I got too much attention from dangerous men, I'd dump them and run away and move on."

"Flooded and crowded" and "lonely" stay with me. The deprivation of attention in her childhood. All the constant moving. As she speaks, I begin to picture a kind of shaky frame, a flimsy container. I think of Zelda Fitzgerald, the tragic wife of F. Scott Fitzgerald, who was mentally ill and drank too much and was said to ride on top of taxis more often than inside them and one particular Zelda detail has always stayed with me—that she was immensely beautiful in person but no photograph ever did her justice, no photograph ever captured her beauty, because she was always in motion. Something about Chloe has this ephemeral, dizzying quality that makes stillness, calm attention, elusive.

"Can you feel steady in this moment, in the here and now?" I ask.

"It's just so hard that Graham is poisoning the kids against me," she says.

"I'm with you," I say. But I don't feel she's with me. Our discussion got so pithy, so heartfelt and meaningful, but now I feel her mind is elsewhere, and here we are again, like a comic sketch of two people in dialogue, missing each other, talking above and around and past each other.

"You think I'm just crazy, like Graham says," she says.

"Did you hear what I said?" I ask, regretting the grouch in my voice.

"Yes. But Graham is just so terrible. Do you not believe me?"

"I do believe you. Can you hear me say that I believe you?"

"Yes. But he's just so terrible, I feel like no one gets it. My brothers are constantly on his side. You're on his side. My kids are on his side—"

"Chloe, I need to interrupt you. You just said I'm on his side again."

"You are, no?"

"No, I'm not. Please, can you hear what I'm saying? I am with you. Let me be with you right now. You seem to be everywhere but here."

"I'm distracted."

"I understand. Let's see if we can get you to pay attention." As I say these words, I turn them over in my mind. Pay attention. How odd that we call it that. As a client, she pays me to give her attention. If you pay attention it suggests that it costs you, the payer, something. So attention is another transaction in life.

"Charlotte, can we have a double session today?" Chloe asks. She's hungry for me to feed her more, even when what I feed her isn't that nourishing or that filling. I'm forced to deprive her, repeating the feeling she has with so many others in her life.

"We have to stop here. I will see you at our next session," I say.

"You're the only person who gets me," she says. I feel sad when she says this. I don't feel I get her. Not right now, anyway. When I'm with her, she feels I'm not, and when I feel disconnected from her, she claims closeness with me. I also feel she doesn't entirely mean these words, given how constantly misunderstood she feels by me.

In between sessions with Chloe, a distressing incident takes place in my own life. I have what's called a threatened miscarriage, and I'm hospitalized. I cancel all my sessions for the following week, sending a generic email saying that something unexpected has occurred.

Chloe replies with fury. "I wanted to tell you something Graham said to me," she writes, "and I cannot believe you've bailed on our session." She misses the following month of sessions, ignoring my messages.

"Are you okay?" I write her at one point, and she doesn't respond. I text her too. I'm furious at myself for worrying about her so much on top of my own health issues. I also realize that a part of me wishes she had the capacity to empathize and ask me if I'm okay too.

She's gotten under my skin, even though I haven't seen her. In my ruminations about her over a period of months, a kind of mental equivalent to bingeing and purging, I realize that some of my frustration has to do with what it means to care about her. Caring seems to come at a cost. Chloe's constantly ravenous appetite for attention from her friends and family has caused resentment, wariness, exhaustion, a lack of interest. Her huge appetite, coupled with her dismissal of what's given, contributes to people not wanting to feed her. And then she feels starved and rejected.

"Charlotte, let's meet," she emails after months of silence. I've chased her, she's ignored me, and when she reaches out, I agree to meet, of course. I'm curious to hear what she has to say and I decide I have something I want to tell her also. I come prepared.

"Don't yell at me," she says, with a coquettish smile.

"When have I ever yelled at you?"

"Then maybe you don't care," she says. "Did you not even wonder if I was alive when I didn't respond to your messages?"

"I did wonder," I say. "And I did care. I do care. I was very worried. And glad to hear from you. And also quite upset. Is that what you hoped for?"

"Yes."

"Chloe, I don't think I've been honest and open enough with you."

"What do you mean? About what?" she asks.

"About how I really feel about our relationship," I say. "I hold back with you, and then I try a little too hard."

"As you often say, tell me more," she says.

She lets me know that she keeps me in mind, referring to when she references this common phrase of mine.

"There's an Aesop fable, 'The Young Crab and His Mother.' Can I read it to you? I have it here."

"Please do." So I do.

"Why in the world do you walk sideways like that?" said a Mother Crab to her son. "You should always walk straight forward with your toes turned out."

"Show me how to walk, mother dear," answered the little Crab obediently, "I want to learn."

So the old Crab tried and tried to walk straight forward. But she could walk sideways only, like her son. And when she wanted to turn her toes out she tripped and fell on her nose.

"Tell me the meaning of the fable," she says, her voice sounding softer.

"I don't want to be a sideways-walking crab with you, telling you to walk forwards," I say. "I keep asking you to make progress, to move things along, but I'm the one who feels stuck. I don't think I've told you that in clear language. I think we are going round in circles. And the fact that I'm going on maternity leave soon means there will be a pause, a planned pause. And maybe you've punished me for that by making me chase you in the lead-up. Or maybe it was because I bailed on a session when you needed me—though I have to say, I canceled for a good reason."

"I don't want to know why you canceled," Chloe says. "I assume all is fine. You're here and you look like you're still pregnant."

"Yes, I'm still pregnant," I say. I wonder if she's disappointed by my confirmation on some level. I'm holding on to what's inside of me, a growing life that will get lots of attention from me, and so much more.

"I want to really, properly give you the attention and focus in this space that you require. I need to meet you where you are, not where I am or where I want you to be. But that's asking something from you too. You need to let me in. You need to let the attention count for something—satisfaction. Let's consider what it means for you."

"First," Chloe says, "I like that you conspicuously care about me. Even when I'm a bitch. Even when I ask you if you don't care about me, and when I punish you. Sure, it was a test. And you passed. You know it, and I know it. Thanks for not bailing. See? I'm getting honest with myself. I'm paying attention. I think it's hard for me to pay attention when I feel so deprived."

"What a thoughtful thing to acknowledge," I say. She is learning about herself.

I think of the pediatrician and psychoanalyst D. W. Winnicott's line: "It is a joy to be hidden but disaster not to be found." She wanted me to keep trying to reach her, and I'm glad that, however tempting at moments, I didn't give up.

"Thanks for scheduling this session with me after I repeated the pattern of coming and going, that binge-purge thing I've done since adolescence. I did it with you. I chewed you up, I puked you out, and here you are, still available, still willing to listen to me. Is it awful, being in a room with me?"

"What do you think?" I ask.

"I think I've shown you the good, the bad, the ugly. And you've tolerated it all, without insisting on retouching any of it. You might have tried to push me places, but when I refused to budge, you stayed with me while I went in circles. So thank you for accepting me. You've celebrated things about me that no one else has ever taken seriously. And you've challenged me on issues I hid from others."

"Thanks for letting me do that," I say.

"Charlotte, you know what's helped in our work together? Since you're always asking what helps me?"

"Tell me."

"You didn't ignore me. You never gave up on me. For me, that's the biggest thing."

YOUR ATTENTION

Wanting attention is human, but it's awkward and convoluted for most people. We feel embarrassed and vulnerable if we ask for attention directly, and we risk rejection, even with those who supposedly love us. We struggle to speak up honestly and admit the longing. We might carry scripts telling us not to show off, not to be demanding, not to be dramatic and selfish. We can believe in our counterfeit modesty at times, and we might even convince ourselves that we don't need attention. Pride and embarrassment can shove us into a ditch of shame and denial, hiding our true longings from awareness.

It can be maddening when people manipulate us in a bid for attention. No need to steal something in the middle of the night that we would give freely in the light of day. Attention-seeking behavior seems unnecessarily complicated. Just be direct and ask! But for someone deprived and desperate, theatrical tricks can feel like the only way to reach an audience. Flame-throwing is protection from the threat of being ignored. Though people resent the drama, fury is still a form of attentiveness.

As uncomfortable as it is to admit the desire for attention, it's also hard to admit that we struggle to continually pay attention to demanding people. We might stop paying attention to one of our children. Our spouse. Our old friends. Sometimes we're simply distracted and preoccupied and we become inattentive. And sometimes we're burnt-out. In any relationship, we might start out with enthusiastic interest, but after a while it can feel futile and unrewarding to dedicate attention to repetitive rants. It gets draining and tedious and feels inequitable. The counterfeit shows of emotion tire us and siphon our empathy. We might want to punish an attention-grabber for conning us into colluding with falseness. Or we lose interest. We want to protect ourselves. We pull back and withdraw the very thing most sought-after: our attention.

We begin to tune out the sound and fury of demands for our attention. We disinvest attention from demanding people, and we also stop paying close attention to our own internal demands. We might obsess and fixate over difficulties without truly paying attention. We think we know how the story goes.

We stop paying attention to our loved ones too, when we think we know everything there. Paying real attention to something familiar and close is hard but wonderful. When someone we care about pays attention to something that matters to us, we feel closer and we feel thought about. It suggests a kind of dedication, a joining gesture that something has personal significance. So make a point of concentrating on an activity or topic that matters to someone you love.

Once something is familiar, it can feel less interesting to us. But what a mistake, whether it's in relationships, jobs, life, the beauty of a corner we know so well we forget to notice. And parts of ourselves and loved ones we've overlooked and taken for granted. It's valuable to observe a detail with affection, notice a trait, detect a struggle, appreciate something effortful. Attention is a form of love and understanding.

Attention is closely related to creativity in celebrating the textures of being alive. Susan Sontag puts it beautifully: "Do stuff. Be clenched, curious. Not waiting for inspiration's shove or society's kiss on your forehead. Pay attention. It's all about paying attention. Attention is vitality. It connects you with others. It makes you eager. Stay eager."

Attention is a kind of energetic attitude. Don't get used to being alive. Be astonished by what you see.

Chapter Six

FREEDOM

The desire for freedom often shows itself through protest and rebellion. We feel restricted, imprisoned, stifled. It's like a toddler's blind fury when strapped into a car seat. What keeps us safe and protects us also traps us. But try explaining safety to a frustrated toddler. It won't help. Distraction might work. From early childhood onwards, a lack of freedom can feel much more threatening to our aliveness than the possibility of endangerment.

Esther Perel writes about the conflict: "From the moment we are born, we straddle two sets of contradicting needs: the need for security and the need for freedom. They spring from different sources and pull us in different directions."

We grapple with wanting protection while desiring freedom. Naming the conflict can help us make room for both in our relationships, but we often sacrifice one for the other and think it's an either/or rather than a both/and.

As we grow older, we might resist, or insist that we're strapped into relationships and commitments. When we choose commitment, whether wholeheartedly or ambivalently, we may at times grieve lost freedom. And if we avoid commitment, that isn't exactly the same thing as feeling truly free internally if we're depriving ourselves of the joys of intimacy, continued dedication and meaningful experiences.

But if we overcommit and overextend ourselves, we can feel trapped and at the mercy of obligations and responsibilities. We resent what we once chose for ourselves and question whether we were ever actually free to choose what now feels punishing and limiting.

Whatever we do or don't sign up for, there's uncertainty about future experiences. Commitments often feel like a choice to limit our possibilities. Our possibilities are always limited anyway, but making commitments can stir up our fantasies of endless potential.

"I don't want to commit to marriage right now, but what if this is my best chance and I miss it?" I got asked this question recently, and I hear variations of it regularly. "If I leave my husband, will my life be any better a few years from now?" Commitment is a gamble. Breaking commitment is a gamble too. We can't know with certainty how anything will be. Commitment generates uncertainty even as it ostensibly offers the emotional safety of predictability. We're always uncertain about future experiences, what will change, how we'll feel (though we might have illusions about all these things).

We long for freedom *from* certain pressures and we dream of freedom *to do* what we please. When we resent our past commitments, we find ourselves grieving the freedom we barely recognized possessing but now have sacrificed—the freedom of potential possibilities. We might ruminate about a choice we could have made or envisage a utopian freedom that will be ours one day. Sometimes we hold others responsible for our lack of freedom.

There can be a liberating feeling of joie de vivre that comes with spontaneous casual encounters with neighbors, shopkeepers, even strangers. Sometimes the lack of structured commitment in a friendship can feel wonderfully plotless and liberating. You meet because you both want to, not because you're beholden. But with no obligations, you're also free to drift and fall out of touch easily. Commitments can remind us of what we value.

Existentialists, most notably Simone de Beauvoir and Jean-Paul Sartre, advocated in a rather extreme, absolute way for freedom in love. Beauvoir wrote that women are taught that finding love is our only and final destiny, and this is ultimately unfulfilling and not enough. Women must work hard to seek freedom, she wrote, as we have underestimated the difficulty and importance of freedom. *The Second Sex* critiques the myths of womanhood. Women easily self-abnegate and overly sacrifice themselves for others, believing that true calling comes from "self-forgetting and love" above all else.

Whatever our gender, ethnicity, sexual orientation, race, culture, or age group, we can all be subsumed by our relationships to the point of forgetting how to be free.

In the early days of a romance, there can be a sense of rhapsodic adventure—freedom to explore in a new way, to discover ourselves as we discover the other, to roam wildly. But in pursuing this freedom, we often have a goal of some form of commitment. We make promises. Mortgages, contracts, or marriage vows, legal or religious, aren't necessarily perfect guidelines for clear and thorough thinking about the meaning of freedom over time in a relationship. We like to lock love down in concrete ways—traditionally, with rings, but also with other concrete gestures, such as the "love padlocks" on the Pont des Arts bridge in Paris. (The weight of those hundreds of padlocks is potentially damaging to the bridge, and so the city sends workers on a regular schedule to remove them.) The Spanish word for "wives," *esposas*, also means handcuffs.

As a relationship matures, we might begin to notice differences in our attitudes towards closeness and intimacy, and there may be disagreements about what choices to make, and when, or if it's even necessary to choose. Affairs, marriages, open relationships, civil partnerships, avoided relationships, infatuations—any choice (including not making a choice) can threaten our sense of emotional liberty. Conflicts around responsibility and dependence emerge. We feel robbed of time, stripped of options and potential, let down, held hostage by unexpected circumstances.

For some, attachments of any kind can feel like a threat to freedom. Caring can be an inconvenience, a distraction from autonomy. It helps if we're conscious about learning how to factor in our need for freedom in any relationship, no matter how attached and committed. If we take an expansive and flexible approach to commitment and freedom, we can periodically update and adjust our terms and conditions, whatever our circumstances and age.

My client Sara, a therapist trainee and freelance journalist, tries to safeguard her freedom by never letting herself commit to relationships. But the rigidity of protecting freedom can become its own cage. We unshackle ourselves in one way only to reconstitute other restrictions and obstacles.

SARA'S SENTENCE

Speaking freely is one of the privileges of therapy. Sara talks about this when we meet. Moroccan by background and raised in both Marrakesh and London, she is twenty-eight years old, lives alone, and works as a freelance journalist. And she's just started a psychotherapy training part-time.

"I'm required to have my own personal therapy as part of the course, so that's why I'm here," she says in our initial session.

If Sara decides to commit to therapy with me, my maternity leave with my second child will interrupt our work, at least temporarily. At six months, I feel melodramatically pregnant, and it's visible and obvious.

"When is your due date?" Sara asks.

I tell her the date of my maternity leave.

"If we do work together, will you be coming back?"

"Yes, I definitely will," I say with a little too much conviction. I'm more confident about my professional plans after the baby this second time round, however difficult. When the words have left my mouth, I realize I've already disclosed a strong view without exactly meaning to. I want to offer balance, and so I clumsily add, "My return date is somewhat tentative—but I will be coming back. And I'm here for another ten weeks. So, tell me about your life."

Sara looks at me with a calm smile. My wish to over-overexplain is insecure and feels connected to my uncomfortably swollen condition. I can barely cross my legs, I have gestational diabetes and must check my blood sugar between sessions, and I'm trying to hold on to everything. I want this baby; I nearly lost this baby. I also want to keep working. I'm trying to ensure that I won't lose my place. It has nothing to do with Sara, and I've already veered off.

We resume focus. She tells me about her course, and the ideas that resonate for her personally. Emotional liberation. Adventure. Unrestraint.

As she tells me about the books she's reading, I'm fidgety and restless. I struggle to sit still, but Sarah and I lock eyes. She seems undaunted by the awkwardness. Therapy trainees can be challenging and rewarding clients, sometimes resistant, feeling forced into therapy, and worried about exposure. I wonder if Sara is judging me or demonstrating her determination to do therapy properly.

We talk a bit about Sara's wish to become a therapist, how it connects with journalism and freedom of speech. She speaks thoughtfully and has a contemplative, deliberate way of expressing herself. She's intense and bright, a little earnest in her demeanor.

"There's a form my course requires me to have you fill out. Is that okay? It's part of the requirement."

"Yes, of course. I've noticed you keep referring to therapy being a requirement. How do you feel about being here?" I ask.

"Um, good question," she says, drawing in a breath and pondering her words. "The truth is, I've never had therapy before, so this gives me an excuse to justify the cost in a way, since it's part of my professional development. It feels less indulgent. But I don't like being forced into things. I make my own choices."

She does slight uptalk, flipping the ends of her statements so they sound like questions. Her ambivalence about freedom and commitment emerge. On the one hand, she feels safer with rules and guidance, deferring responsibility to authority. On the other hand, she rebels, and resists being told what to do. She tells me about her professional choices, her wish to push forward and live her own life without being trapped by a man or motherhood. "Settling down" is a dreary expression, she says, and something she will be sure to avoid. She doesn't want to feel bound to anyone else. She believes in open relationships, though she isn't polyamorous. ("Too many rules and a whole set of beliefs, polyamory," she says. She twists her hands in her lap. Her silhouette is distinct: part grace, part strength.)

I say that hopefully she'll find therapy liberating, even if it's required. She's free to speak without censorship, so hopefully she'll feel unrestricted in that sense. Then I point out that she was also free to choose her therapist. Why me?

"A couple of things drew me to you," she says. "Convenience. I live less than ten minutes away from here. So there's that. But also, I read that you've worked in Senegal. I figured you'd be open-minded about Muslim culture." There's a confidence in her voice and a hesitancy in her face. "I'm no longer religious. But I was." She feels caught between cultures and beliefs. "And also, when I emailed you asking for an appointment, you said you'd be going on maternity leave. You didn't say when, but I knew there would be an interruption if we work together. I liked that. Long-term commitment freaks me out."

We talk about the importance of feeling free in therapy and not feeling judged.

"I'm hoping you won't judge me the way an Islamic therapist would. Or the way an Islamophobe might. It would be useful if you get it a little bit, where I'm from."

I stop myself from trying to demonstrate any special knowledge about her background. I hold back from trying too hard.

"My background isn't the main thing for me. I want to feel free to discuss whatever I want, and even if culture and religion come into it, I don't want it to be defining; I want that to be my choice."

"That's understandable," I say.

"I guess I'm intersectional. Intersectionality . . . do you hear that word a lot?" Sara asks.

"Yes," I say. "How do you feel about it?"

"It applies to me, but it's the most overused word on my therapy course. I'm so . . . boxed in. It makes me claustrophobic. Everyone is careful around me. In the group discussions. In everything to do with race and ethnicity and marginalized groups. They talk to me with such care and consideration, it makes me awkward."

I ask her about feeling awkward.

"It's like I'm a little girl. I'm the token Muslim girl. Even though I'm not practicing. I want to be a psychotherapist so I can help people talk about things that are difficult. What you can't talk about anywhere else. I thought therapy would be daring, full of badass people talking without any censorship. I don't want to keep it safe and careful. I chose this course because it seemed interesting and bold. I imagined provocative, open discussions and pictured it being a bit exciting. Well, it's swarming with overly cautious, super-considerate people. No one in the group says anything remotely controversial to me. It's so vanilla."

She had fantasized about the freedom that would come with psychotherapy training. She feels the course sanitizes discussion for her.

"I'm not committing to next year until I have a better sense of what this training is like," she says. "But I'll commit to our work together up until your maternity leave. I feel free doing that."

I ask her what freedom in this context means for her. How would she define it?

"Just being myself, I guess. Feeling that I'm allowed to be myself, you know, fully." She tells me about the political rights she's advocated for, freedom of press and women's issues in Morocco. She describes the writing assignments she's had and the adventures that are possible because she's not tied down. Externally, she's advocated for freedom. Internally, she's in flight.

She describes leaving Morocco as an adolescent after her mother died. "It was like when you take an avocado stone out of an avocado. The rest of the avocado goes bad without the stone. My dad, brothers, we didn't make sense once she was gone. Without my mother, I needed to get out of Morocco. I couldn't stay there."

Sara moved to London and lived with an aunt and cousin in West London. She fell into a rough crowd but got good marks. She began to wear a headscarf but never a full hijab, starting when she became pubescent. "I became more religious than my family, weirdly. No one else wore a headscarf in my family, but I wanted to." From the time she was fourteen, she'd behave well whenever her headscarf was on, but occasionally she'd give into temptation and pressure. "I'd take my headscarf off," she says, her eyes intensifying.

"And?"

"And then . . . anything really. I'd wake up in strangers' beds, on night buses, in so many crazy places. I'd drink, take drugs, mess around with guys. I blacked out a bunch of times. I once woke up in a field outside of London. In the middle of nowhere. I don't remember how I got there or anything about the night. I'm lucky I didn't end up dead in a ditch . . ."

She describes what it was like when the headscarf was on.

"I was safe. It was like nothing bad could happen to me. Got good marks. Didn't mess around. No alcohol. Nothing. Never. No way. I could never do something bad when my headscarf was on. It wouldn't . . . even have felt possible."

The headscarf protected her from herself, in a way, as well as from outside forces. I ask about the timing of wearing a headscarf and her mother's death. Was it a transitional object, a way of having, and also rejecting, a maternal cloak?

"Coincidental," Sara says. "But I knew you'd say that. Maybe it felt like authority, the covering. In a maternal way, a bit. But I also didn't like having it on all the time, so I'd take it off. It was just on and off. Day and night."

The headscarf determined a split, a bifurcated identity.

"You're not wearing a head covering now," I comment, suddenly conscious of my using mismatched language: switching from "headscarf" to "head covering" feels potentially inaccurate. "Let's have a deal," I add. "I don't want to be like the people on your course, sanitizing or overly editing myself as I speak. But I'll probably get stuff wrong. Can we agree that you'll let me know if I misstep or say something that's culturally misattuned? I'm struck by what you said about wanting uncensored conversation."

"Sure," she says. "I want both of us to speak freely. You need to be yourself if you're going to help me be myself. And I need to be myself. I guess that's the real reason I'm here. . . . To answer your question, either term is fine—headscarf, head covering. I stopped wearing it completely when I got my first journo job. The other girls at the magazine had straight hair and no one covered anything. Short skirts and sexy legs and makeup. All of that. One day I just took it off in the morning, put it in a drawer, and didn't put it on again. That was it."

We explore what it was like for her to stop wearing any kind of headscarf, and (somewhat to my surprise) she describes the loss of liberation in pursuing what she thought would free her. "I've rejected a lot about my Muslim upbringing. I don't share most of the attitudes towards women that my mother had, and my father and aunties still have. But wearing a headscarf protected my freedom. It kept me from being objectified. There's all this stuff about how restrictive and oppressive headscarves are and all the controversies at schools you read about. But I'm . . . torn. I've written about how veils in general can feel sheltering and protective and, in a way, liberating. They keep us free from harm. And I personally liked hiding my dirty hair under it. But also the veil kept me from doing stupid things."

She pauses and looks pensive. "But when I'd take it off in my teenage years, I thought it was freedom, but in a scary way. Those situations, I don't even remember half of them. It's all like a dizzy blur. Not in a good way."

The release from restricted containment to boundless liberty overwhelmed and endangered her. "So do you feel you freely chose to take it off and fully stop wearing it, or were you pressured?" I ask.

"We're always pressured. Show me one person on this planet who isn't pressured in some way, even if the pressure is to have fun."

"What do you feel pressure about?"

"I feel pressure to be free. It's so important to me that I hold on to my independence. I can't give it away. It's hard-won. But it means I'm not able to care about anyone or anything. I can't. If I care, I'll lose my freedom."

I mull over her comment. *If I care, I'll lose my freedom.*

Did she care about her mother, and lose her? "Yes," she says. "I cared and lost. Not doing that again."

"Do you care about yourself?" I ask.

"Hmm. Not sure," she says.

We spend several minutes coming back to the issue of caring or not caring, and whether detachment is a free choice, and if it's freeing. It seems connected with losing her mother. Avoiding the vulnerability of intimacy and closeness might protect her freedom in some ways, but doesn't it limit her freedom to engage fully? Her reluctance to commit also seems tied with the sense of abandonment from her mother. The cost of maternal commitment and care were too much. Never again, she says.

"I can count on myself. I'm responsible for my own life, and that's it. I don't need to take care of anyone else or get attached. And if I'm a psychotherapist, I'll observe people but I don't need to get overly involved. I want to observe but from across the room. I don't need to get closer." She's reiterated all that she doesn't need.

By the end of the first session, Sara and I agree to work together, and I reiterate that we will soon be disrupted by my impending maternity leave. She says the finite nature of our agreement suits her better.

Over the course of our work together, Sara talks a lot about rules. Cultural rules, religious rules, customs, requirements. The rules of psychotherapy also come into focus when we explore the significance of self-disclosure and whether she feels free to talk about her innermost vulnerability with her training group. "They think they know me because I've given them some red herring cultural traumas. But it's not real intimacy I'm giving them," she says.

She describes competing pressures and temptations: how, in her early twenties, she tried to protect her sense of purity by having anal sex instead of vaginal; how she's looked for loopholes and ways of reconciling conflicting impulses. Different ways of rebelling and conforming to her inner sense of authority. She bends rules.

I get bigger, and our break comes closer.

At the start of one session, Sara arrives looking bothered and intense.

"I met this guy, and I think I like him," she says. "I actually really like him."

"Oh! And? How do you feel about it? I haven't heard you talk about liking someone before."

"That's because I haven't. I'm deformed by what I'm feeling already. The experience is too strong."

She seems unmoored by liking him, as though it's unbalanced her entire system.

"We all choose our restrictions, I guess," Sara says. She points to mine. "Don't you ever feel like your baby is bored, just trapped inside you? It must want to get out."

Never had that occurred to me. I assumed in utero contentment. I ask her to say more about her question.

"I feel bad for the baby being so dependent," she says. "And for you too. You're dependent on the baby being okay. See? Caring messes with freedom."

She's right, of course, that when we have more to care about, we have more to lose. We're vulnerable to things going wrong, not just for ourselves but for our loved ones. Her insistence on not letting herself care hardly feels carefree.

Is Sara letting herself care about the therapy or herself? She says no. Sara might experience another form of loss by playing it cool and making her world colder, but it's the story of how she coped with losing her mother. We're attached to our stories of coping with trauma. We cherish whatever we believe got us through unbearable pain. We think that we survived the terrible experience because of our story of glory. Sara's story of glory for dealing with her mother's death may have been her bid for freedom and independence. So any attempts to challenge this story could feel like a threat to what helped her survive.

A few weeks later I've expanded even more. I do, admittedly, feel claustrophobic in my unwieldly third trimester. Though I don't feel the baby wants to escape my body, I'd like to have a little reprieve from myself.

Sara feels pulled and pressured in different directions. The guy she likes is Moroccan, not at all religious. But she's suddenly missing the headscarf. She misses the ease and clarity of having the barriers in place.

"I miss the protection, and simplicity," she says. I ask her about protecting herself now. It feels impossible.

"I'm . . . um . . . I'm kinda trapped," she says. She avoids eye contact.

She often describes entrapment and restriction. But this feels different.

"I'm pregnant, and I don't know if I'll keep it," Sara says flatly.

I'm surprised by her news momentarily. We look at the conflicting longings, the meaning of keeping the baby or terminating. She asks me if it's strange for me to hear her contemplate getting rid of a baby when I'm clearly towards the end of growing one. I say it doesn't feel strange to me. What about for her, seeing me pregnant while contemplating what to do about her own pregnancy?

"It's weird. But fine," she says. Sara sees entrapments and enclosures in most attachments and commitments. Safeguarding her independence matters most for her, she tells me. She's worked hard to be free. She doesn't want to give it up. "I'm a *flâneur*," she says of herself. "I wander and look around, but I don't need to overly involve myself in just one thing. I can keep on walking."

She winces at the commitment of motherhood, the obligations and endless responsibilities, the loss of independence. She seems not to want to have a baby, at least not now. Sara says she likes this guy. She doesn't elaborate. She hasn't told him she's pregnant and she might not ever tell him. She's not up for the hassle of dealing with his reaction. She's overstretched already, she says, crossing her arms. She's disturbed by her own reckless behavior. She hasn't protected herself and now she must deal with this situation. She needs to decide what to do. She says the choice is obvious. And it's only hers to make. That's the part she values but also resents. She feels the weight of responsibility in having to decide.

"I can't care so much. I need not to care," she says. "I need to detach myself."

The next week, Sara doesn't show up for our session.

I email her. I phone her. I never hear back.

She's ghosted me.

Free to come and go.

FINDING FREEDOM

Once, for a podcast, I interviewed the journalist Erwin James, who served twenty years in prison, about how incarceration had shaped his life. He described the feeling of release: "It was a sunny August day, and I could go left, or I could go right." The freedom to choose left or right means just about everything. But freedom itself can be terrifying. We have the freedom to make mistakes, get into danger. What's promising is the freedom to understand our restrictions and limitations, to think about the boundaries and explore what draws us to construct cages.

Some of us are intoxicated by the idea of freedom, but when we are strongly attached to anything in life, we cannot be entirely free. It's not just responsibilities and the demands of commitment that tether us; it's also the fact that the moment we're attached to anything, including life itself, we have something to lose. Things can go wrong, and we're vulnerable to getting hurt. Caring adds value and meaning to our lives but it also costs us—and not caring costs us too.

"Freedom is what we do with what is done to us," says Sartre. Whatever form it takes, we all want freedom and it's usually a struggle. We feel restricted by rules, family, religion, cultural pressures, time limits. Relationships of any kind can liberate and trample us. Sometimes we rebel so fully, we're imprisoned in another way— simply by rebelling and doing the opposite. There's an adage that when it comes to social rules, you can live in conformity, rebellion, or freedom.

Part of the problem with freedom is our own internal mistrust. We seek and resist freedom and safety in surprising ways. We can trick ourselves into thinking we're doing as we please, when we're psychologically tied to voices of authority we've internalized. We might partially want independence, but we also revert to the familiarity of being told what to do, and we doubt ourselves.

Erich Fromm, the humanistic psychologist, captures this tension: "Is there not also, perhaps, besides an innate desire for freedom, an instinctive wish for submission? If there is not, how can we account for the attraction which submission to a leader has for so many today? Is submission always to an overt authority, or is there also submission to internalized authorities, such as duty or conscience, to inner compulsions or to anonymous authorities like public opinion?"

Beauvoir and Sartre used the formal "vous" to address each other throughout their long relationship. They emphatically championed freedom by marking their distinctions and separateness. But Beauvoir called Sartre "the greatest success" of her life. And Sartre wrote to Beauvoir: "I have experienced the world with you." The mercurial authority of love finds us.

Even when we live in the supposed free world, where we can do what we want and make our own choices, we rarely feel completely free, and often because of the voices in our head judging us. As the neuroscientist Christof Koch puts it, "Freedom is always a question of degree rather than an absolute good that we do or do not possess."

Awareness of emotional freedom alerts us to opportunities. A degree of internal freedom is almost always available. The problem is that we haven't been taught how to pursue freedom in healthy dosages, and the meaning and definition of "freedom" is confusing. Adrienne Rich puts it, "In the vocabulary kidnapped from liberatory politics, no word has been so pimped as 'freedom.'"

If we give away and sacrifice our freedom too readily, at a later point of regret we can freak out. We can find ourselves behaving like **sheeple**, sleepwalking and sheepling along at work or in our relationships, and then we may panic and begin to run away without understanding that this is what we're doing. Secret spending, affairs, drinking and taking drugs, indulging in unhealthy habits—even the compulsion to look at our phones incessantly—can all be signs that we long to escape where we are in the present moment. Conscious awareness of freedom in all its forms can help us prioritize moderate dosages.

What you think of as freedom may not match how other people think of freedom. Consider the varieties of freedom and continually ask yourself what kind of freedom you want. The freedom we want at twenty isn't necessarily the same freedom that's available at sixty (though we may fantasize). Update and amend your opportunities for freedom. Adjust the terms and conditions of your commitments, to make space. Be flexible and imaginative in how you get freedom too. Sometimes it's just glancing up at a patch of blue sky. Other times the freedom of life is dizzying. Find your edges.

Chapter Seven

TO CREATE

When I was eleven years old, my teacher gave the class an unusual homework assignment. He told us to put aside thirty minutes that evening and just imagine something—anything. A girl in the class peppered him with anxious questions about this assignment, seeking clarification, instruction, guidance. He refused to be more specific and said the point of the exercise was to let her mind wander. It wasn't about getting a good grade. There wouldn't be grades. She became increasingly upset. A straight-A student, she wanted to get it right. She just did not understand this exercise. Eventually she burst into tears.

"Just tell me what to do!" she cried.

When I met up with her a few years ago and we looked back at that experience, she said he was the only teacher who had ever invited her to be creative.

Society doesn't really nurture the creative spirit in daily life past childhood, when it is ordinary for children to be given art materials or invited to write stories or sing and dance without any consideration of attempting perfection. Imagination, play—these are things for children. Children are told to "play." Playing is essential to learning, but adults are rarely instructed to do this. Playing and creating both involve imaginative and impulsive acts, a willingness to make it up, to invent, to take leaps, to let go of certainty. In play, even if there are some rules and guidelines in place, there's mystery and discovery, the possibility of making mistakes, changing course, not knowing what comes next. After childhood, many people just don't feel safe enough to "indulge" in creativity and play.

If we expand our sense of creativity and what it can mean for how we live our lives, we can add texture and nuance to our daily experience in countless ways. Being playful, allowing yourself to imagine things that are well outside your own experience, allowing yourself to engage in silliness or to revel in the pleasure of quotidian tasks such as cooking or housekeeping, is to give yourself new opportunities. The first step towards a fuller engagement with creativity is choosing to be deliberately creative in defining it for yourself and in recognizing opportunities to take a creative approach, to renovate the familiar, to (in the words of poet Ezra Pound) "make it new."

I'm often asked why it's so difficult for people to change, and how therapy can help. We all get stuck. Creativity—and playfulness—can lift us out of the mud. It requires courage, uncertainty, being genuinely open to new thoughts and feelings and experiences, even surprise. Perhaps most essentially, the hallmark of creativity is flexibility. New creative strategies can feel risky if we're unconfident and insecure. We cling to familiarity, to the illusion of certainty.

The poet W. H. Auden wrote in *The Age of Anxiety*: "We would rather be ruined than changed . . ." His words speak to some part of us that fights change to the point of martyrdom, even when we want it desperately. Perfectionism can store away secret one-day fantasies. We feel blocked. If not internally, we are obstructed by circumstances. We stick with what has reliably failed. Productivity easily fills the space for creativity and play. Especially if we don't feel inspired or excited. We run through tasks and obsess over societal definitions of progress and growth. Fallow periods are valuable in life too. I know a writer who calls the times when she isn't actively producing pages "rotating the crops."

Therapy itself is a creative collaboration. We attune ourselves to the worlds of others while also paying close attention to our own responses. We listen for subtle notes, make links, offer insights and curiosity, invite reflections and associations. We use metaphors, look at symbolic meanings, recognize larger themes from a wide-angle perspective, and explore details with a zoom-lens focus. It is an intensely idiosyncratic endeavor in some ways. Each relationship is inimitable. Two people come together to create something unique.

When we script our stories beforehand, tell our stories, and leave with the same exact understanding of the stories, that's not a creative process. What's creative is when we tell or retell a story and discover something, hear a hidden note, however big or small. We see a theme or pattern, an angle, a connection, a feeling, a thought, maybe even something mysterious.

We can be playful and creative in the lives we're already living, by seeing and experiencing the world in new ways. And sometimes when we're afraid to play, our bodies are creative. In my work with Rosie, a young woman struggling to have sex, her body is highly imaginative and symbolic in expressing her intimacy blockage. Rosie wants to create new life. This means something different than either of us expected. We need adequate safety so we can take risks and discover something new. The flexibility of Aristotle's Lesbian rule comes to mind—bending and adjusting to the particulars of experience. Her resistance to play, playfulness, is at the heart of our work together.

ROSIE'S ROOM

My instant feeling when I meet Rosie is that she's rigid. She speaks with exaggerated precision, and her way of simply being in the room instantly intrigues me. She sits still, with the stiff, uninflected upright posture of an Irish dancer: her arms never move, and her upturned palms are awkwardly resting in her lap. Her inelasticity unsettles me.

"Apparently there's nothing physically wrong with me," she says. Rosie, an administrative assistant in her early twenties, has been married for a year, but the marriage has still not been consummated. She wants to get pregnant, but every time sex is attempted, she tenses up and nothing happens. She has been diagnosed with **vaginismus**, a condition where vaginal muscles tighten and make penetration impossible or incredibly painful. In the words of novelist Edna O'Brien, "The body contains the life story just as much as the brain." I'm curious to know what Rosie's body is expressing.

The referral came from a private gynecologist I met once at a hospital fundraising event. I appreciate the referral and I'm particularly interested in vaginismus—a brilliant metaphor for the essential tensions of closeness. We all have moments where we snap the door shut. Or we're denied entrance to someone's inner world.

All human beings, whatever gender or age, can seek and resist closeness with the body, the mind, other people, and the space between. Sexual difficulties can symbolize an incredible panoply of our ways of relating, illuminating the barriers we put up that prevent us from taking in and giving.

I'm primed before I meet Rosie, already engaged and curious. My opening questions are strategic. I know I need to go slowly. *Opening. Slowly.* Even the words in my mind feel symbolic.

I ask Rosie to tell me about herself, about getting married, her upbringing, her feelings about sex, the struggles that led to her receiving this diagnosis. I say it will help if I can get to know her and develop a sense of her life.

"Um, okay," she says, staring at me. "The doctor gave me dilators to use at home, and my health insurance authorized six sessions with you. If I do both these things, will that fix what's wrong?" she asks.

"Therapy isn't exactly about fixing," I say, hearing myself take a deep breath before plunging in. "It's about understanding and working through issues. Vaginismus is very treatable, and talking really can help." As these words leave my mouth, I'm already deeply bored by the sound of my voice. What I've said comes out flat and sounds like a defensive disclaimer in the fine print of medication instructions. My first attempt to engage her is uninspiring and narrow. We're off to an anemic start.

She asks if this problem is common and what it's about. I tell her that every story is different.

"A vagina in panic" is one description. People can panic about the panic, suffering in silence, feeling ashamed and embarrassed and frustrated, not knowing where to go for help. The issue is shared across religions, cultures, educational levels, and age. It can come and go, and it can be chronic.

I'm glad she's here and reaching out for help; that's already an encouraging start. Psychosexual issues can get lost in a kind of lacuna somewhere between medicine and therapy and relationships. Not knowing where to go, what and who goes where, how to put things together, can be literal and figurative when it comes to sexual difficulties.

We are yet to discuss anything personal and specific to Rosie. I ask her what she'd like from therapy. "To make new life," she says. "I saved myself for marriage. My husband, Michael, did too. We met through the church. And we planned marriage and starting a family, and it's not happening. And I'm nearly twenty-three. I thought I'd have a baby by now." She seems very determined to stick to her plans. She has a fastidious quality that makes her seem like a little girl and an old woman at the same time. She comes across as more innocent and inexperienced than most twenty-two-year-olds, but also much more sensible and adult.

She's small and thin, and attractive in a tidy, organized way. She has large blue-gray eyes, dark hair worn in two plaits, and precise, pointy features. Her speaking is clipped, staccato. Though her words are polite, she looks pugnacious and exasperated. She hasn't said anything to substantiate this, but I feel there's a rigid toughness to her. What is she warding off?

Rosie grew up in a highly religious Christian household, and her parents are both missionaries. Her father is an evangelical pastor and they moved around. Rosie spent parts of her childhood in Germany, Kenya, northern France, and Brighton. When I ask about siblings, she says she's the eldest child but she's not sure how to count them because of the number of foster children and non–blood relatives considered to be family.

"In our household, we took in everyone. We've always been welcoming," she says. "We didn't make distinctions about who was really related. *Mi casa es su casa.* Wherever we were, people would come and live with us. Some of them would stay for a few weeks, but others stuck around for years. And, as missionaries, the more the merrier for bringing people in."

And now her vagina is protesting. No open-door policy! Entrance denied!

"How was that for you, moving from place to place, having so many people in your house all the time?" I ask.

"A lot of work. And mess. A never-ending cycle of laundry. But that's just how it was. And being the eldest, I was put in charge, and constantly cleaning up and looking after everyone. I kept track of homework, housework, chores, meals, schedules. It was endless. I did most of the drudgery of organizing stuff, but there were people and things everywhere, always."

Blurred distinctions quickly emerge as a theme from her upbringing. Lots of rules and responsibilities but an absence of clear boundaries. Grown-ups were larger-than-life (Rosie's father) or like children (Rosie's mother). Children were more like parents (Rosie) and other children, some unrelated, were turned into siblings. Strangers became family. And family could disappear. The landscape of her childhood is like emotional quicksand, with no sense of who is coming or going, which way is up or down, what is stable and consistent. There is no sense of a secure base, a steady foothold. Rosie's sturdiness and clearheadedness is admirable, but it has been her survival defense; it's come at a cost.

In Rosie's words, "We also had lodgers. They came from all over, and I'd see someone new sitting at the kitchen table. I'd look over and think, *Oh, that person will probably be here for a while.* We had room in our homes and our hearts, wherever we were, because of Dad's role at the church. We were blessed to have enough to give back."

Some of what Rosie says sounds directly inherited, the parroted party line, while other observations seem more like her own. An example of her personal voice: "People would suddenly appear. You know, like in a dream. You don't question why people are there, or why someone suddenly vanishes, or what's happening. It's just how it is."

She starts with details of shared beds, shared meals, not knowing which toothbrush belonged to whom. And then she describes her mother's alcoholism, her crashing around at all hours, drunkenly waking her to meet strangers, telling her stories she didn't want to hear. Rosie was adultified and parented her mother from as far back as she can remember. She describes her mother as "a sloppy drunk, always sobbing or laughing too much. Floppy and exaggerated."

Rosie herself seems the opposite of floppy and exaggerated. Her rigid comportment and tight, careful voice seem to illustrate her reaction formation to her mother.

"Dad I trust," she says.

She shifts ever so slightly in her seat, and her face settles.

"He's strict but fair. He's the one who taught me about morality and God. He wasn't around as much as Mum, only because he's always served the community with such tireless devotion, but whenever we spent time together, I'd listen and follow his guidance. I still do. I've always complied and done what he asked. Except for one time. But only once. Apart from that, I've been as good as a good Christian girl can be."

When she was ten, one of the lodgers crawled into bed beside Rosie and fondled her. He rubbed his penis against her bottom and ejaculated on her body, and though he didn't penetrate her and she hadn't gone through puberty, she was nevertheless petrified that he had impregnated her. Describing this traumatic experience to me, she remains frozen. Rosie didn't tell her mother what had happened. "There was no point. I knew she'd turn it around somehow and I'd end up having to make sure she was okay."

But a few weeks after the incident, she did tell her father. She felt she had to. He responded with rage. The lodger had already left by then. They never spoke about the incident again. Rosie carried huge shame and guilt for failing to comply with his standards of acceptability. "He always said that if you touch a rose, it loses its luster. He picked the name Rose knowing I'd be a beautiful flower, but he told me to save myself for marriage, and I did. Other than that one time, I never stepped out of line."

I feel sad that she thinks of this assault as a moment when she stepped out of line. Is her aversion to being touched connected to conflicting beliefs about losing her luster?

Rosie has distanced herself from her mother in recent years, and when they do speak, her mother rants and cries, and Rosie usually regrets taking the call. She enjoys her father's calls. "But since I got married, Dad and I speak less often. Michael is my family now," she says.

In her present life, she shows an intense need for order and cleanliness, rules, boundaries. She was never fully allowed to be a child. A child who could explore, dream, play. Make a mess. She wasn't protected and made to feel safe and cared for, emotionally or physically. Sex is about all of these things.

She tells me about her behavior again, as though she must defend her integrity. "I got good marks, did my Bible studies, looked after the kiddos and housework, and I never got into trouble. It was only that one time—that was it."

I jump in and say that what happened to her with that man wasn't her fault in any way, however it felt for her, whatever the details, and she's blaming herself. My point is so obvious, I almost don't say it. But the unsaid often needs to be said when it comes to sexual trauma. I don't feel my words reach her or that she believes me. She's unresponsive to me, and I don't want to force her to revisit this immensely significant incident if she's not ready. She's got it fenced off.

She seems admiring and protective of her father. He tolerated her mother and endured her chaos. "He's always said Mum is baroque. He's got a way with words."

"I can tell you have his gift of language," I say.

"My dad's way with words—that's why he's such a charismatic conduit for the Lord's messages. And he's so sensible. He's a humble leader. He helps so many people."

I feel she hasn't taken in my response to her and has needed my sense of her to go right back to her father and his greatness. It may be her discomfort about being in the spotlight.

Her family asks when God will create a child. "We all pray." And then she adds: "Ironic, right? The daughter of missionaries can't even do missionary position."

Some of her insights and observations are astute and bold, even as she is immensely defended in other moments.

She's been the dutiful daughter, but her role sounds matronly, performing the invisible work of endless household tasks and cleaning up after others. She's been the wife and the mother, the hospitable caretaker. But her vagina is refusing to grow up. The etymology of the word "vagina" comes from "sheath," or "scabbard," which means covering, protection. I think of how her vaginismus is helping her remain protected in some way, even if it's blocking her from intimacy.

"This situation, my issue, this is not what we planned," she says, her lips pursed in a way that looks almost anal.

I ask her how she feels about changing plans.

"Michael and I always stick to our plans. We are compliant, good people. He works very hard, in insurance; he's a risk analyst. It's only sexually that things aren't working properly. That's what I need to sort out." When I ask about other forms of intimacy, kissing, cuddling, touching, she says that she doesn't enjoy being touched. It's not that it's painful, but it's irritating. "Like mosquitoes," she says.

"Ever since we lived in Kenya, I always felt like people touching me were just as annoying as the mosquitoes around us. We had those mosquito nets on our beds, and I wished I could get a net to wear when I had to be around people."

I feel like I've stumbled across gold when I hear these sorts of remarks. My face probably shows it.

"I'm a closed flower, not living up to my name," she says. "Maybe Dad was right and I lost my luster from that one time. A rose that can't blossom."

A rose that can't blossom or doesn't want to yet? I wonder.

She describes Michael as "perfunctory," and when I ask what this means, she explains that he ejaculates very quickly. "He's efficient in all ways." With money, food shopping, household practicalities, and, apparently, sexually.

How is their communication? Do they talk about sex? Are they intimate emotionally? "Well, we've spoken about my coming here and he knows I'm getting treatment. If that's what you mean, yeah, we are close."

I feel my questions have landed in a clunky way. I'm blocked from my own creative expression. Am I experiencing any of the awkwardness and self-consciousness she feels, the struggle to discuss sex, think about sex, approach the issue in an engaging way? I'm interested in her symbolic and imaginative play with language, and her deadpan delivery. She's quite remarkable in her observations in some ways, but she's rigid about what she'll let in. It's hard to get comfortable or playful.

"Michael and I get stuff done. We're both super-organized and functional." She speaks in a mechanical way, reporting details without showing any affect.

Her comportment, and her contained narrative, are a striking contrast to her chaotic childhood. It's as if her lack of a secure base externally has pushed her to construct something sturdy and steely within. And it's a struggle to let go, to take in, to negotiate between her internal world and outside forces. Her husband's penis might feel like yet another encroachment of her space, of her privacy, when she's never had protected boundaries and clear lines of demarcation. Taking him in and making a baby could feel like an unbearable threat if her inside world—her vagina—is the one space that's entirely hers and hers only. And taking me in could feel threatening.

Rosie's administrative job seems consistent with some of her traits. She likes organizing and systemizing. This can be creative, but is it for her? She says she gets exasperated with her boss and colleagues when they fail to cooperate. She wants clarity about processes, order. One plus one equals two. Nothing less. Nothing more. This includes our process in therapy. She asks me what's next.

I begin to tell her about the process, including the logistics and practical details, but she's uneasy as I explain that an important part of what helps in therapy is the creative possibility of conversation without a fixed agenda. How can she possibly prepare and organize her thoughts for this? Spontaneous moments can be liberating and fascinating and can lead to substantial breakthroughs. Therapy cannot be entirely scripted on either side. Once the boundaries are established and in place, there has to be space to wander, play, and tolerate uncertainty. If we choreograph every moment, it shuts down creativity. She looks bemused when I say some of this to her. What I want to say is: *Let me in, let anything out!* But I don't.

I try to shift the focus from her plans to her feelings. How does she feel about sex, procreating? It can be hard to fully explain the desire to conceive, and Rosie answers immediately: "Having babies is what people do. And we're married now. It's a sensible, reasonable thing to do." She lowers her eyes at me in a way that feels disapproving.

"My wanting a baby makes good sense," she adds. "I'm married and this is the next step."

I nod but say nothing. I think of a line of Picasso's I loved and obnoxiously quoted as a teenager: "The chief enemy of creativity is good sense." Does she have room for creativity with all that is sensible and reasonable? I want to give her space to consider.

"How do you feel about wanting a baby?" I ask.

"I don't really get what you mean. It's not unusual to want a baby," she says.

"It's not unusual to want a baby, but nor is it what everyone wants, and it can be complicated and bring up all sorts of feelings," I say. "You've been motherly in your family, to your siblings, to your mother. And this room is a space where you can look at how that's been for you, what you want from your life."

"I want new life," she says.

"New life" reverberates. She's shown something internal and genuine here. Wanting "new" is creative.

I am a demanding therapist. I want therapy to spark something and change life in some way. In the words of the pioneering psychotherapist Karen Horney: "There is no good reason why we should not develop and change until the last day we live." This means something different for everyone. I cannot know exactly where we'll go or how we'll get there. Rosie needs space for flexibility so we can cocreate something together. I struggle to explain this.

For the first few sessions, Rosie is unusually revealing in some ways, but she keeps me at arm's length. She describes things without seeking my insight or opening up discussion. She reports facts as though there's a requirement to hand over documents. She doesn't express interest in reviewing stories or looking at them. What is she interested in?

"Sensible" is a word Rosie uses lots. She's done her best to plan and script what will happen, to make sensible choices and prepare for each moment of her life, including marriage and motherhood. But playfulness, desire, where art thou? I want to know what her body is communicating. I know this sounds extremely peculiar, but I find myself admiring her vagina for rejecting her modus operandi.

What is the standoff telling us? Is her body trying to reclaim a state of being a little girl, when she didn't get to be a child in her childhood? Is her closed vaginal door a protective barrier to the intrusions she experienced? And does the danger go both ways, not only for what she takes in, but for what she might let out? Her carefulness, her governed narrative—is she suspicious of, fearful of, what would happen if she loosened her grip?

Between sessions, I notice the cherry blossoms, the beauty of London in the springtime. New life everywhere. Rosie has, in her way, communicated something bold and daring, but not necessarily about having a baby. It's about creating a life of her own.

In the next session, Rosie arrives with a look of frustration. She's polite but curt. We are halfway through our agreed time frame, and she still hasn't had sex or made further attempts with her husband, nor has she masturbated, when I ask. The question doesn't make her wince, as I half expected, but nor does it spark interest. She has diligently followed her homework of trying the smallest dilator and she succeeded with that insertion. "It's like Russian dolls," she says.

"Interesting comparison," I say.

"Heh heh," she says. The words come out with no affect. She doesn't go further with the idea.

"How did it feel?"

"Fine," she says.

I ask her if she ever masturbates. "I try not to," she says. "At our church they call it interference. God will see if I interfere."

I ask her what this is like for her, feeling seen by God if she does something wrong. She might think she wants to have sex, but she's steeped in her fear of pleasure. I keep thinking about calling masturbation "interference." What else in her life feels like interference, literally and emotionally?

When I ask her about her experience of therapy so far, her feelings from our sessions, she repeats the answer she gave to a question earlier: "Fine."

Nothing less. Nothing more.

This does not feel creative.

"This is your space," I say.

"I would like to tell you about my week," she says.

I tell her to go ahead.

"Everyone is useless. It's just one thing after another. I'll tell you about the dry cleaner," she says, her big gray eyes brightening.

"Go on," I say.

"The dry cleaner charged me £12.50 to repair a jacket that came back completely unfixed. Infuriating."

"Gosh, sounds it."

"I was livid, and I sent it back so they'd better sort it out," she says.

"I'm wondering if this is possibly a metaphor for how you might feel about other areas of your life," I say.

"Um, no," she says.

I've pushed too hard again, too soon. "Okay, I get that. I just wonder if there's a pattern of you feeling that things aren't working as you'd like," I say.

Still no.

She describes other household frustrations. She complains and vents in detail. She's physically small, but she fills the space with concrete complaints about her week. I notice myself feeling cornered but also left out. Is this how she feels in her life, or how she makes others feel?

In our next session, she tells me again about the dry cleaner. She reports it in the same way as the week before, using the same words and details.

"It's so irritating," she says.

"It sounds irritating indeed. You actually told me about this last week," I say. I don't always point out repetition. Repetition and retelling can be reparative and soothing, familiarizing and a way to absorb new ways of understanding. But I don't think Rosie's telling me about the dry cleaner again is particularly helpful. It doesn't go anywhere.

"Do you think it speaks to bigger frustrations, perhaps, for why it's taking up so much residence in your thoughts, these problems?" I ask.

She grimaces. She tells me about a delivery mishap. A barista who messed up her order. A problem with her ink cartridge. A person who skipped the queue. A bus driver who took a long route. A colleague who made a scheduling blunder. I want to do something with her complaints. She's interesting, razor-sharp, and I'm sure there's more here than the surface level of our discussions.

This is my misstep. I go on about how therapeutic conversation involves uncertainty and not-knowing, but my emphatic approach cuts her off. I need to allow for surprise, discovery, mystery, at her pace, not mine. These are essential creative ingredients. Flexibility. The Lesbian rule! I need to attune myself to the particularities of the situation and let the shape emerge.

It's only when I realize, in conversation with my supervisor, that I've been uncreative in forcing Rosie to be creative that the work starts to progress. There are therapeutic dictums about trusting the client's selection of material. Do not set an agenda or steer the progression of the work. We can, however, encourage people to see things in a new light. I want therapy to be life enhancing. I don't want to change this part of myself. So here we are, both refusing to budge.

"Our roof has a leak and our landlord still hasn't sent someone to take care of it. People can just be so incompetent," Rosie says.

By "people," I assume I fall into this category, and I feel ineffectual. Filling her sessions with complaints, packing in grievances—where's the space for intimacy or fun?

"It seems that nothing is going your way, with all of these incompetent people," I say, still adamant in trying to distill the chapter heading of her grumbles.

"Obviously," she says. "Arghhh. The landlord's failure to sort this out—it just really set me off."

"Where do you express your frustration? How do you process your negative feelings?" I ask.

"Here," she says.

She's right. She's doing what she wants. But I'm struggling to accept that this is enough. Still set on making the space playful and creatively rich, I am on a treasure hunt for fun, mischief, play, along with illumination. I'm like a sleuth wanting to decode her complaints and see if they're clues to hidden longings. But maybe there's no mystery and this can't just be "solved."

Rosie doesn't seem to want to hurry her treatment along—not the sexual aspect, nor in any other way. Her pattern of negotiating her inner world and the external world continue to seem emblematic of her conflict about growth and change. On the one hand, she has expressed wanting to grow new life and make a baby, but she's keeping herself small and constricted. She can transmit but not take in, and she draws tight circles around her stories when I attempt to tamper with them, trying to penetrate, get inside, go somewhere.

I keep trying to steer her to the bigger issues, the underlying feelings, but I feel as though I'm subsumed in the granularity of her complaints. I've labeled her in my mind as what a former supervisor of mine called TAT (The Aggrieved Type). TATs carry grudge lists of life's burdens. We can all be TAT, and usually there's a sense of not being witnessed that is part of what makes us latch on to frustrations and obstructions. We need to show off our surviving of life's paper cuts. But there's more to it than that. Critiquing and complaining can feel less daunting than creating something, and I think she's warding off her aggression. Her complaints and her bodily protest communicate this. If I say this to her, will she freeze up further?

I have no sense of who I am to her. Am I her intrusive and imposing mother? Her doctrinaire father? Another invader? An inept service provider like her husband, the dry cleaner, her colleagues? The work shouldn't be about me. But still, the therapeutic relationship is about two people, and I have no clue how she experiences me.

I want to hear about her struggles. I want to make a meal with her, but her complaints feel like little packets of insipid snacks. Her irritations have grown in our time together. I hear about house chores, the fiddly dishwasher, the dumb pedestrian who got in her way, the online purchase that was a rip-off, the delivery mishap, and numerous other irritants. The irritants matter, to some degree, because all material matters, but it's chronic and consuming with Rosie.

Something remains out of reach: she keeps me at a distance, and she doesn't want us to go deeper. Whether she gives abstract statements about people being annoying, symbolic insights, or concrete specifics, I feel banned from playing with it in any way.

She still hasn't asked for feedback, interpretations, insights, links, much of anything. Maybe she's asking for agreement when she complains, or is it disagreement she wants? She's critical, but I don't even know what therapeutic success would look like for her. At this point, I'm not sure she wants her vaginismus to improve, or to discuss the matter at all. My determination to help her is pushing her away. Our dynamic illustrates her internal conflict around closeness and intimacy and blocking as her vaginismus plays out metaphorically in our relationship. I feel restricted. She hasn't let me in. And when I try to talk about it with her, she rejects me further. But she keeps coming back and she wants something from me and from therapy. "I want to stick with this," she says. "Stick" seems to be the key word here.

I'm tempted to stop trying so hard. I start imagining her husband's poor stamina, his premature ejaculation. I wonder if his symptom came first or hers, and how they're linked. I feel she's castrating the therapy, **femasculating** me. Whatever you want to call it. When I try to build something, she knocks me down. I'm stymied. It's like a creativity block. A procreative block.

What I overlook in the moment and realize only on reflection is that she has expressed a wish to tell me about her week. This is what she wants. When I discuss her further in supervision, my supervisor talks about the clients who bend us out of shape. They test boundaries, push limits, unsettle us in all sorts of ways. Rosie is making me feel oddly shapeless and invisible. I feel different with her than with other clients. On the other hand, what doesn't bend may break. I don't want to break. I'm still determined to figure out how to work with her in a way that can be effective.

In our fifth session, I point out that this is our penultimate session, since we've planned on having six sessions. She asks if we can extend our work together. This is the first bold request she's made—a deviation from her strict path—and I'm struck by her expressing something she wants. I agree that we can continue, and we negotiate a reduced fee she can afford past our sixth session, when her health insurance will stop covering the cost.

Though she still pushes me away when I call attention to our relationship, her way of being in the here and now feels like disavowed aggression.

"What is that you're wearing?" she asks in our sixth session. She's noticed me! I'm here, I'm a person! In a body! Before I've had a moment to respond, she adds: "It looks like someone slashed your neck." And now I'm dead. The necklace, incidentally, is a chain with a string of little red rubies. That necklace won't ever look the same to me.

On another occasion, she tells me the zipper on my jacket looks like it will cut my face. This is all part of the work. She **complisults** me, claiming innocence in remarks that feel hostile. Rosie struggles to acknowledge her aggression, but my enduring survival means something too. She's having an impact on me, even in the frustrating ways, and even in the ways she changes my perception of a beloved necklace (and that jacket, which I haven't worn since). Points for her creativity!

In our seventh session, a very peculiar thing happens to me bodily in the room with her. When our time is up, I stand up to let her out, and my left leg is completely asleep from the way I've been sitting—and I fall. It's as if my sturdiness has completely folded and my body has given way. It's mortifying to fall in front of her. I feel like roadkill.

"Are you okay?" Rosie asks.

"Yes, I am, and I'm so sorry! I'm embarrassed," I tell her, struggling to stand up. "My leg fell asleep. But I'm fine." It takes a while for sensation to return. How long, I'm not sure, because my self-consciousness is so powerful that I can't think straight.

"I'm glad you're okay," she says.

This moment changes something in our dynamic. Though I'm embarrassed, it's a jolting admission of collapsing. I've lost control.

I am flummoxed that this happened. I tell my supervisor about it. I would normally notice when a limb starts to go fizzy if I have been sitting in the same position for a long time. Where was I when this was happening? Disembodied? Dissociated? Trapped in some way? Mirroring her frozen comportment? Floppy like her mother? There's something about the paralysis that seems connected to the block between us.

The following session I admit to Rosie how embarrassed I felt by my fall. I talk about what happened. "My leg fell asleep and I didn't even notice until I stood up. It's as if I was frozen," I say.

"It's fine," she says. "I'm glad you're okay."

"I feel frozen in our work sometimes. Stuck," I say. "I'm going to risk annoying you, but I've wondered if this is how you feel some of the time. Paralyzed. Cut off from a part of yourself. Possibly collapsing."

"Stuck. Yes. I don't know what motion would look like," she says. "So, do you feel paralyzed by me?"

"Sometimes I do. I feel restricted by our conversations, and judged by the words that come out of my mouth. It's hard to work under threat, and the feeling I have when I'm in the room with you is that I'm getting it wrong. I feel I'm trying, but maybe too hard. Sometimes you give very concrete descriptions of problems, and you play with language in a fascinating way, but when I try to engage, or even respond, you push me away. I guess I want to do something with your concrete descriptions too. Use the concrete to build something. But if I take the material you bring and try to go somewhere with it, it's as if I'm snatching it from you and offending you."

"I feel you're hard on me," Rosie says. "It's like you're pushing me to dance with you, and I don't know how to dance," she says.

"I really hear you. And I think that's a powerful, imaginative way of describing where we are. I'm trying too hard to respond to your statements, to have a retort, a solution, an interpretation. Gosh, if you don't want to dance and I keep trying to force you to dance with me, how is that for you?"

"I don't know. I appreciate it. Even though it also frustrates me and overwhelms me. Please don't stop trying," she says.

"Okay, but I don't want to be forceful or overwhelming, and it's interesting that you experience me that way. Let's figure out how to get in step together."

"I really don't know how to actually dance; that's the thing. I said you're trying to get me to dance symbolically, but I literally don't know how to, and never have. Ever," she says.

"Ever? Around the house, as a child? At school? Just silly dancing?"

"Nope. Never. I have never danced. Not once. My brothers and sisters did, and Mum and her friends. But I always found them so foolish and silly. I never did it. And when Michael and I got married, we didn't have a first dance. We had everyone link arms and do a group thing that wasn't us dancing. He doesn't know how to dance either. But he's pretend-danced, around the house. I haven't."

"This seems like such a good place to start. Letting yourself dance, moving, being silly. Let yourself dance badly! See what happens. How about trying it when you get home?"

"Okay, what song? How? For how long?" Rosie asks.

"Anything! I'm sure you can think of a song—any song—and just let yourself bop around, by yourself, for as long as you want."

"Okay," she says warily. "When you fell, were you embarrassed?" she asks.

"Yes, I was, but I survived. And you've survived my collapsing too. We fall apart sometimes, and get messy. I think I've been impatient with your complaints because of my own desire to make these sessions meaningful for you. But maybe they are—not in the way either of us expected. It matters that you can tell me about your week, your day."

"Hearing you say that back to me makes me realize how small my life is, though. I want more. I'm so frustrated by the things that go wrong."

"Your frustration is interesting. I think your destructiveness, your aggression, is also part of your creativity."

"I've never thought of myself as creative," Rosie says, looking dubious.

"I experience you as creative. But it's as if you talk yourself out of it. The block, your vaginal block, the emotional block, could be about this. There's so much about productivity, compliance, ticking boxes, getting through life."

"And you're the first person to tell me I might be creative," she says. "Why do you think that?"

"Your aggressive remarks, your veiled attacks—they're quite imaginative. The comment you made about my necklace. My jacket. Your symbolic use of language. You've got a vivid mind."

"That's a first for me, hearing that," she says. "I guess I like that you think it's possible for me to be open. Michael once told me that being with me is like hugging a porcupine. You haven't let me kill you with my spikes."

"Intriguing that you feel your spikes could kill. Do they protect you by attacking anyone who tries to get close?"

"Yes. I'm so tired of it, though. Charlotte, I'm beginning to realize I've never felt safe enough to play."

"Understandably," I say. "Children need some security to play freely, and your childhood may not have given you that."

"No. I felt nervous and watchful all the time. I had to be that way. I didn't have any privacy. I always wanted my own room, my own stuff, but everything got shared and taken or went missing. Wherever I've gone, whoever has come and gone from our house and my bed and with my clothes, my inside world is the one space that's mine and mine only."

"Rosie, I'm fascinated by your stark awareness and willingness to understand yourself. It's new. You're doing it—you're making new life."

"Children knock down buildings with more enthusiasm than they have building them," she says. "I've always been struck by that with my siblings—the way they knock things down. And I've been the one to clean up the mess. Maybe I wanted to knock something down as a way of playing. So that was part of my feeling that you fell because of me."

I ask how this felt for her.

"I felt bad, thinking I'd somehow knocked you down, that you fell because I had you in my grip. I wanted to rush over and make sure you were okay. Maybe I feel aggressive sometimes, but that doesn't mean I want to actually destroy you."

"I'm here," I say.

We look at how she's hoping to become the mother she didn't have. But she's also intensely ambivalent about having a child when she didn't ever get to be one herself.

"I want to play. I want to learn how to play. Is it too late, at the age of twenty-two? I want to let loose."

Letting loose says a lot—for both of us.

Rosie and I both started off parsimonious and rigid, each unwilling to budge an inch. I thought I was generous and industrious, giving her my time and thoughts, and she believed she was doing the work, but we didn't really give ourselves the chance to experience something in a new, imaginative collaboration until now. We've been filing problems, and each other, into strict inflexible systems of understanding. We need motion, flexibility, movement, playfulness—creativity—to unstick ourselves. We're getting closer.

I'm the person who finds out about her day, her week, her life.

"When we return home and 'tell our day,' we are artfully shaping material into story form," writes the philosopher Iris Murdoch. She explains how this is our way of "constructing forms out of what might otherwise seem a mass of senseless rubble." I realize that Rosie is telling her story to me in a way she couldn't with her drunk mother or her stern father. Or her efficient husband, who may not give her space or show interest in hearing about her day. For Rosie, telling me about the dry cleaner, the missing chopsticks, the delivery blunder, the irritants—this is a way of narrating her life. And she needs me to be available to hear about these details.

Finally, something is shifting, but in a way I haven't anticipated.

In the following session, Rosie arrives and reports that she had sex with her husband. She says offhandedly that she had multiple orgasms. I'm dubious but don't say this. I ask her about her experience. "I didn't really have multiple orgasms, but I feel so boring and uptight. I'm like a burnt-out reporter covering dull news, and I want that to change. So I used my imagination," she says, deadpan.

"How was it in your imagination?" I ask.

"It was exciting. The truth is, we did have sex. And it wasn't great, but it happened. And he ejaculated very quickly, as usual. But he managed to fully penetrate me at the same time. So that's solved the problem."

She looks dejected.

"What's on your mind?" I ask.

"Could I have a few more sessions, please? Even though I don't need to be here anymore . . . It doesn't make sense, but I like finding out about myself."

"By all means, keep coming," I say.

"No pun intended," she says. And then she actually laughs.

We sit together with the sound of spring rain pelting down. It's a soothing sound, feeling safe and dry where we are, just two people together in a room, comfortable and open.

CREATING AND PLAYING

Mozart made scatological jokes in pun-filled letters to his cousin. Seriousness and playfulness are allies. We can express ourselves in interesting, imaginative ways. We can play. We can invent. We can be silly. Whether in the form of doodling, building something with our hands, solving a business problem with divergent thinking, planning a menu, arranging flowers in a particular way—we can take pleasure in our own daily creativity. Every day, the smallest moments are expressions of who we are. Of course, there are many aspects of life that require conformity and rule following, but it's all too easy to feel limited by the well-worn grooves of a busy life. It's important to stay in touch with your creative instincts, whatever form they take.

Try to be a meaning maker, not a ticket taker. When we automatically follow the beaten path because we think we're supposed to want certain things, we can feel stuck and blocked. Cooperation requires some ticket taking, but we can make meaning out of situations where we feel obligated or pressured by prioritizing what matters to us. Maria Luca, a formative lecturer and psychotherapist in my training, once talked to me about her career path. "I wanted to become a builder, and I became a cleaner," she told me. "The higher I got managerially, the more I was just mopping up. Not creating." She stepped down from her position of senior authority as head of an entire therapy institution, giving up her position so she could be a therapist and a teacher, and an academic. "I was done cleaning up messes," she told me. "Time to build." She let herself change her mind.

We have life admin, work demands, social pressures. It's important to notice and celebrate what we've achieved, but also to realize that productivity isn't the same thing as creativity. Be willing to surprise yourself and experiment with going off the beaten path in everyday tasks, whether it's the way you dress, make a meal, or write a card. In the words of the cultural anthropologist Margaret Mead, whose outspoken personality made her a legendary speaker: "Cooking the daily midday meal is repetitious, but preparing special foods for a feast is creative." Not every meal can be a feast, of course, but when life feels full of obligations and responsibilities, it's important to add sparkle and make ordinary moments into occasions when possible. Few of us have enough creative space unless we claim it for ourselves.

There's a paradoxical aspect to creativity. You need to be alone to create in certain ways, but in other ways, gathering, engaging, joining up with other bright minds, can bring about the magic of synergy. So, rather than isolate yourself, treat yourself to encounters with other sparkling minds you can draw from. A conversation can be creative.

Limitations and boundaries facilitate play and creation. Cinderella's fairy godmother tells her to return by midnight. We need time limits for magic. Framing and restricting can galvanize and contain. Too many choices, too much space, too much time, can overwhelm and block and drain away any urgency to engage and create. So, come up with limits for yourself, define the edges—whether it's making a meal with only a few ingredients, writing a story with only a few prompts, or setting a material restriction or a clock limit for a familiar task that challenges you to do it in a new way.

Even when we have space, shame and fear shut down play for adults all too easily. We stop dancing because we're self-conscious.

We feel silly playing a game we think we've outgrown. We're afraid of doing things ineptly, of making mistakes. We're worried about exposing ourselves, even to ourselves. And we can even feel embarrassed to admit enthusiasm for something.

Our creative powers can deflect into hidden thoughts and feelings, saturating our fantasies and beliefs. The vividness of anxious catastrophizing, for instance, is often highly imaginative. Jealousy is imaginative too: we grab on to wisps and construct scenarios. Creative expression can shine a light on our fantasies and help us deal with reality. See if you can note some of the ways your mind creates theatre, so you can appreciate the color of your inner world without being at its mercy.

Rosie didn't think of herself as remotely creative, but she was. We all are. Whatever your circumstances, see if you can reconstitute any of the material of your life in a creative way. When Rosie started therapy, she said initially that she wanted to create new life, but this ended up not meaning a baby—not for now, anyway. The new life she created was her own. There may be restrictions in your life that you have not chosen. Consider ways of turning what you have always experienced as liabilities into possible assets. And, conversely, consider how something that you've characterized as an asset might also be burdensome.

If you insist, you can have creative moments every day just by observing and being curious. Express yourself imperfectly. Change your point of view about an issue. Take in something new and let out something personal. Experience something fresh.

Chapter Eight

TO BELONG

Early in my career, I worked bedside with a young woman in intensive care who had fallen off a balcony at a party. Now, at the age of twenty-two, she had to accept that she'd never walk again. She wept from her hospital bed. "Where will I belong?" she asked me, her eyes looking shocked. "No more dancing. Ever."

Her story moved into a space within me. If my work pulls me away from my personal life at times, it's because I want it to.

Belongingness has become a media darling, swelling in popularity. Known to promote employee retention and productivity, workplaces cultivate belongingness. Schools nurture it. Communities promote it. The desire to belong exists in every culture. The social psychologist Abraham Maslow placed belongingness in the pyramid of needs; we're social creatures and we like to be part of groups, at least sometimes, whether it's friends, family, coworkers. Community gives us support, protection, sometimes purpose. We're bolstered by endorsement and acceptance. But there's a darkness to the reality of what it's like for people who don't belong. Promoting a sense of belongingness doesn't address the crisis of not belonging.

A strong therapeutic relationship is not always enough. People may feel safe inside the room, but they leave and go into the cold night. They end the online session and return to the ostracizing environment when they open the door and step outside the room. When people in therapy convey the desire to belong, it's worth exploring. The yearning to belong can be compensation for earlier experiences of exclusion. A deferred wish for the belongingness that didn't fully happen in family, school, culture, nationality. Sometimes it's deferred obedience to the oppressive culture, or a desire to individuate.

The crisis of not belonging, or no longer feeling a sense of belonging, can bring people to therapy, even when it isn't manifestly recognized or stated in the first meetings. It shows up as a feeling of alienation.

We need to talk more about not belonging. Not belonging can be a crisis, a catastrophic feeling of loneliness and despair, and it's stigmatized. The popularity of belonging makes the pool of not belonging smaller and sadder, or at least it feels that way. "They're faking it, some of them, their complete sense of belongingness, right?" a client asked me after a work retreat. An interesting possibility. She felt choked by the pressure to belong, by the simplistic expectation that she'd want to belong to her workplace, or could.

"Never tell people where they belong, or where they want to belong. Assume nothing," Desa Markovic, a vibrant systemic therapist, says. "Invite them to tell you." Being asked where she was from annoyed her: her accent clearly marked her as foreign and the question suggested she didn't belong here.

I've romanticized not belonging. The loner artist, the exile, the odd one out—I've seen not belonging as noble and original. I'm hardly original for my naïve admiration of the noble and spirited outsider. I didn't see how problematic my romanticization of not belonging could be until I recently confronted my bias, and I was startled and embarrassed.

The issue of not belonging, and the desire to belong, emerged in surprising ways in my recent experience with Dwight, a Black man in his late forties. He came to me following the discovery that his wife, a White woman, had cheated on him with her ex-boyfriend, also White.

DWIGHT'S BLUES

"I'm fine, can't complain," Dwight says through a tight smile. His voice is very quiet and deep, and I often have to ask him to speak up. He's tall and exceedingly handsome. A onetime lower-league footballer in his late forties, he now works for an international online music platform as a product designer. He's crackling with an unusual mixture of energy and timidity. Though he's described the events of his wife's infidelity to me, he seems to hold back from letting himself experience the full force of feelings during our sessions. I'm not sure where, if anywhere, he lets himself feel fully. He's both tempted and reluctant to go deeper. It's as though he takes me along different paths, but we usually end up at cliff edges. No way. Step back. Wrong direction.

He calls it the "blues," and he doesn't want to go there. His father had the blues, and he barely got out of bed for most of Dwight's childhood. It was as if the family lived underwater, quietly drowning in the spiritless gloom. Dwight was embarrassed by his father; he found the sadness feeble and weak. He's defined himself in contrast. He takes pride in not letting himself flop like his father.

As he tells me about himself, he has the expression of an onlooker. Peering with slight judgment, he stands back from himself as though his survival demands the distance. He's determined to steer himself away from sadness. The blues are where he's come from, but there's no way that's where he's headed. He's in therapy, he says, "to keep being positive."

Over a period of months, I have a sense of anticipation with Dwight. We are reaching towards something just out of sight. There's something—an implacable, undefinable quality—in the faraway look in his eyes. He's reserved and private, and we talk about this. He's always been this way, but especially recently. He's told none of his friends about his marital crisis, and he's withdrawn himself socially. Jessica, his wife, has broken off her affair, and they are attempting to repair and recover. Dwight is determined to hold on to a sense of hope. He and his wife are in couples therapy with a colleague of mine, and Jessica has life coaching. They have two little girls and they'll "make it to the other side"; they have already. "We'll come out stronger," he tells me. He's never had therapy before this crisis. He's grateful and is a "convert," as he calls himself.

From the start of our work, Dwight has insisted he's over the affair and has forgiven Jessica. He believes in peace and forgiveness, he says repeatedly, and he insists on positivity. That word again. He sometimes brings in poems about forgiveness and seeing the bright side of life, and he likes to read quotes on the subject. Gratitude seems to be the keystone of his mindset. Not being angry or sad is part of his philosophy, his faith, his determination to be different from his bitter father.

"My dad felt the light never turned green for him. He had a running list in his head of lifelong grudges." Back to the blues. Morose, pitiful, depressing. Dwight's father has "nothing good to say about where he's from, or where he could go." Dwight identifies much more with his "sunny-side-up, cheerful" mother. He gravitates to his mother's joyfulness like a sunflower turning towards the sun, he says.

Dwight's parents split when he was a teenager, though they never legally divorced. The dissolution of his childhood family pains him still. But just as he approaches the distress in our sessions, he quickly shifts gears and goes back into the action mode of positivity. All green lights for Dwight. He and Jessica are moving onwards and upwards.

"We're different," he says. "We've always been different. From each other, and from where we're from. Not just because she's White and from Liverpool, but our personalities too. But it's our thing, this yin and yang. She's chatty and likes to plan stuff. She's the sociable one. I'm the quiet, calm guy. She gets easily upset, and I'm not someone who dwells. I steady her. It works well," Dwight tells me. "We belong together." And then he adds: "Yeah, I feel lucky, and there's a lot that's going right." His manner has a coolness I can't fully fathom. Incredibly pleasant but one step removed from me in our sessions.

Differences and distinctions have bonded Dwight and his wife—as long as they stay in their character lanes. There's no urgency, but the more Dwight cheerleads, the more I want to explore the "blues" he's trying to avoid. I really do love hearing about what's going well. I want to hear about the good times and not just the dark times. But therapists are like truffle pigs when it comes to vulnerability: we go hunting and rooting around until we find what we're looking for. We need to get to the pain, at least a bit, so we can begin to work together on making life better. He's alerted me to real pain, but we keep edging towards it and back again. His father's sorrow seems oceanic, and it's as though Dwight is fighting for his existence in pushing this away. I feel piggy, sniffing for more.

Dwight is the peacemaker with his parents and family—Jessica's family too. He's usually very able to fit in with groups, he says, and takes pride in getting along well with everyone. And with himself, with whatever is wrong. It's a challenge to get beyond all the peace he insists on.

When I ask about how his sex life is with Jessica in general, he says that their connection is about more than sex, and who has time anyway, with two young children? It's fine, he says. Not a problem. "I've always handled uncertainty well," he adds. What an interesting leap. I'm not sure what to make of this, and he moves on to the certainty of looking at the bright side of life.

The mantra seems to apply consistently: Do not hold on to negativity. It's as though I'm seeing a duel between his ideal self, "the sunny-side-up" Dwight, and his scorned self, the "blues." He references this part of himself only to explain that he doesn't want to give it airtime.

There's a psychotherapy cliché that's true: what we resist will persist. In fact, better yet, that the thing you avoid is *the* thing. Name it to tame it. In our sessions, I continue to feel a kind of reticence from Dwight. What is he distancing himself from? When I ask, he often returns to his wish to be positive in life. To stay on the sunny side of the street. Does he think that visiting the shady side of the street will take him to some dangerous point of no return?

"I don't want to go there. I can't," Dwight says with a wry smile. "I'm an introvert. Getting me to speak my mind with you—it's already a big deal. I don't say this much to anyone. Maybe it doesn't feel like a lot to you, but for me it is."

It's a sharp reminder of my professional bias that my everyday emotional home is foreign and rare for others. It's only in supervision that I realize that Dwight goes places every day that are foreign to me, and I still feel reluctant to acknowledge it: the issue of race!

I talk with a Black colleague, Dr. Victoria Uwannah, about issues of race, and whether it's worth bringing up if the client hasn't. I admit to her that I haven't yet. And not only have I avoided the issue, I've been pushing Dwight to talk about his pain, the blues, the difficult stuff.

I hear the smile in Vicki's voice. "It can be an invitation," she says. "You can throw it in there and see what people do with it." I ask her what she thinks of matching therapists and clients racially. She says most of her Black clients seek her out for her Blackness.

"I believe that the majority of Black clients who intentionally seek out a White therapist are struggling with issues of identity or fear of judgment from a Black therapist." She reiterates that I should bring up my awareness of difference when we're in the room. "Discussing these issues openly can aid a Black client in feeling seen and validated."

What's clear, from my discussion with her, is that I'm the one who has been running away from this more than Dwight.

I ask Dwight how he feels having therapy with a White woman.

"Well, you being a White woman, like Jessica, maybe it's connected," he says. "But also there are more White therapists available. It's not all psychological. I liked your style of working. Not everything is connected to race."

He pauses, crossing his arms, uncrossing them, looking at me in a way that makes me feel he's gearing up to say something difficult.

"I've told you I'm not that sexual at the moment, and I haven't wanted sex for a long time, not since Jessica cheated on me. But I've forgiven her, and I want to have sex with her again to show it, and I can't. We've tried a few times, and it's bad. It just doesn't happen. Like smashed avocado on toast. That's what it made me think of, trying to get it in there. And it's making me feel . . . pretty shit. I don't know how therapy can help me with this, but it's a sign that I don't belong in my life in some way."

As he says the words, he seems bathed in shame. He looks down to the ground, his head hanging low, like a schoolboy admitting a failure.

Viagra hasn't done the trick, he says. "It's like I'm pulling back from Jessica, even though I want to forgive her. Why am I doing this? What am I withholding? I don't get it."

We look at how he might be libidinally disinvesting on some level, not trusting his wife sexually, not feeling it's safe to be inside her and have intimacy. It's notable that they haven't had sex since he found out about the affair, and though Jessica broke it off, and they want to have sex, his body seems not to want to. "I'm protesting, I guess," he says. "But it's hard to really say what's going on, what this is about. Jessica apologized and ended the affair. I don't know what I'm waiting for."

"I like that you're asking these questions. I want you to feel safe enough to express whatever feelings you have," I say.

"But it's not safe in other places," he says. "It's just not. And I'm so used to people seeing me the wrong way."

He looks at his hands, and he's now stock-still, almost frozen, except for the occasional blink. I feel that trying to catch his gaze at this moment might make him self-conscious. I choose not to call attention to anything about his body.

"I'm curious to know what the right way and wrong way of seeing you means," I say.

"I'm not sure you get it," he says. "It's not your fault. It's just how it is. For all the hype these days about authenticity, vulnerability, those two buzzwords, they're bullshit. I can't be vulnerable. I can't be authentic. I told Jessica about some financial problems right before she cheated on me. I'm pretty sure my vulnerability screwed me. And my authenticity . . . what does that even mean? If I'm authentically myself, I'm angry. And I don't want to be angry. It's not just that I don't want to be angry. I cannot afford to be angry. A Black man cannot. And I can't explain that to you. It's just how it is."

"You've explained a lot already, and of course there's more you can't explain. Is that part of why you picked me as your therapist, so you'd reinforce your positivity and remind yourself of how to be in a White world?"

"Probably. A Black therapist calls bullshit on the positivity stuff, especially after being disrespected by my White wife. That's what I imagined. But you've been so . . . understanding. Maybe it's your wish to make me feel comfortable."

What hubris to think that therapy can magically put Dwight at ease. "You're naming what's happening. Do you do this anywhere else?" I ask.

"Nope. I guess being shy and avoiding speaking up can be a problem. I don't speak up at work. I don't speak up with most people. This happened with Jessica. It takes a lot for me to confront people, and when I do, I'm often too hurt. . . . But my hurt is mostly inwards."

One simple definition of "depression": anger turned inwards.

Internalized anger happens even more if negative emotions and any expression of them are banned, denied, prohibited. Dwight looks at me with tentative eyes, as though seeking my approval. "I'm expressing myself here, though," he says.

"Yes, you are. Do you feel like you're confronting me too? Do you feel hurt, the way you've just said you do when you speak up anywhere else?"

"I do feel hurt. But I don't think it's by you. But it's your people. And I'm worried about being offensive."

"Please let yourself speak freely," I say. "I can take it."

"It's new for me, all of this. I've never said these things to anyone. Back to the introversion thing . . . I process things on my own, apart from people."

"I wonder if you feel unsafe processing with people who might use your disclosures against you," I say.

"Yes, it's that in part. But It backfires when I do open up. It's hard to speak up if I don't know my thoughts and feelings at those moments. I mean, even when I do know, I can't show my real self. It's just not totally safe to be authentic, to admit what's really going on. I'm a Black man. I'm constantly misunderstood. However tame and cooperative I appear, I'm two seconds away from people perceiving me incorrectly. That's reality. That's the dangerous real world. Come on."

Of course, he's right. And I'm oddly left out. I am not part of his world, even when I try. And my empathy and curiosity and attentiveness don't make me feel effectual. I feel impotent. This happens in therapy when we realize the limits of our worldview. The experience he has of being in the world is profoundly challenging in ways that my empathy cannot solve.

I've been so avoidant of my own blues about difference and belonging and the state of the world, I have tried to relate to Dwight, to see the sameness, to overlook the oceans between us.

Dwight is constantly proving what he isn't as much as what he might be. And I'm constantly proving that I'm with him, joining him, when I'm probably not. The world doesn't permit him to fully express himself. And I feel desperate to give him a sense of safety so he can show himself here. I can't force him. My hyper-respectfulness is more than try-hard correctness: it's actually been alienating.

If I'm asking him to uncensor himself here, I need to do the same. "Dwight, I'm being a try-hard, wanting you to feel comfortable with me. You worry about being misunderstood, and I'm misunderstanding you, telling you I get you. I keep wanting you to feel you belong here. Let's go the other way in: you don't belong here. I don't belong here with you. We're not the same or from the same culture. But we both want to belong, not just in general but here, doing this work."

"I want to say that, just for the liberation: I don't belong here. Working with you. I don't belong with Jessica. I don't know what belongs where anymore. Nothing fits."

"How do you feel saying that?" I ask.

"I'm kind of lost. I thought I had figured out how to navigate life. Jess and I, when we began dating, we loved our differences, and our world opened up because we weren't the same. Man, we had chemistry in the early days. When we were getting to know each other, we were like magnets joining together. The force of our love steered us. You know that feeling of being so united with someone, it's like you're confident enough to conquer the world together? That's how it felt for me. Jessica was so relaxed in this culture I'd never felt comfortable in, and I was cozy with her. It was as if marrying her gave me me a worldwide passport. I could go anywhere and feel at home. And then, bam . . . I remember the feeling so clearly, when I realized I was not at home, these were not my people . . . the first time I showed up at one of Jessica's family dinners, after discovering her cheating on me. I felt betrayed by all of them. And scared. I've hidden from letting myself freak out. Yes. We are not the same. We don't need to be. But that's part of our chemistry . . . we embraced our differences. . . . But, man, do I miss the way we connected in the early days. Like magnets slotting into place, we both trusted love and let it steer us. It was like 'Yeah, I'm not really a part of things. These fuckers aren't really my people. I'm not one of them anymore.' And maybe I never was. I do still hate her a little."

The following week, Dwight says that he doesn't fully belong with White people, but neither does he belong with Black people. "I've got two mixed-race kids. I've left my people, whoever they are, or were. You know how I talk about the blues, not wanting to go there?" he asks.

"Yes."

"I went there with Jessica, and that's why she cheated. I can't prove it, but I feel it. And I'm angry. Jessica begged me for years to show vulnerability. 'Be vulnerable' were her exact words. She said that to me so many times. She wanted me to open up, get closer, share my wounds with her. And when I finally did, she didn't like it. I remember where we were sitting. It was a Sunday evening, and the girls were asleep. We were in the living room, reading the papers. She put down the papers and told me to stop reading. 'Let's talk!' she said. She's always saying this. She asked me how I was, and instead of saying I was fine, I showed her my vulnerability about money stuff, and she freaked out. She didn't admit it, but I could see it. And she pulled away from me—maybe not at that exact moment, but I feel like that's where things began to go wrong between us. You might tell me otherwise, and she might not admit it, but women think they want men to show vulnerability, and when we do, they hate it. I'm telling you."

His words stay with me, and I can't fully process them in his company. I say this to him. I guess I too can be introverted! Is it introversion or saving face?

The following session, I acknowledge some of this to him. "You're right that vulnerability is complicated. We're full of mixed messages. You're not the only man to tell me that women think they want to hear about vulnerability but actually they react badly when men do show it. Jessica might have thought she wanted you to show vulnerability to her, but your money concerns could have activated her own anxiety and insecurities."

"I see what you mean. The context. Oh, man. Sometimes what I miss isn't how close we were. It was the belief that we could be . . . I really believed in us. We belonged together. And even the hard stuff felt possible. It feels impossible right now."

"That must be hard," I say.

"Yeah, Team Jessica and Dwight. Her cheating with an ex who's White. I haven't thought that's part of the story, but maybe it is. Fuck."

We sit together in silence. Dwight's face suddenly looks pulled apart, almost in a deranged way. His eyes look haunted, and his eyebrows are knitted in a kind of anguish I haven't seen him allow himself to feel in our sessions before now. This is the look of pain. It's a relief, even though it's hard. We are together, and full of differences and solitary bits of ourselves, but so together. There's something generous about his willingness to trust me enough to see this.

"I'm lonely. I want to belong to a team again. But I'm not sure I ever will, or ever fully have. I'm questioning so much. Why do we want to belong? What's it about?"

"I think it's about longing to feel at ease and recognized," I say. I'm finding my way. "It's more than just being acquainted with people. It's about acceptance and support."

"Yes, but with an individual? A group? Who is *your* tribe?" He tilts his head and gives me a sidelong look.

"Can we stay with you?" I ask.

"Where do *you* feel at home?" he asks. "Please. And thank you. It's helpful to me if you're willing to share." His voice sounds impeccably polite.

"I feel at home everywhere and nowhere in a certain sense. That's part of me. I relate to different cultures, but never entirely," I say. I enjoy being part of things, and think of various groups where I'm somewhat comfortable with but never fully: psychotherapy modalities, mothers, groups of friends, cultures, schools, families—whatever it is, there are aspects of groups I relate to, but inevitably I feel like an outsider to certain features of most groups and systems.

"How do you deal with that?" he asks me. "The part that doesn't entirely belong." I try to acknowledge it. It can even be something to celebrate. I don't ostracize myself for not belonging or force myself to pretend I belong when I don't.

Is anyone entirely and fully at home in just one place, ever? Maybe, but not most people I know. We have blissful moments when we feel we fully belong, but it's usually partial. The best we can do is accept that we belong and don't belong partially in multiple places. "Lucky," he says. I ask what he means by "lucky."

"Your being an outsider is more privileged than my feeling like I don't belong. When I cross the street at night, I hear the sound of people locking their car doors as I approach. It's just different."

"Yes, it is," I say.

Dwight settles into the sofa, looking comfy and cozy. "I look at you and I assume you belong. You belong in the armchair you're in. You belong in your profession. I imagine you belong entirely in your family, with mother groups, with shrink groups—fuck, even in WhatsApp groups. So knowing that a part of you doesn't feel entirely at ease in any one group, I kind of like that. A lot."

"I'm glad," I say, and we smile. "I do feel I belong here in this armchair," I say. "Working with you. But I also now realize all the ways we are in different worlds outside of this space. I don't like it, but I'm beginning to get it."

"I'm an outsider in my own home now. I used to feel I could be myself with Jessica, in bed at night. And now we are just so damned far away. Alone. Lonelier than actually being apart."

"Tell me about the loneliness and feeling far away from her," I say.

"She's just on another planet from me. We don't look at each other anymore. She feels like the enemy."

"You felt betrayed by her. She became the villain of your story, at the same time that you have continually insisted that you've forgiven her."

"But I *am* over it."

"Are you? I get that you want to be. And if you want to forgive her, if you want to get past this, you can. But it takes time to let go," I say. "I think you're wanting to. Maybe you're ready to stop punishing her and punishing yourself. The protest is tiring you."

"It is. No wonder I'm not interested in Black protests. I've been protesting in my own life. Jessica fucking cheated on me. With a White guy. And I'm not fully over it yet. Maybe I haven't yet forgiven her."

"Dwight, I have never once heard you say what you've just finally allowed yourself to say: that you aren't yet over it, and you haven't yet forgiven her. Bravo."

"Why bravo? Isn't that all obvious?"

"Not at all. You have constantly and persistently said that you're over it and you've forgiven her. One of the major steps for recovery is admitting that it's not okay—not yet. You can forgive her, but first you have to allow for where you are. And this is where you are."

"Well, I like that. I've tried to be cheerful like my mother. No complaining. No misery. It helped me have a good attitude as a footballer. And in other ways. But not when it comes to getting over my wife cheating on me with her ex-boyfriend. A bit of sorrow is allowed. And then recovery."

"I like that. All that you've just said."

"I think I chose a White female therapist so I would have special access to her world. I thought you'd invite me into her way of being. I didn't want a Black perspective on her."

"That's interesting. Do you think Jessica and I share the same viewpoint?" I ask.

"Not really. Now that I think about it. You're nicer to me than she is, obviously, but she's my wife. And your niceness isn't always that helpful."

"Tell me how I'm not helpful. It's useful for me to know," I say.

"Being too nice is an insult. It's like you don't think I have the capacity and strength to tolerate being challenged. It's only recently that you've begun to be demanding. That makes me feel more secure here, like I actually belong here, doing this work with you."

"I will continue to be demanding, then," I say. "My desperation to put you at ease—I totally get what you mean. I'm glad we've ruptured and repaired. I hear myself still trying too hard, pushing for success, even as we discuss my therapeutic failures. But we seem to be getting somewhere."

"I hope so. Everyone has seemed so far away. There's this distance with Jessica. We're both somewhere else. She's apologized for the affair, but I don't believe that she's sorry. I think she feels it was warranted. And she's sulking that she had to shut it down. She ended the affair for the girls, really. And for her image. But she's still there, in fantasy land. She thinks she should be living fabulously and belongs in some other life. When it comes to belonging. I realized this. I've always thought that Jessica belonged to everything—to the White girl club, English middle-class, private schools, members clubs. The fashion scene she was part of. But exclusion is always there. I mean, our daughter asked what 'private' means the other day. She's five years old. What 'private' means. Can you believe it? What a question. Her friend at school talked about a private compound on some holiday, and she wanted to know what this meant. Explaining the difference between private and public is hard. But a good question. It's fucked-up, how we group ourselves and hold on to status in desperate ways." Dwight pauses to catch his breath.

We look at each other and pause. There's more to say, but we sit in a comfortable silence together without needing to say anything more at all right now.

WHERE DO YOU BELONG?

Never tell people where they belong. In my romanticization of not belonging, I didn't see Dwight's fear. I saw his reluctance, his avoidance of pain and sorrow, but I didn't catch his terror. The blues were a frightening echo from Dwight's childhood—when he was helpless, vulnerable, and dependent, and his father's sadness nearly drowned them all. Dwight was petrified of falling into this abyss. Or re-creating his father's role and becoming the guy he'd sworn he'd never be. Seeing the blues in a new light disconfirmed his dread that where he was from would determine his fate.

I had an idealistic approach towards belongingness with Dwight at first. I had a perfectionist vision of making him feel better. When he said he wanted to stay positive, I thought he needed to go to his pain, but I didn't go to my own discomfort. For all the horrors and injustices out there in the harsh world, inside my consulting room I foster respect, insight, safety. I want people to feel comfortable, that the space is theirs, that they can make themselves at home. It just doesn't work that way. The world comes into the room. And we leave the room and take therapy out there too.

Admitting what we don't understand, searching for our own biased positions, recognizing the limits of our repertoire, help us belong to our own selves. Pretending to grasp experiences of difference when actually we don't will obstruct emotional safety in a therapeutic relationship. Admitting what we don't know and would like to find out about is a more helpful starting position. We can continue to commit to relationships and cultures where we don't fully belong, but it's helpful to have clarity.

Systems and cultures are flawed in so many ways. We can't always control how we're defined, how we're typecast and portrayed, and there's deep injustice and unfairness in life. James Baldwin made this fascinating remark in 1971 in a conversation with the anthropologist Margaret Mead: "You've got to tell the world how to treat you. If the world tells you how you are going to be treated, you are in trouble." We're easily in trouble. We get excluded, stereotyped, associated with groups we don't want to belong to. I asked the psychologist Frank Tallis how he feels about not belonging: "Not belonging has its benefits." There are obvious evolutionary reasons we seek belonging to groups, but development also requires the discomfort of not conforming. "If you rigidly stick with the group where you already belong, you might feel safe but you won't go very far.

At times, you might feel alienated and at odds—with your own sense of self and with the people around you—but if you can feel comfortable in being all that you are, you can experience not belonging with more ease, even with delight at times. It's about being comfortable with all that you are, even the awkward, clumsy, oddball moments—especially those moments! Think about all that encompasses your existence. Be patient. Fitting in often goes against belonging. It's self-presentation, performative, often insincere. Belonging is genuine.

Chapter Nine

TO WIN

The desire to win can be crafty and contradictory. Winning motivates us to learn and grow, but in subversive ways it also makes us children again. Even without our full awareness, so many relationships have a crust of rivalry.

"Do you think that it is such a great pleasure for me to stand in your shadow for the whole of my life?" the psychologist Alfred Adler asked Sigmund Freud. Originally friendly colleagues, Adler and Freud eventually became feuding enemies. Adler carried a faded postcard Freud had sent him years earlier that he'd whip out to prove, should anyone inquire, that Freud had invited *him* to meet, and not the other way around, as Freud told it.

Each was apparently threatened by the other, and for years they volleyed sarcastic, caustic remarks.

Still holding a grudge even after Adler's death, Freud wrote to a friend: "I don't understand your sympathy for Adler. . . . The world really rewarded him richly for his service in having contradicted psychoanalysis." A triumphant match point in their relentless rivalry. Did either win the battle? They both seem smaller in their emphatic sense of threat and their ongoing attempts to diminish and dethrone each other. Their petty acting out is astonishing, given that Adler coined the terms "inferiority complex" and "superiority complex." Adler maintained that we start life feeling inferior and we spend our lives trying to prove our superiority. How ironic that neither Adler nor Freud seemed to have insight or equanimity about their years of rivalry.

Therapy is hardly the situation for direct competition. But it's a brilliant space for examining the covert games we play. Secret longings to win trot into conversations. We struggle to celebrate a friend's soaring work achievement. We elaborately explain how unenvious we are of a flatmate. Our disparaging judgments of a sibling sound like too much of a protest. We catch humblebrags in midair and notice the overtones of shame in how we imagine other people see us. We consider what our rivalries are *really* about.

Official competitions are probably the clearest opportunities for trying to win. With explicit contests and tournaments, we understand the rules, the score is visible, there are judges and referees, and—however volatile and conflictual the game—there's a defined finish line or highest score. Winning and losing are clear.

But the lines are blurred in games between people. Starting in childhood, so many of us feel the need to prove ourselves. Sadly, we usually do this by showing our superiority to someone else. In so many ways, we ask, who is better? Who is bigger? Who has more? *Mirror, mirror, on the wall* . . . Our desire to win is rationally entangled. "She's going to be a heartbreaker!" is a line so easily said about dazzling children. Think of what it suggests— that people will suffer because of the child's "winning" personality or appearance. Can we win without others needing to lose? Hot on the heels of compulsive winning is the urgent threat of inadequacy.

Our wish to win is one way we try to cope with inequality and scarcity. We may be responding to limited supplies of parental love, money, opportunities. But even when we do have equality, we can still feel the threat of a rival that disturbs our sense of equilibrium, safety, and abundance. There's a sense that there isn't enough to go around. Scrambling for security and safety, we waste energy trying to knock out opponents.

Role suction draws us into awkward conversational dynamics, and, without calling attention explicitly to the competition playing out, we swirl into games of betterness. The terms and conditions are often unspoken and changeable. Angsty competitions between people have no set rules and can be open-ended. Strange games of betterness can pull in anyone, and it's shocking to feel it happen with some people and not with others. **Compersion** with one person, competition with another—rivalry forms in surprising ways.

We compete with ourselves too—the contest between the life we're actually living and our fantasized life of imagined possibilities. Whether our unlived life is a house of horrors or a utopia full of triumphant glory, it helps if we're onto ourselves. It's when we're not aware of our tricks that we tend to act badly.

We can get drawn into thinking we need to prove ourselves, no matter how small the stakes, and it can go on for decades. We're inconsistent about what we actually want from our rivals, and we're often competing with phantoms from the past along with what's at hand. The desperation to prove superiority can overwhelm our perspective and sense of self.

However irrational, we often want updates about a rival. It can be out of fondness and nostalgia for the history, the underground system we've had all these years for positioning ourselves. It sounds wrong, and usually is, which is part of what keeps us from fully admitting it—even in therapy, it's hard—but rivalries carry secret wisdom for how we've defined and understood ourselves through them. We've probably lost ourselves through them too, trading in our integrity for small, petty wins. With rivalries from our youth, we've been through so much together, sidelong glances apart. Seeing a rivalry in a new light, updating ourselves too, can be victorious.

When relationships become hostile zones of combat, the threat of mutually assured destruction increases. Couples can seek security but jeopardize it in their fight for superiority. *I'm right and you're wrong* becomes the driving force. Cooperation gets hijacked by competition. Sometimes there are endless competitions for who has it worse, a pernicious bid to win at losing. Who does more chores, who works harder, who is more burdened, who has less free time, who suffers most? Very often, when rivalry becomes adversarial in a relationship, there's an aching sense of deprivation, and an unmet desire. But rather than acknowledge the true wants, the modus operandi is to attack.

Meet Gabriel and Samantha, a couple in their early thirties. They're here because they can't stop arguing. They both claim that the other started it. Whatever *it* may be. "I told you so" is another line that gets said frequently. They use playground warfare with deadly seriousness. And they both accuse the other of being wrong—in big ways and in small details. They're vividly aware of what's disappointing and problematic in the other, and though they love each other, they're rarely loving in their present lives. They stab rather than stroke each other conversationally.

Their arguments are on full display, but the notes of their rivalry get lost in the sound and fury. I ask how they recover and resolve their arguments. They don't. They jab and chip away and shout. And they leave the mess and hurt behind.

They used to repair their ruptures with elaborate affectionate gestures. "We'd genuinely reconnect, and it felt euphoric," Samantha says. But they're too cross and stubborn to make generous gestures. They're each trying to teach the other lessons. And they both refuse to cooperate or learn. Up until the moment they start therapy with me, their fights are chronic, their ruptures are unrepaired, and their points aren't listened to. It's a hostile standoff. They're jammed in a game of not budging.

TAKING THE PATH OF MOST RESISTANCE:

I feel anxious when I'm facing them in the room. I'm pulled into the rushing traffic of their snipes. There's a sense of urgency in their race to nowhere. Gabriel has an agitated way of speaking. He has black stubble and a vivid, earnest face. I look at Samantha's attractiveness, her beleaguered expression, and I wonder what she looks like when she's smiling. Neither of them has any kind of plan or purpose other than putting the other down.

They've been together for eight years, and they're both determined to make their relationship work. They live in East London in a small flat they bought a year ago. Gabriel's parents split when he was five, and he was mostly raised by his grandmother. Romanian by background, he moved to the UK for university and works as a biomedical engineer. Samantha is British, raised in London, and her parents separated when she was eight. She works in marketing at a small media agency.

The story of their relationship started off with courage and individuation. Adamant not to follow in the footsteps of their parents, Gabriel and Samantha formed their own little two-person family together. They don't think they want children. They don't feel the need to get married and feel it's no guarantee of commitment. They each offer descriptions and characterizations with confidence.

"Oh, and very importantly, we have two snobby cats," Gabriel says. Samantha laughs and agrees.

Their flat was meant to be an exciting mark of adulthood, success, and self-expression. But it has loads of problems, and this giant responsibility has burdened them.

Neither of them is remotely excited about their work. Even in passing reference, Samantha's expression becomes bovine, and she emanates malaise. Gabriel is completely frustrated by the organization he works for, and he's stopped caring. They seem resigned to sticking it out only because they don't know what else to do and they need their incomes.

I ask them what interests them, what they enjoy together and separately. Samantha likes going to flower markets. Gabriel likes cycling. But he hasn't gone lately, and she's stopped bothering to go to flower markets. It's as if they're not fully participating in their lives; they're getting through them.

I ask them about having fun. "We're too busy fighting," Samantha says, rolling her eyes. "Not much fun." Gabriel shushes her for being so negative. They have fun. Life is not that bad. He doesn't want me to get the wrong picture. She has a resting sad face, he tells me. She's bringing him down.

"Holidays" are their idea of fun, and they say this in unison. They live for holidays. They work for holidays. But normal life, not so much. The story of so many.

What's extraordinary, but also eerily familiar, is how they resent each other for life not being a glorious holiday. It's as if each of them holds the other responsible for the facts of life. They turn on each other for not fixing whatever is wrong, and also for depriving the other of some kind of utopia.

I ask what their visions of utopia look like. One ongoing holiday? What emerges is scathing criticism of the other. Gabriel wishes Samantha weighed less. Samantha wishes Gabriel earned more money. These criticisms become explanations for why their lives aren't as they should be. I wince as I witness their snipes and try to think about the underlying desire. They don't truly want to destroy each other and, if anything, seem hell-bent on keeping the other engaged and up and running to keep the fight going. They seem drawn to diminishing each other, lowering the other's worth, in some kind of scramble to prove superiority. I don't want to go into the granular detail of their arguments. The details are often distractions and become nuanced debates about who is right and who is better.

They will pick up any stick to beat each other conversationally. They are far better acquainted with what's wrong in their life together than with what success might even look like. Samantha's captious critiques are mind-blowingly specific. She rehashes details of Gabriel's laundry mistakes as though I'm the laundry police investigating a felony.

"I just can't deal with it anymore," she says. She looks appalled as she describes his failures. Gabriel looks wounded. He pulls back, literally moving a few inches away from her. Their sharp intellects don't help them comunicate effectively. They use withering expressions and insult each other with cutting articulateness.

Gabriel soars in the clouds in his critiques. Lofty and vague ideals of romance collide with the harsh disappointment of real life. Samantha should look a certain way and act a certain way. Respectful, beautiful, fun. It's an extremely old-fashioned sense of femininity, and I struggle not to react, and I don't want to collude. Discussing it in supervision reminds me that if he's old-fashioned in his terrible disappointments in Samantha, his sense of manhood may be hugely wounded also. And indeed, there's something about his bruised sense of self, his feeling small, that pushes him to one-up her and refute her.

He knocks her down when she talks about politics. He calls her out for getting a fact wrong and gets out his phone to look it up quickly. He declares that he's right and she's wrong.

"You're both wrong," I say. "Trying to gain points for cleverness doesn't seem to be helpful."

Samantha asks what I mean.

"Some of the childlike lines you used at the beginning of the work—'You started it' and 'I told you so'—I feel these lines reverberate throughout your disputes. You're like bickering siblings feeling wronged by the other. You get drawn into the weeds of one-upping each other and knocking each other down, and I think that, rather than engage in this **Pyrrhic victory**, we need to clarify the direction of travel—the goal of our work together, and your relationship."

We talk about Pyrrhic victories—successful battles that are so taxing, both sides are diminished. If they destroy each other with their insults, what will be left of their relationship?

The relationship is my focus more than confirming the winner. When I say this, Gabriel responds, "I thought I was winning therapy." We laugh, but I suspect he means what he's said.

I return focus to what they want from the relationship and what success would look like. They respond with criticisms of the other and no ideas for what they could each do to contribute to their relationship together. They're novices at compromising and experts at putting each other down.

"Experts at putting each other down. Ouch, Charlotte," Samantha says.

"Ouch to me? Or ouch to each other? You're the ones wounding each other."

"Harsh," Gabriel says.

"Yes," I say. "There's a lot of harshness in this room. And you've come for help, so I'm hoping we can find a way forward."

Maybe I need to be the bad guy occasionally, to reconnect people by giving them a shared target for one thing. But being the new object of scorn isn't a long-term solution either. This couple needs to find a new path.

Relationships often need The Story of Us. What's their story? Compromising isn't sacrificial, and they both need to hold on to a sense of self, or maybe develop and revise a sense of self while allowing for influence from the other. "Our story is something about being best friends," Samantha says the following week. Gabriel agrees. "We were on the same side. It was us against the world, in a positive way. We turned on each other."

Gabriel thinks he could have picked a "better" partner. Someone hotter, tidier, nicer. Someone more loving to him. He sighs
at the ideal he dreamt of. It's nostalgic, his longing. He thinks
of oaky cold winters in Romania, studying hard for exams, his
grandmother's spongy amandine chocolate cakes. He longs for the
dream he had of what life could become. A beautiful and loving
wife was the plot and purpose of most of what he believed in
and hoped for. His fantasy of love is so intimate in his mind, in
his reservoir of memories, he thinks his ideals are real—or should
be. He thinks his fantasies of love and marriage should become
reality. "I'm proud of my standards," he tells me. But hearing his
own thoughts come out of his mouth, he's also astonished by the
expectations he's had—not just of Samantha, but of himself. They
both want each other to be the way they used to be. They don't
just want this; they demand this, as though of course this must
happen. But they're also bothered by how little they've changed.
What is progress? Their arguments feel like motion, but they're
circular, not linear.

"Don't hold this against me, Samantha, what I'm about to say . . .
I think I'm afraid. I'm worried that I'm completely ordinary. And
fighting with you is draining, but it's also been the only thing I really
care about."

A delicate turning point. I gently suggest: "Can we turn your
duel into a duet?"

The line runs in my head throughout the week. Turning a duel
into a duet is a concept we can work with. A different letter makes
such a difference. At this point in our work, the two essential ingredients are encouragement and clarity. We look at what a duet might
mean.

"With any kind of duet, each person sings a different tune but
is aware of the other's tune, and accommodates it," Samantha says.

They did this in the beginning, learning about each other's cultures and upbringings, and wanting the other to do well in life.

Something got stagnant. Their constant fights are for air and space and resources in their lives. It's got much worse since the pandemic began. Brexit too. The living-space issue, limited time, financial pressures, the struggle for residency in every sense. Though they are actually fairly close to being an equitable couple in many ways, the small differences matter hugely. And they picked up a game of winning small points of superiority. Petty spats about rightness stand in for the vague and lofty feelings of inadequacy, and the sense that life should be better.

Personal growth for each of them matters, as does considering the other person's point of view. Their attitudes need some pep.

They're both burdened by the expectations of relationship "shoulds": "It shouldn't be so hard for us to be happy, baby. You know what I mean? You're so impossible. It shouldn't be this way," Gabriel says.

Samantha also believes that their relationship should be easier. "If he loves me, he should make me feel cared for," she says. "It's quite basic and obvious." This includes specific gestures such as making her tea and paying bills. What's obvious to each of them is unintuitive to the other, and they're cross that they have to explain and clarify what should simply be known already. The fantasy of an easy relationship comes up often for people, and floridly for this couple. The effort required in a long-term commitment demands more of us than we expected. But while holding on to tales of easy love, we also make relationships much harder than they need to be. Their struggles are more aligned than they realize, but they come from different places in every sense, and they're impatient and intolerant. They're taking the path of most resistance by fighting to win small battles without understanding the war.

The constant conflict seems to be a transposed expression of their unmet desires. Rather than openly request more from each other, they belittle each other. They're negotiating and trying to secure their worth and status. They're both fighting for their rights—for emotional citizenship and for respect. But their way of trying to gain more individually is to take away from the other. Each diminishes the other in a bid for more. They're locked into this dirty and destructive fighting pattern, depriving and denigrating each other, but what is their aim?

In a conversation with the writer Katherine Angel, I ask her about choosing what's painful, choosing what hurts us. I tell her it's an issue that comes up in therapy regularly: choosing destruction over health. This couple is self-destructive in their constant put-downs.

"Sometimes, we chase what is dangerous and dark precisely because that's what makes us feel alive, or real," Katherine says. "And it might be gratifying in some way."

For a long while, every time I meet with Samantha and Gabriel, their lacerating criticisms continue. As psychologist Marshall Rosenberg put it, "Criticism, analysis, and insults are the tragic expressions of unmet needs." What do they need? I think of Katherine Angel's remarks about chasing danger because it makes us feel alive. Her insight applies to so many of my clients—if not all of us—in some way. But this couple in particular is upsettingly bored by their lives. Their flat is a responsibility. Their jobs are simply obligatory. Their lives have become chore lists. They need to feel alive. Fighting has been their life force. But the jittery adrenaline of fighting is wearing them done.

I suggest that they update their roles and responsibilities. As individuals and as a couple. It's something we do at work, and it helps to do it psychologically too. They're both holding the other responsible for their own well-being, and they each feel beholden and ripped off by the job share of their relationship. Gabriel accuses Samantha of exaggerating and Samantha accuses Gabriel of minimizing. Both distortions are disputes over who does what. They struggle even to share reality at times.

They go away with this assignment and return with written-out descriptions. The central themes are recognition and acknowledgment. But it doesn't come easily to voice these needs.

"I feel like **Rumpelstiltskin**," Samantha says; it's a childhood favorite for her. She's suddenly aware of the poor plight of Rumpelstiltskin himself. She now identifies with the fable's eponymous gnome. She's worked hard, spun straw into gold, and she's gotten no credit.

In her bid for recognition and overdue credit, she's attacked Gabriel and put him down, as though that will compensate for the ways she feels undervalued.

"I feel like Rumpelstiltskin too!" Gabriel says.

"Copycat!" Samantha exclaims. "He gets all his good ideas from me," she tells me. "But I'll take it as flattery. I want peace."

"You need encouragement to rework your story so that you both stop spinning gold into straw," I say.

They've done things the hard way: they've struggled to celebrate each other's wins, and they've pounced on each other's flaws instead. They've taken paths of resistance and nearly destroyed each other in order to feel alive and adequate.

It turns out that when the constant games of criticism and one-upmanship stop, they're left with their own minds and lives.

Sometimes we struggle to face ourselves. Gabriel and Samantha find their edges in softer ways. Softness is soothing even though it's also a little dull. Sometimes, success is a little bit dull. And sometimes dullness is success. Their lives won't be nonstop glorious holidays, but they can be healthier and happier than living out the misery of a Pyrrhic victory. Their duel can be a duet.

WHAT WINNING MEANS

Winning can be powerful, but the same thing that makes us feel powerful can also be our downfall psychologically. We can destroy relationships and diminish our power when we indulge our pugnacious, petty, rivalrous side.

The biggest problem with rivalries is the unclear purpose. Without an end point, without boundaries, it's unlikely that there can be much fulfillment. Without a declared winner, we don't know how or when to stop. Charlie Chaplin said, "The key to a great performance is knowing when to exit." You can also apply this to rivalrous games. When we start one-upping each other and needing to be right instead of understanding, we've gone off course. It's not particularly fulfilling to constantly prove one's betterness. There's rarely victory in any kind of substantial way. Consider what it is you want from the situation, where you would like to go. Look out for Pyrrhic victories and consider what you may be losing by insisting on winning each point. Decide for yourself when you want to exit a duel or bow out of a rivalry.

Winning doesn't shield us from loss. As Simone de Beauvoir puts it: "If you live long enough, you'll see that every victory turns into a defeat." Victories that come from diminishing others often feel like a scramble to protect vitality. Constant denunciations are a response to the searing threat of loss—the loss of self most of all.

It's a joy when we feel safe and we don't need to prove or compare ourselves. But it's also a joy when we feel safe enough to admit jealousy and envy, to acknowledge threats and recognize how much we are secretly desperate to win. Clarity and honesty about these uncomfortable feelings gives us more agency.

If we're unaware of rivalrous dynamics, we can feel insulted by a sense of being unseen and unappreciated. Clients in therapy talk a lot about withheld praise. Why didn't a sibling, a friend, a colleague, a parent, express how proud they are of them, how happy and excited they are about their achievements, skills, all that they've become? Refusing to be impressed is in itself a competitive gambit, a passive-aggressive way of lowering the value of an opponent by elaborate not-noticing.

Compersion is the lovely antidote to *Schadenfreude*. Joy in someone else's success—it's a rare and beautiful state of mind when we feel delight for another human being. It can even feel generous to show joy and acknowledgment when receiving a thoughtful gift. It's sharing joy and letting another person feel significant. But to get to compersion, we might have to work through our own darkness.

Along with outward contests, we can be self-envious and rivalrous—competing with versions of ourselves when we felt better, were more triumphant or more accomplished, or were thriving fantasy constructs of ourselves. We can also gloat about a success and show off to our younger selves. Self-competitions can be motivating or menacing.

When we're obsessively rivalrous, we're battling constant threats. And when we feel particularly threatened or deprived, someone else's success can give us a terrible sense of discontent. The writer Gore Vidal, known for his snarky and withering zings, captured a dark truth: "Whenever a friend succeeds, a little something inside me dies."

And it can also be a breakthrough to recognize our *Schadenfreude* (the German term for joy at the misfortunes of others) and voice our honest feelings of threat. We don't like this about ourselves. But other people doing well can evoke confusing reactions in us. It's an old feeling. We want to win, and if someone else is winning, what does it mean for our chances of doing well and having enough? And if someone else is losing, will this help us succeed?

Most of us are ambivalent. On the one hand, we want propinquity to success: it feels contagious, in a good way. It's a sign of how well we are doing if our friends and loved ones are thriving. Having energetic, interesting friends is something many of us want and cherish. We also, in a positive and lovely way, may genuinely wish for others to succeed. We want our friends to be happy. We want our siblings to do well and have fulfilling lives. But there are some valid reasons it might be a little bit hard at moments when we see others flourishing.

Compare, despair. We feel on some level that another person doing well will take something away from us. A colleague who gets a major professional break will somehow take the place that would be ours, even if it isn't an explicit rivalry. So much goes back to the early experiences of love we received. These memories may have been the basis—at school, in social situations, in family life—for why it feels hard for us, however secretly, when others get what they want. We feel there simply won't be enough to go around.

When we constantly catastrophize and imagine terrible things that could happen (but mostly haven't), we can habitually play the anxious and rudderless game of "What if . . . ?"—envisioning scenarios that could go wrong. Or we ruminate and play the torturous game of "If only . . ."—convinced that we can replay, undo, and redo where it all went wrong. We play repetitive games based on the fantasy that one day we'll prove our glory to someone who doubted us, failed to appreciate us, made us feel small and helpless. We dream of making up for our own past hurts and inadequacies. Clients often reveal fantasies of winning that will prove to the doubters how wrong they were.

Our convoluted rivalrous feelings are often about our unease with egos. We wince at a friend's cocky delight when something goes well and, watching from the sidelines, we remind ourselves that we wouldn't dare put ourselves out there so brazenly. Most of us have been fed mixed messages about the right to have ego. Whatever our circumstances and upbringing, we can find ourselves pushed and pulled in the sway of cultural tides. Empowerment, confidence, self-esteem, body positivity—these are lovely and good things (though our embedded beliefs and personal histories might clash), but ego is treated like a dirty word. Not to mention narcissism . . . "Too much ego" is still a withering message that quiets us. Stay safely away from ego—that lethal enemy! Ego has a reputation for causing trouble, danger, confusion. "The dangers of ego" is an expression we hear, and most cultures give mixed messages about the acceptability of ego. We're easily conditioned to hide and deny ego—from others and even from our own awareness. Banished egos come out sideways—through others, through insisting on winning in small ways, through anger, frustration, judgemental envy. "Ego" means self. It comes from the Latin word for "I." It can mean self-respect and recognition. It can be a breakthrough when we scrap our faux modesty and, in the privacy of therapy, we simply enjoy being who we are. If not now, when?

"I'm delighted with myself. I did brilliantly. Well done, me. I see that I'm skilled at doing this, and I have done an excellent job," a fifty-five-year-old said to me. "I want to do this more." She enjoyed appreciating herself. The scent of her ego felt socially contraband, like a mischievous secret. But she embraced it. "This feels like a win," she said.

Consider the meaning of "winning." The definition changes and the rules vary. It's up to you to revise your roles and play games that feel successful to you, whatever that may mean.

Chapter Ten

TO CONNECT

Our desire to connect is as central to human existence as eating. It's caring and considerate. Salve for alienating, threadbare experiences. We can form connections and reconnections throughout life, at any age, any stage, if there's a mutual participation and openness. We connect with friends, colleagues, strangers, in therapy. Without connection, it's hard to know how we could think of ourselves, if we could even conceptualize ourselves at all. Of course, disconnecting happens in all these places too. There's nothing more disconnecting and connecting than secrets. The loneliness of a hidden secret can be hideous, as can the indiscreet exposure. But when it's possible to tell someone the untold story, to hear it, there's a kind of alchemy in human connection.

I remember vividly when my second child began clapping at around seven months. He exulted at the sight of his hands coming together, and he instinctively started mirroring people clapping their hands. Clapping in unison made him jubilant. He would try to catch my gaze, and when he did, he'd beam with delight. We both beamed. His face would light up when I marveled at him, and he would gaze back at me. The rapport we experience is both outward and inward. We look outside ourselves and join in. Clapping is such a distinct human gesture of appreciation and coming together. Our desire for connection is about the dichotomy of separateness and unity.

Attention and connection are about feeling seen and heard. But shouting may get attention without forging a connection. Connecting is about joining in a shared experience. It's about mutual participation. I see and hear you, and you see and hear me. When we engage wholeheartedly, authentically, we feel a togetherness that makes us comfortable in our own skin and helps us understand each other and make sense of life. Connecting is how we care for each other and process our experiences.

The primal dance begins at birth, when newborns bond through touch and being fed. Connecting with others and with parts of ourselves brings fragmented bits of experience into an intelligible, coherent narrative. How we develop and relate to the world, how we discern our differences and similarities—this is how we define ourselves.

But connecting can be difficult. We can't wait to tell a beloved friend a hilarious story, but when we do, we get interrupted, or the friend doesn't laugh. We send a text message and don't get a reply. We seek validation about something we've experienced, and we feel rejected or ignored. Disconnection can be like the sound of one hand clapping. We turn away from admitting deep pain to the people who love us because we're horrified, embarrassed, afraid. We feel unnoticed. Misunderstood. Paranoid about an awkward or flat social encounter that wasn't what we expected it to be. We feel uncared for, unrecognized for how we would like to be seen. We're haunted by memories that suddenly feel unacceptable.

A strong connection is valuable in a therapeutic relationship. The therapeutic space is an emotional laboratory where we can observe and work on issues. Connecting and finding and reshaping the stories we tell ourselves and the untold stories we've carried is a tremendous part of the work. We can deepen our understanding of past events, see things in different lights, come to terms with haunting memories, have transformative experiences in the here and now, and make meaning out of certain struggles.

Astrid, the woman who trusted me with her story, was in her sixties when she came to me for therapy. I love working with different age groups, though most of my clients are younger. I connected with Astrid in a way that felt superficial initially but turned out to be significant. Astrid wanted therapy and found it terrifying. "There is no agony like bearing an untold story inside you," wrote Zora Neale Hurston. Astrid had an untold story that she tried not to tell and needed to. Telling the story changed her, and hearing it changed me. She defined and redefined the meaning of connection.

ASTRID'S PRESENT

We make assumptions, and I'm no exception. I try to keep my eyes open to fresh experience, to meet people and allow for discovery and surprise, to suspend judgment and not stereotype people. Psychotherapy has a history of imposing theory on individuals, and it's a great mistake to think we've figured people out, especially when we barely know them.

Therapists are particularly invested in first impressions, because the assessment session often contains notes that we hope will turn out to be full of foresight and clever and apt observations. We also assess for risk and suitability, to cover our bases and decide if we need to refer on or if further support is required.

We jot down some of these notes in the session, or after, and if we plan on continuing to see the client for more sessions, the assessment notes might just be for ourselves. If we are making a referral, we might give the assessment notes to a colleague. Our descriptions vary, depending on the intended reader. We are always constructing stories and piecing together and assembling details in our own subjective way. Perspective shapes what we see. However hard we try to just focus on the people we meet, we inevitably imprint and impose ourselves to some degree; the dynamic in the room is created by the people in the room, including the therapist. We are professionally trained to catch our projections and spot the ones coming from our clients, but therapists' backgrounds, cultures, personal lives, appearances, training, moods, dispositions, idiosyncrasies, all come into how they view and relate to people, and how people experience therapy. This is what makes the process intensely personal and individual.

We are not mind readers. We observe and engage and construct. And we miss stuff. I do my best to meet people where they are, allowing for material to emerge rather than impose labels. But I form first impressions quickly, and I got it wrong with Astrid. I've decided to forgive myself for my inaccurate immediate impressions, since we all tend to form them, and the important thing is the willingness to revise and update. Since therapy is in large part about reworking stories, we need to rework our stories about clients too, and it's liberating and expansive to admit that our initial sense usually isn't the full picture. Not even close.

I got it wrong, and I also got it right. My first impression was of her togetherness. She was so polished. This turned out to be true and completely misleading.

The assumption I made was that she was as together as she looked, that she wasn't in real trouble.

Astrid arrived early for our first session. The receptionist alerted me and said, "There's a lady here to see you." She added in a whisper: "She's so stylish!" I introduced myself and offered Astrid a glass of water, which she graciously declined, and I told her I'd be back in a few minutes. Even in this flash of a moment, I took in her refined appearance. She was so orderly and clean, with a small scarf around her neck and another scarf tied at the top of her structured handbag. When I welcomed her into the room a few minutes later, I discovered the layers of her ladylike presentation: the raincoat she hung on the coat stand, the floral umbrella, the bowed shoes and matched earrings and necklace. (She almost always wore these; they were inherited from her grandmother, I soon learned.) Astrid's style was a big part of what it was like to sit across the room from her. The clean lines and bright colors and pretty features formed a feeling of visual order. *She's so put together,* I thought. The meaning of being "put together" is complicated for some of us. Her visual coherence mattered to her; it masked internal chaos.

Astrid sought therapy now, in her early sixties, "to connect." She explained: "I have a history of going for scoundrels. Please help me pick someone decent. I want a companion." I asked her what "connecting" meant for her. She told me about her ex-husband, the father of her child, and how they'd never been particularly close, despite years of marriage and family life. He cheated on her, they divorced, and he remarried twelve years ago, while she had some short relationships and a series of failed romances in the years following. Her recollections, even when wistful and sad, had an undramatic and accepting quality. Her English had the silvery fluency of many Scandinavians. She enunciated certain words, like "scoundrel," with green-apple crunchy exactitude.

What about other sources of connection, outside of romantic relationships? She frowned a little. "You know, I want a nice man I can care for, who cares for me." Her mother, "a prim churchgoing woman whose hair was always pinned up," encouraged her from as far back as she could remember to find a man to love, a man to take care of. "My mother had a secret mischief. She adored skiing and musicals. Those were the two places where she had great fun. But even then, the most important thing was dedication to a man. *My Fair Lady* was one of her favorite musicals, and the message she drummed into my sisters and me was to bring Henry Higgins his slippers. Those were words we lived by, and still do."

At this point I felt a little shiver of deep affection for Astrid. I loved *My Fair Lady* and know the slipper line well. But what a screwy message! Henry Higgins is proud of his fixed mindset, while Eliza Doolittle, despite her name, does everything.

Astrid was surprised and pleased that I knew the reference. "Your generation doesn't know musicals," she said. "Maybe there's hope after all."

Therapy isn't just about liking what we see. We might not like parts of ourselves, or each other. We need to look at the soot and the grime as well as the pastels. But at this moment it was sheer pastel. She liked me. And I liked her. What a sunny, pleasant moment.

I was struck by her attractiveness, and I felt curious to discover her depth and intensity.

When I asked her about her sense of self, she gave me characterizing descriptions, as we do. She'd been a midwife for decades but she'd recently retired. She grew up in what she described as "wholesome Copenhagen—a little bit *Sound of Music*," but without the rolling hills or wealth.

"My sisters and I spent summers in Jutland, wearing pretty dresses and making art. We were very virtuous and innocent when I think of it now." She moved to London to have an adventure. Though her finances were quite modest, she could afford to rent a little flat and take horticulture classes. She no longer felt burdened by endless responsibilities, and she finally felt a kind of freedom, so coming to London was her "big third act." She admitted she was inspired by Jane Fonda.

She struggled to let the conversation just be about her. The lopsided nature of our relationship felt awkward for her, as it can for many. She spent a lot of time noticing her surroundings, paying close attention to what she saw in the room, and in me. "That's a nice painting behind you," she commented. "And I like these cushions."

I asked her questions about her inner self, and she responded with a comment on how I was dressed and my accessories: "I love that you always wear earrings. The one other time I tried therapy, I spoke to this woman who was very drab."

When I pushed her to tell me about her feelings and thoughts, she answered with awkwardness, interrupting herself to ask me if I was comfortable in my seat, which wasn't nearly as cushioned as the one she sat on.

"It looks bony," she said. "I worry about you sitting in that thing all day. You should ask for a better chair, or at least one that matches the comfort of where I get to sit."

She was right. I spent my days as a therapist sitting in a wooden chair that came from an office cupboard. It was a really uncomfortable chair.

She wouldn't let it go. "Charlotte, you're thin, so you don't have cushioning. You're going to develop back problems if you continue to sit in that thing. Looking at you is making me worry. I'm a nurse, trust me!"

I felt embarrassed by her concern for me and deflected the focus back to her as much as possible. Her comment about my body made me feel childlike, and not just physically. She alerted me to my immature ways of relating to authority.

Her concern for me, her mentioning her medical expertise, her awareness of aesthetics—all these things contributed to my sense of her character, her values, her interests. And her deflections and ways of bringing the discussion back to me and the room were of course revealing, telling me how she was in the world and in her relationships.

I continually reminded her of her aim: to connect. This meant connecting with herself first. She was telling who she was, even if it felt indirect: part of being Astrid meant astutely noticing her external environment—other people, surface details—even perceiving the internal experiences of others, but not her own inner life. She could imagine my discomfort in that chair, but she struggled to verbalize her inner world. Astrid habitually focused on other people, making sure others were okay, and she was deeply uncomfortable when I tried to keep it only about her. She fitted the cliché that doctors and nurses make tricky patients.

I was honored that she wanted me to be helpful to her. I wanted her to like me and find me impressive. We quickly formed a rap-

port, and I felt delighted, and I think she did too. Our work was
sparkly, and she told me she'd always wondered what it would be
like to have a daughter, and that her daughter-in-law was so frosty
with her. I felt both daughterly to her but also motherly, in that
odd way that can happen in **transference** where real age and emotional ages come together. The grandiosity way that's possible only
at fantasy level. I could connection was protected by the boundaries. Our conversations mostly made me feel delightfully polished
and in command of myself. Except for her detecting my masoch-
ism with that chair. I'd fine-tune certain moments, but mostly I
went with the pace and flow of discussion. We danced well together. These are embarrassing things to admit, and it's taken me
years to discuss the shadowy ego sides with my supervisor, in my
own therapy, or even just admit it to myself. But if I don't admit
these things, I'm hiding and avoiding important issues that shape
the therapeutic relationship.

For several sessions, Astrid and I had a delightful time. It just
wasn't difficult. She fussed over me, and I fussed over her, but we
mostly just chatted about her life without really discussing it. Until,
finally, it wasn't just me in that chair having a painful hour; Astrid
let herself feel hurt, and the real story emerged.

When we meet for our next session, Astrid has less than her usual
poise and seems nervous. She has on a velvety headband and crosses
her ankles like a dainty debutante. She opens her notebook and
places it on her lap.

"I don't want to lose my train of thought, or my nerve, so I've
written down some prompts to make sure I tell you certain things,"
she says. Her voice is trembling, and I can see that her hand is shaking. I want to put her at ease.

"This is your space," I say. "Let yourself just be here and say
anything you want."

"That sounds nice. Okay, okay, that sounds nice. How are you today, Charlotte?"

"I'm fine. But, please, Astrid, tell me how you are."

"Okay. The real reason I came to see you. It was, as I said, to meet a nice man, and I still want that. . . . I feel a lot of embarrassment. I got myself into a bit of trouble. I told you I had a history of dating scoundrels. Well, there was one in particular. Charlotte; I can't believe I let this happen, though I don't quite know how to tell the story. It's hard for me to find my words." Her voice is staccato.

"I understand," I say. "Give yourself space to just let the words come to you. We will bring it all together." I can see that she's distressed, anxious, already reliving something unprocessed and painful just by mentioning that something bad happened.

"Okay, I'll just say some bits and pieces, and you can help me assemble it, please," she says, her voice gathering strength.

"Absolutely."

"It began at a dinner party a few months ago, a gathering of some of the midwives I trained with, and there were several colleagues there too, and a distinguished, charming Australian surgeon who sat beside me. He said he always liked nurses better than doctors. It was a lovely evening, and before I left we exchanged details. I wasn't sure I would ever hear from him, but he emailed me that night, and I replied, and then he replied again the next day, and over the following week if felt as if we were developing something of a connection. A handsome man, a couple of years older than I am, very confident, very knowledgeable. Well-read, divorced a long time ago, a son living in the States. He was flirtatious but never vulgar or anything like that. He told me he likes skiing and going to art exhibitions. Well, so do I. We had a lot in common. So we agreed to have dinner, and we had a marvelous time, and then he suggested something for the following weekend—I was so nervous, but ready and game, and I liked him very much. So we drove together to this lovely country house hotel in the Lake District.

He had picked it out. It seemed picture-perfect. Do you know the Lake District?"

I nod but stay silent in the hope that she'll stay focused on the difficult story she is trying to tell me.

"Well, I recommend this hotel, if you're ever looking for a little weekend getaway, though I won't be going back there. But you might like it. Do you go away for weekends?"

"Astrid, you know I'm fairly relaxed about self-disclosure, but let's stay with your story, please."

"Okay, okay. James. That's the name of this man. Oof. Even saying his name, I feel a waft of something." She pulls in a loud quick breath. "I don't want to feel anything just yet. I want to get through all the details first. He seemed so kind and attentive. I felt like we had a connection. I was nervous, but also a little giddy that we were having this romantic getaway. We had dinner. I drank a glass or two of red wine, two at the absolute maximum; I wouldn't let him refill my glass. We shared chateaubriand, medium rare. I said no more wine for me; I was starting to feel tipsy, but in a nice, warm sort of way. We were in a little corner of the hotel's restaurant, with a window looking out on a beautiful view. It was all going so well. It was romantic. I felt happy. That's what's so flummoxing. I can't piece it all together." Her demeanor in this moment becomes strict and controlled, and she has a headmistress quality of correctness.

"I'm not telling this well," she says. She looks at the corner of the room with a mineral-hard stare. Her angular face looks pained and cross, as though she's reminded herself of something wretched. I haven't come close to her vast interior world until now.

"Astrid, tell it however you can."

"I want to tell it exactly as it was. Now that I'm here, digging this up, I need to get it out. But I don't know how the pieces come together. It doesn't make sense."

"Don't worry about that yet, the piecing-together bit. Just let yourself continue," I say. When people have experienced trauma, they can feel incredible pressure to tell their story in the right way, as though the performance were the part that matters. A lot of this comes from the horror of what's happened, the incredulity that it really did happen, the frozen voicelessness of shock and the fear that it won't be believed or they'll be blamed. And most of the time they've struggled to believe what happened and have blamed themselves already. Telling an untold traumatic story, even in therapy, can feel terrifying.

"We went up to our room. So sweet, just charming. Very nice people run this place, a family. Everything around us was out of a picture book, everything I dreamt of when I was a child in Denmark, imagining the English countryside from all those Beatrix Potter books I read, and so many movies. Heavenly place. I'm repeating myself, okay. I'll get there. I was nervous to go back to the room after dinner, but I thought, 'Let's just see what happens.' I thought my nervousness was because I hadn't had sex in so long." Her voice softens when she says "sex." "And dating, well, it's so intense and uncertain when you meet and then you get closer, and now it's going to the next level. I'm out of practice."

"I understand," I say. I wait. I don't want to ask if this is the whole story, but I'm just not sure. It reminds me of times when I've opened gifts in a bag and can't tell if there's more at the bottom, but I don't want to seem greedy or dissatisfied by conspicuously scrounging through the tissue paper to check if there's more.

"Well, that's it," she says. She looks down and pauses. The planes of her pensive face are striking at this moment. "That's the last thing I remember. Until I woke up on the cold tiled shower floor, and there was blood everywhere. And my head . . . I felt a throbbing pain. And I felt pain all over. Bruises everywhere. I was numb, but aching."

"Oh, Astrid," I say, suddenly feeling a surge of distress. I knew something bad must have happened to her, but I didn't see this coming. Nor did she.

"I knew I needed to tell you this," she says. "I wanted to." She gets out a tidy little square tissue from a pretty floral tissue case and unfolds it with precision before blotting her eyes carefully. I wish she'd just use the box of tissues placed in front of her, but she's so prepared with her planner and her tissues and her clothes and her scarves and her belongings. She maintains herself in all these ways.

"I'm glad you're telling me," I say. "This sounds dreadful, and traumatic."

"Yes, it was, and I haven't told a soul. I've just been so . . . embarrassed . . . I'll come back to that. I want to tell you as much as I can. Anyway, when I finally pulled myself off the floor, I wanted to call for help, but I didn't. This is the part . . . this is the part I don't understand . . . this is the part that's eating me up." She begins to choke up and struggles to speak through her tears.

"It's so hard, all of this," I say. "I really feel for you. I'm with you."

"Oh, Charlotte. I need to hear that. That you're with me. I don't get it. James was lying on the bed in a terry robe, reading a magazine. A travel magazine. He was just lying there, reading about some luxury destination. I crawled towards the bed, my head badly bashed, in pain, blood everywhere. I dragged myself up on to the bed and lay down next to him. And he said nothing. And I said nothing. I think I was stunned. I didn't call for help. I didn't phone the police. I don't understand. I just don't understand. I need to tell you the rest."

"Please do."

"I looked up at him and I asked him what happened. You got drunk, you naughty girl. That's what he said. I didn't! I know I didn't, but I tried to go with this idea. And I slept in that bed with him that night. I can't believe I crawled into the bed beside him, but I did. And the next morning, I woke up, my head so sore, and I don't know how I slept at all, and we dressed and went downstairs to the hotel's lovely breakfast room. And we had a pot of coffee, and we ate pastries, and then they brought us the full English breakfast, and it was all like a magazine article about a lovely country house hotel in the Lake District. We went on a walk in a wooded area nearby. And we took photos of flowers. He was very knowledgeable about flowers and kept identifying them. Oh my God. I did all of this. I went along with all of this. We took pictures of ourselves on this walk. Look, look at these photos."

She shows me the photos, holding out her phone with a shaking hand. There she is, with a wide, frozen grin on her hollow face, her hair stuck to her cheek, a visible gash and slight bruising on the edge of her forehead. The tweedy man in the pictures looks pleased with himself. His arm is around her. I feel a kind of seething rage towards him, the rage she didn't let herself feel at the time.

"Astrid, I'm so sorry. I'm so sorry this happened, and I'm so glad you're talking about it now."

"I cannot believe I didn't call for help, or report him, or even say something to him. How did this happen? It's not just what he did to me. I know he drugged me. I know he had sex with me when I was unconscious."

"How do you know?" I ask this carefully. I'm so afraid of questioning her in a way that could possibly sound skeptical or challenging.

"Well, there was semen dripping out of me and running down my leg along with blood. It stained the sheet on my side of the bed, which was so embarrassing. I felt out of control. And I was completely unconscious, knocked out cold."

"Oh, Astrid."

"I don't know why. I would have slept with him. Awake. He didn't need to drug me. Why? The worst part for me . . . is that I pretended it was all okay. Everything was fine. We had a lovely weekend away. I pretended even to you, just by not telling you about it. Even now, I want to minimize it and make it all just go away."

"This isn't sex. This is rape. This is violence," I say.

"Yes, that's true. You're right. As a nurse, I know all this. And yet . . . and yet. I cannot believe this happened, and I normalized it, I minimized it, I pretended it wasn't so bad. I did all these things. I'm shocked by myself as much as I'm shocked by this man. It's not okay, what he did. It's not okay. I'm shocked."

"What he did is really not okay. Not okay at all." I'm shocked too. I'm truly shocked by the story. I hear about rape and violence, abuse and trauma, all the time in my work, and in some ways, even though I'm calm and used to it now, I'm always shocked by it. I believe it, and I know it goes on all the time, but I'm still shocked, and I think I want to be. It's shocking because it's so unacceptable. I hate that this happens. And it happens constantly. More than we know. More than we read about, more than what ever gets reported or told. More than therapists even find out about.

Astrid and I together examine what stopped her from calling out for help, from phoning the police, from reporting this man. "I remember feeling embarrassed. The hotel was so quiet. If I called for help, or told someone what happened, or phoned the police, imagine disturbing everyone there. The people who ran the hotel were so nice. I didn't want to make a scene." Not making a scene stops us from speaking up in so many ways. The underside of what society has taught us, has taught women, about politeness, perhaps. "I was brought up with a belief that it's not ladylike to shout. And to have good, old-fashioned manners, being 'ladylike,' is the most important thing. The ultimate compliment."

I ask her what's embedded in this identity of being ladylike.

"I think back to my mother telling my sisters and me to sit up straight at church on Sundays, sitting there with our hair plaited, singing along. Don't talk out of turn. Don't dispute. You know, don't rock the boat. Don't call attention to yourself unless you're asked a question. All these things our mother said, and some of it her mother might have said to her—Mormor probably said it to us too when we were little girls."

"Gosh, I'm thinking of your telling me in our initial session how your mother always said that Eliza Doolittle must bring Henry Higgins his slippers. You were telling me a lot with that detail, even if we didn't fully realize."

"Oh, goodness, I forgot I told you that. But, yes, bring men their slippers. What do you think that means in this context?" she asks.

"You tell me."

"It means do whatever it takes to please men. Be agreeable and attentive. Engage in conversation agreeably. Smile." Astrid looks off into the corner as though combing through a catalogue of realizations.

"And what about the darker stuff, when things go wrong? What then?"

" 'Keep things pretty' was a big one in our family. Orderly. 'A tidy, pretty home is a tidy, pretty mind.' 'Don't get too angry. Or aggressive.' Oh, Charlotte, I cannot believe I'm realizing this stuff only now. I feel as though suddenly I'm opening my eyes to something," Astrid says.

"This is shocking, the experience you've had," I say. "It was only a few months ago, right? You may still be in shock. *I* feel shocked. It's a terrible thing that happened. Let's just allow that it takes some getting used to, to let this story settle, to bring it into something coherent."

"It's been nothing but fragments," she says. "These fragments I've pushed away sear me like flames. That's the sense I have—flaming-hot shreds coming at me, pestering me. I could be gardening, talking with someone in a shop—doing anything—and the smallest thing can suddenly remind me and set off flames again. What's happening?"

"It sounds as though you're having flashbacks. You've stored traumatic memories in a heightened, sensory way, and you're on high alert for threat."

"I have these memories, too many memories of some of it, and too few in other ways."

"That's often the case with trauma," I say. "We feel we remember too little and too much. You will begin to bring the pieces together.

You're already doing that, and you're discovering the story. Be aware that you may still be in a state of trauma. Don't rush yourself, don't pressure yourself. Recovery won't happen instantly, but it will come together. Be kind and patient with yourself, please."

"I like that. Okay. I can do that. Thank you. It will come together. Okay, okay. You know, I'm not very good at noticing when something is wrong for me. With others, yes. I notice things."

"I know you do. You see your surroundings and others with such acuity. You do it here too, with me. You were right about this uncomfortable chair! And I'm here to help you, and you still find it hard to speak up for yourself."

We talk about her feeling fake in her encounters with her son and his wife and child. But she doesn't want to tell them what's happened. Not yet, anyway, until she's made sense of it herself. And the story is hardly over. She shows me subsequent communications she's had with James. They've exchanged emails and photos.

"And there's this," she says with a shudder. "This part is really bad. I had sex with him, consensually, one time after all of this happened. We went on a date! Why did I do that? Why?" Her face is wide and electric.

It might have been a wish to undo the trauma, to make it okay, to normalize, to mend things, to make it something that wasn't a horror story. She kept thinking she could fix it in some way. "I wanted to make it right," she keeps saying. As she tells the story, she begins to answer some of her questions about herself, and she gathers strength and insight about herself, even if she remains baffled and irate.

"I'm too old to be assaulted. Who assaults a woman in her sixties? I feel very embarrassed, as though people would think I think too much of myself to think I could be a rape victim at my age. I think I saw him again to try to make some sense of the whole thing. You know, that he would make it all okay somehow. What was I thinking?"

Her shattered self-worth saddens me. And I can see how she went back to him to try to comprehend something incomprehensible. It's often the desperate wish to understand the people who have caused us pain that gets us to go back to them for more. As though the wounders are holders of wisdom and reparation. We think the people who hurt us can make it better. We sometimes think they're the only ones who possibly can.

"I think I went back that time, met him again, thinking that I could make things better if I got this bad guy to actually be a good guy. That way, this bad thing isn't so bad anymore. Does that make sense?" Astrid asks.

"Yes, it really does," I say. "But the bad thing that happened is still bad. And nothing can make it un-happen."

"It's still bad." She shakes her head, allowing herself to feel it. "And when I think about how it was, having consensual sex with him, I don't even think I was present. It's like I was just there, going through the motions. I don't think I felt anything. But I didn't even think about what I was feeling. I was so busy trying to make the situation okay. And it wasn't okay. It was never going to be okay."

"It was never going to be okay. You have survived something dreadful," I say.

"Yes, I did. It happened. This happened."

When people survive trauma, there's often a period of realization that something bad really happened. It's both simple and complicated to accept this basic fact.

"I want to press charges against this terrible man," Astrid says the following week.

We contemplate the process of what reporting the rape would be like for her. When she considers the complexities of the sequence of events, and the challenges, having to tell and describe every detail to the police, she realizes she doesn't want to face pressing charges. The photos of them the next day, the friendly emails they exchanged, the consensual sex ten days after the rape—it all makes her case nearly impossible to prove. She knows this, and I know this from guiding others through the very flawed justice system. At this moment I think of an acronym I came across once for empowering people in dealing with sexual trauma: LIFE—listening, informing, facilitating, and educating. I'm furious that I can't do more for her. I can hold space for her and support her and contain her, helping her make her own choice in how to deal with her experience, but the system is still punishing.

"I know that pressing charges can be retraumatizing and doesn't always lead to anything close to victory. Not pressing charges is deeply upsetting too, and there's a sense of great injustice," she says.

I agree. It can be brutal and impossibly hard to decide what to do.

Astrid decides she doesn't want to fight a battle she'd probably lose. She recognizes how this could diminish her further.

"I don't want more pain. I can deal with the pain here, with you, but I don't want the pain of the system. Is it bizarre that I love coming here, as painful as this has been for me to talk about?" she asks.

"I don't find it bizarre. Maybe it's a relief that you've gone so far here."

"Yes. I feel a little bit proud. I enjoy our sessions," she says. "I even put on my Sunday best sometimes just for the occasion. And even though I don't see you on Sundays. You know what I mean. It's nice to have a reason to put on a pretty dress.

"I like this room. It feels safe. So calm. And beautiful. And professional, now that you've gotten your new chair."

"You were right about the chair. I'm so glad to have this new one," I say.

"There's one more thing that bothers me. May I say?"

"Go ahead."

"I love the flowers. You have these pretty fresh flowers each week, in a little vase on the table. Everything I've learned from therapy is about realness, fragility, new life. Flowers are lovely at any age, until they're dead. That's part of why I love them."

"*Flowers Are Lovely at Any Age, Until They're Dead*—good title for memoirs."

"Yes!"

In a way, we are talking about life itself, who we are within the systems, policies, showing our real opinions, and in another way we are completely sidetracking. We laugh. I realize that some of our surface discussions are scenic routes to where we need to go.

With all the possible perspectives, it's just the two of us in the room, and it's up to us to make meaning from this situation.

The next week, Astrid arrives at the session with a potted rose-bush in her arms. "This is for you, Charlotte. Well, it's for both of us, really. I would like to officially donate this to the room. May I?"

"Yes, you may," I say.

By accepting the rose bush, I hope that I am honoring Astrid for the trauma she's survived—and all the other people who tell their stories in this room.

"I like the idea that, even with all the sorrow, there's always beauty," Astrid says.

"Yes. There's always beauty. This room is about real growth. And our chat about flowers; it too is about that in a way. But also you've let in the darkness. You haven't just kept it all sanitized and pretty."

"I love gardening for that reason. The soil is so honest, the grit, the earth, and we get on our knees to bring these beautiful things to the surface. That's what we've done here. It's hard. What I really want, Charlotte, is to connect with a nice guy. I even tried to persuade myself that this might be possible with a man who drugged me and raped me while I was unconscious. I so badly wanted it to be a different story than what really happened. I was trying to reshape my experience into something okay, even though it wasn't okay."

"What happened wasn't okay, and it wasn't real connection, or anything that could be shaped into it, but wanting to connect is beautiful and completely worthwhile, and possible," I say. I know it's possible because she's allowed for connection here, with me.

We've had shared experiences, shared meanings, and she's let me see her many different parts and layers. We've connected fragments and found threads to make sense of what it means to be Astrid.

"I somehow believed that if I cooperated and pleased this man, and didn't make a scene, and did all the things I was meant to do, I would get what I wanted."

"Do you still want what you thought you wanted?" I ask.

"Good question. I have my mother's voice inside my head, telling me the only way to live a meaningful life is with a nice man. But of course that's not the case. And I'm glad you've pushed me to feel horrified by this man's terrible behavior. I may not have seen it clearly as it was happening but I'm seeing it now. My first impression of him wasn't the full picture. First impressions, wow, they can be misleading."

"Yes, they can be," I say.

"My first impression of you—may I tell you what it was?"

"Of course." I'm deeply curious.

"I thought you might not be as smart as you are," she says. "You looked too stylish to be intelligent. Isn't that just awful of me to admit? I'm so conflicted, because I also liked you for your appearance. But I held those things against you also. I stereotyped you."

We all stereotype. We all make assumptions. I made assumptions about Astrid; she made assumptions about James, and about me. Sometimes our first impression is accurate, but often we need to keep assessing.

With Astrid, there are many layers that matter, and appearance is part of the story. "I feel superficial, but deeply superficial," she says. "Maybe it's deep, maybe not. I've hidden behind my appearance my whole life. Always so put together. I thought it would help me, and it has, in certain ways. But it stopped me from speaking up and sometimes being a big old ugly mess. I could never be a big old mess with my mother or my father, or even my sisters, and various people from my past. Not even with my own son. And certainly not with men. I've been lonely for a long time."

Astrid goes on to form new connections, and she reconnects with some people from her past. She feels less alienated from herself, and she tells her sisters, and eventually her son and daughter-in-law, about her traumatic experience. Most of my clients are in her son and daughter-in-law's age range, and I imagine hearing about this story from their perspective. With all the discussions and cultural changes around consent and gender, Astrid has given me insight about some of the embedded beliefs and complex struggles of her generation.

We decided to end our work soon after she fell in love with a man named Axel. They met online, they formed a relationship rather quickly, and so she planned to move to Stockholm, where he was from. She was excited for her move and for her life ahead. Having a tidy and planned ending to the therapy with me felt consistent with our dynamic. She needed our work to be a coherent story, with a beginning, a middle, and an end. And she was a little bit of an incurable romantic. I didn't need to solve this for her, even if I felt cautious on her behalf.

She told me about their plans. They would live in his house in Stockholm, but on weekends they planned to escape to his cabin in the mountains. She described the grass roof, how they'd go tobogganing, pick cloudberries, eat reindeer. Axel volunteered as a mountain guide for disadvantaged children. They wanted to enjoy themselves and give back. This was her revised third act.

She kept thanking me at the end of our work, telling me she wouldn't have ever found love if it weren't for me. I know this isn't entirely true; it's fantasy, projection, idealization, transference. But there was no dissuading her, and she wanted to hold on to this story. "You helped me face myself. That's a very big deal where I'm from. I've never really been my innermost self before," she said. "And you made me feel lovable. You didn't say it, but I feel you viewed me as someone who could be loved and give love."

"That's true," I say.

"Here's the really odd part for me. The part of love that I didn't anticipate. I needed to hate, I mean really hate, to let myself then love. I hate that monster of a man for raping me. At first, I hated myself. All the clichés applied. I blamed myself, felt disgusting. And then it shifted when I told you about it and realized what had happened. I never understood the power of denial . . . but now I do. It took a while for me to see that I am not a disgusting person and he did something terrible."

"Yes, everything you're saying: you're not disgusting, and I'm sad that you felt that way, and glad that you no longer do, and he did something terrible."

"I'm still angry when I think of him, and I hate him. I hate him! Maybe that will change. Time will tell, but hating him has been useful to me. It gave me room to love. Feeling bad about myself—it took up all this space inside me. I was always pushing it away and covering it up, not just about what happened to me, but going back further. Much further. I might even be using the rape to explain everything. Putting all of life's troubles on him. Is that unfair of me?"

"Unfair for whom?" I ask.

"Good question."

"What happened to you is dreadful, and if you can make lemonade out of these lemons, do what you want," I say.

"Yes, do what I want. I am. I came to you wanting to connect. As you pointed out, I was disconnected from myself. And connecting here and seeing things in a new way—it's given me room to connect with Axel in ways I didn't imagine before. It's madness, that I needed to hate in order to love. But I've never been allowed to hate anyone except myself my whole life. Not my ex-husband, certainly not my parents, not my patients, my children, no one. And finally, I could hate someone. And you hated him too. It freed me to love. Thank you for getting so worked up about what happened."

"Just keep looking after yourself. All the attention you give others, thinking about their comfort—please check in, internally, and ask yourself if things hurt or feel safe or are what you want. Just keep asking yourself those questions. Your views matter. Think about your own slippers."

"Ah, the slippers! I get the reference. I promise I will."

Two years after we'd ended our work together, I was surprised to receive a pair of sheepskin slippers from Astrid. And a jaunty card included a photo of her with Axel, standing in front of their grass-roof cabin, looking happy and healthy.

This story has an upbeat, bouncy ending. Too good to be true? I was a little unconvinced, seeing that perfect photo of Astrid and Axel. But why? Astrid's third act was painful and ultimately transformative, leading to her longed-for connection. I realized that, despite promising myself I would never let my profession dampen my enthusiasm, I'd become suspicious of happiness. **Cherophobia** is the clinical term. I looked at the photo and read the card again and decided I could trust her effusive report as much as I trust stories of sorrow. Astrid had what she'd wanted and she was enjoying her life.

ONLY CONNECT?

Connecting is a deep-seated social drive. Throughout life, we seek human encounters, look for links, form bonds. We can have moments of connection with people we barely know. We can connect with strangers or hidden parts of ourselves. Sometimes, connecting is a deeply felt sense. It can go beyond words.

Perma-connecting is the new emotional superfood, but disconnection is inescapable in some cases, and we're not very comfortable when that happens. We pretend it's not there, avoid it, turn away further, or we freak out and despair. We need to normalize disconnecting. As human as it is to turn towards each other, it's also human to turn away from each other at times and to detach from parts of ourselves when something feels unbearable. Astrid struggled to voice her story. Her traumatic experience had alienated her. It can be painful, lonely, upsetting—but it happens. If we expect disconnections, we can learn how to mend and recover with more ease. Acknowledging failed connections can be a liberating relief. It happens constantly—in the workplace, with friends, with relatives, with therapists. Surviving disconnection does not mean we must feel isolated and unmoored. It means we need to accept the limitations and imperfections of all relationships. We might reconnect and we will also inevitably make new connections.

Connections usually come from a variety of sources. No one gets all their needs met through one person, whether that's oneself or another human being. When we take a flexible, expansive view of life, we're receptive to connections from a bigger range.

Allow for diverse sources. Be discerning. Don't try to connect with everyone you meet. Constant over-connecting can feel exhausting and emotionally promiscuous. Forcing a connection can feel false and leave you with vulnerability hangovers. Don't expect full connections with everyone you love at every moment.

If you're carrying trauma, shame, a source of pain, it takes courage to open up and connect with someone. When you feel safe and comfortable, revealing something private can bring you to a place of acceptance. When you tell your traumatic story to someone you don't feel connected to and thought or hoped you would, be prepared for a feeling of unease. It happens, and sometimes you don't know if you'll connect with this person until you're already telling the story. We form connections by showing vulnerability and opening ourselves up, so we can't always predict how connected or disconnected a conversation will feel.

If you feel no connection with your therapist, find a new therapist. If you feel disconnected occasionally, speak up and see if you can work through it. Rupture and repair might bring you closer. Connections don't go in straight lines. My connecting with Astrid meandered. We tolerated the uncertainty. Connecting can mean "taking a line for a walk" (as artist Paul Klee said about creativity at the Bauhaus), threading and bringing together and gathering and discovering along the way.

Chapter Eleven

WHAT WE SHOULDN'T WANT (AND WHAT WE SHOULD)

I once had a ski guide explain to me that he took his wedding ring off while instructing certain female clients, to prevent them from coming on to him. "They would want me more if they saw that I was unavailable." What this says about attraction and rules is staggering—his own issues included, of course. He and his wife eventually split up, and I'm not sure how she felt about his policy of taking his wedding ring off before lessons. It's an example of we want what we're not supposed to want.

"No" is a deeply fascinating and complicated concept. "No" can be encrusted with shame, pride, excitement, anxiety. When did you last say no to someone, or someone said no to you? What was it like for you? We are conditioned to say no to things we secretly want and yes to things we don't actually want. We internalize conflicting messages of yes and no, and we sift through competing wants. We are constantly showing and hiding parts of ourselves, negotiating the rules of desire. We're pressured by all the shoulds in life: we feel burdened and restricted by responsibilities and expectations. Breaking the rules is a thrilling, terrifying temptation.

"No" can be a terribly tricky game we play without full understanding. It can be a turn-on, not necessarily for the person saying it but for the person hearing it. "No" can be eroticized in part because it's not always fully meant or entirely believed. The ambiguity can be exciting and dangerous.

It's complicated to understand the meaning of yes and no, regardless of gender and gender dynamics. But I do think gender has to be acknowledged in this discussion. In the words of the journalist Leslie Bennetts: "Although the term 'slut-shaming' is a modern invention, women have traditionally been indoctrinated to see their own desires as shameful and unfeminine. It's only in recent years that feminist activism has encouraged women to shed those stigmas and claim the freedom to explore their own sexuality, but the process remains difficult and painful for many people."

We break the rules of yes and no in our aggressive and sexual fantasies and dreams. We have sexual fantasies at one time or another that are at odds with our values, our choices, our lifestyle. Dreams have no censorship in this way, and we can dream about having sex with all sorts of inappropriate people. We might wake up horrified by our filthy inner workings, astonished to consider that some part of us might actually desire something completely wild and even repugnant.

Most of the time, we don't act out our taboo and illicit fantasies, and we don't fully want what we fantasize about. Rape fantasy is a classic example of wanting something at fantasy level. The forensic psychotherapist and writer Anna Motz has talked with me about the embedded beliefs around sexual pleasure. If a woman fantasizes about being raped, she's the object of irrational, devouring desire, and she's given no choice but to have sex. She can have sexual pleasure without initiating or even revealing her longings. And, of course, the fantasy is entirely different from actually, truly wanting this to happen. A rape fantasy does not mean you really want to be raped.

Some fantasies are harder to let go of. If the person you want is unavailable or unapproachable, you might want them all the more. You know you shouldn't keep obsessing over an ex, or a dead person, or someone who has rejected you, hurt you, but when someone is off-limits or turns you down, you can feel oddly attached.

We want people who are out of reach because we don't believe we are worthy of real reciprocal love. But we might also harbor grandiose ideals, visions of potential, along with a sense of inadequacy. The desire for what's out of reach appeals to our split sense of self. We can project endless fantasies and possibilities. The relationship can remain idealized, which can feel safer and prettier than the disappointment and vulnerability that comes with reality. You can preserve and even immortalize ideals if you keep your distance, uncontaminated by real intimacy. We sometimes want what we shouldn't because we are less trusting, or less excited, with what we can actually have.

Sometimes our attractions are misleading, dangerous, inappropriate, at odds with our values. Inwardly and outwardly, we can feel oddly drawn to danger, destruction, people, or situations that aren't good for us, aren't healthy. We might feel attracted to what's taboo, out of bounds, transgressive. We're tired of being good all the time. We crave mischief.

"Yes" is also a complicated word. You might say yes to a job offer, a marriage proposal, getting pregnant, because you feel you should do these things, but you don't necessarily want to. Saying yes too quickly, too keenly, can be a turnoff. So we hold off saying yes at times, even when we want something. And we struggle to say no when we feel guilt-ridden, pressured, conflicted. We know we cannot possibly make it to a friend's dinner, but we don't want to say no, we just don't, and think that maybe we'll make it somehow. So we say yes when we should really say no.

Katherine Angel's book *Tomorrow Sex Will Be Good Again* explores consent culture beautifully. With consent culture, we are meant to say what we want, identify our desires, say yes or no as a complete sentence. Say what works and what doesn't, do this, don't do that. But let's look at what might keep us from saying the word "no." People-pleasing, especially when there's a power difference, can make "no" very hard to say. You might bend over backwards at work or in a friendship, say yes to overwhelming demands, make yourself available at odds hours, and overdo it. Some of us go above and beyond, however stressful and subsuming it is. You might not want to say no to your boss, but you might not want to. You're also glad when you're asked for a favor, even if you also complain about how inappropriate and wrong the whole thing is.

Human beings can be self-destructive as well as self-preserving. Most of us have some kind of attraction to harm—towards others, towards ourselves. At different phases throughout life, we might drive dangerously, treat people badly, steal, cheat, drink too much, eat unhealthfully, smoke cigarettes, avoid or reject something that's good for us, take drugs, sleep with inappropriate people, spend money unwisely, feel drawn to reckless or harmful people, seek closeness in the wrong places, or mistreat ourselves in ways that can damage our health and stability. We want what's good for us, and we want what's bad for us. It's pleasure and pain, life and death, good and bad, all rolled into a series of contradictions that touch us to the core.

We seek comfort, safety, and security, and we ostensibly strive to make healthful choices while still yearning for something else, something opposite. We are often at odds with ourselves about the meaning of danger, ambivalent about what we really desire and value, and this plays out when there's an impasse, a block of some sort, a deep, unresolved obsession.

Seeking danger is usually about potency, fantasy, expansion. We feel a surge of vitality when we push limits, bend rules, test safety, and somehow survive. We feel exceptional when we go against the grain and transgress. Knowing we have the capacity to misbehave, and even blow up our lives, both excites and terrifies us.

For many, maturity means avoiding harm when possible, set-tling down, growing up, and making responsible choices over reckless ones. We commit to relationships, houses, professions, even ourselves—vowing to self-care, do yoga, pursue worthwhile things. Perhaps we still misbehave the odd time and enjoy scandal from afar: we snack on salacious gossip, books, and TV shows containing twisted plots. We are fascinated by horrifying news stories. The contrast reminds us of our safety, like the cozy feeling of being warm and dry and hearing a storm outside. But a little part of us seeks destruction and danger.

It's flummoxing that we can feel strangely attached to sources of suffering. We want to flourish and feel content, so why do we find ourselves drawn to pain in weird ways? There's a lure in the familiarity of the old story that we must suffer for love, that our pain holds special wisdom for us, contains meaning we need. It can take the form of a connection to a past trauma.

Trauma changes who we are—we don't know who we'd be without it—but the meaning can change. We may feel helpless and victimized at times, responsible at others, empowered—all of it. We do not need to let our traumas define us, even if they're part of us. Trauma might shut us down or open us up at different moments. We can think we're over something and get reactivated. We can feel shame and realize that we're still not okay. Sometimes we're simply fine; we feel genuinely recovered, strong, healthy, and at other times it's as if we're right back there, however long ago it happened, whatever the circumstances. "Trauma always happened yesterday," the philosopher Francesco Dimitri put it. We might even occasionally miss it.

ALICE'S SECRET SIDES

Alice and I have worked together intermittently for twelve years—my longest therapeutic relationship yet—before and after both of my maternity leaves and through her first one as well. Alice is thirty-nine years old, reasonably settled down, with a decent husband and a beautiful one-year-old daughter. She has exceptionally fetching looks. There's always been something surprising about her prettiness—as though the arrangement of her features just so happens to be attractive, and her unexpected beauty makes it more apparent. She looks incredibly exhausted today, but healthy. Exhausted from being up with her baby and working hard, not exhausted from two-day drug benders.

I met Alice in a place of darkness and danger, when she was secretly in the throes of a traumatic and tumultuous affair with Raffa, a married film director in Paris. There was sexual violence and copious drug use. When she first started therapy with me, I was scared for her, and she was isolated. I was, at various times, her only form of support, though we worked hard to cultivate a safety net. With great difficulty, Alice extricated herself from Raffa, and we've spent a long time processing what happened. We've dealt with the aftermath of this highly charged, traumatic affair she kept secret. It was both formative and scarring. Together, we've worked towards her recognition of the horror, the damage, the shame, the pride, the sorrow over the violence and assaults Raffa inflicted on her. She has learned to embrace the beauty of healthy attachments and the possibility of real and lasting love. We've helped her recover.

Leaving Raffa is just one of the many ways I've witnessed Alice transform and grow over the course of our work. When she first came for therapy, she worked for a designer eyewear company for whom she spent half the week in London and half the week in Paris. She described countless tales of her boss's diva dysregulation, but she had some form of Stockholm syndrome in both her work and romantic situations. The diminishment she experienced from Raffa, and her boss, fed her overall sense of worthlessness and disgust— "disgust" was a word she used often to describe herself—and intensified her compulsive desperation to be liked. She left her boss shortly after she left Raffa, and said adieu to Paris, to the whole life she'd been living. She started an organic soap company, and it's still going strong. And she got involved with Simon. For a few years she struggled with his alcohol use, his slowness to commit, his excessive need to go to festivals and act like a student although he was well into his thirties. "Simon just needs to grow up," she would say. She worried he never would. He seems to have got there in the end. They're married and have a child. And he's responsible.

We have worked through a lot of her past—the violence she experienced from her father in her childhood, her mother who never protected her. She no longer takes drugs—not because she's entirely committed to sobriety but because she's still postpartum and feels she has too many responsibilities for drug use. She's dealt with tricky friendships and self-esteem issues, and she's tried to protect herself and make healthier choices in so many ways.

"But I need to be honest with you," Alice continues. "Screw therapy and all the health it promotes. That's how I feel right now. I miss the darkness."

"Okay. I'm glad you can be honest. Tell me more," I say.

I find these moments of therapy exhilarating: the unvarnished candor of intimate conversations in the safe container of the therapy relationship. We can be bold and real and bizarre and deep. And Alice and I have gone way past platitudes and polite chitchat. Unlike ordinary social encounters, in this space, there is no imperative to edit or follow conventional manners, and we don't even have to pretend to keep things tame; we are here to talk about difficulties. I feel trusted by her to have been allowed in. She lets me understand her inner workings, and she's unusually open. But she's obstinate and determined to make up her own mind and resist being told what to do by others.

"I'm an **askhole**," she says. "I ask for advice and then I don't follow it."

"I like that. Did you come up with that term, 'askhole'?" I ask.

"No, I heard it somewhere. But it's so good, right? You're welcome to use it. So, I'll be an askhole now and tell you about my dilemma . . ."

Some of her decisions are immediate and urgent; others are longer-term. She is constantly torn between one thing or another thing and makes hand gestures of weighing up scales. It's often an either/or. This or that. She also has the habit of doing air quotes when she tells stories about herself. And often at serious, genuine moments, as though she must make light of herself or feels embarrassed if she takes herself too seriously.

"I want to be with Raffa again. Should I leave Simon and be with him? Don't answer," she says.

"I won't," I say.

"I'm spinning . . . my candor and confidence—it's also deceptive. I don't know why it feels deceptive. Does it feel deceptive to you?"

"Candor can be a mask. Whatever your candor is, it's not definitive. You have different sides."

"Yes. That's it. And of course it's not definitive. I give the false impression that what you see is what you get," she says.

I ask her how that is for her.

"It makes me feel lonelier. No one fully knows me. I've been deliberate in choosing what I show, but I'm on my own with it all."

I don't know her all that well either. I've felt deeply connected to her for all these years, and in some ways I have special access. But my viewpoint is partial. And sometimes I wonder if she lies to me. Her stories can feel pleasing, even when she's demanding—the little therapy valentines. We've formed a shared idiosyncratic language, full of expressions, pet terms, and associations.

"I'm confused and baffled and not as straightforward as I thought I was. Right now, I feel uncertain of myself in some pretty big ways," she says. "I'm in a weird place."

"Tell me where you are."

"It's just Raffa. Filling my head. Can't get him out. I'm thinking about him morning, noon, and night. Even though our relationship was disastrous, I'm missing him right now." She lets out a graceful yawn and continues. "He was a terrible, very cruel, and destructive guy."

"Yes, he was."

"More like a minotaur. More bull than human. It makes no sense. It's been so many years since we were together, since I've even seen him or spoken with him, and the whole thing was grotesque. It's monstrously wrong on so many levels. We've processed this. I've healed. I know better. But . . ."

"But?"

"But . . . I feel like somewhere along the way, maybe since Simon and I decided to commit and settle down and stop taking drugs and have a baby, he has learned how to be kinder to me, more empathic, more dependable, less objectifying. We've worked through so much and repaired these earlier wounds. We know this. We know it's good and healthy. And Simon's such a loving dad. I'm so grateful, I really am."

"You can be grateful and also feel other things."

"I've done all the right things . . . but I keep replaying the first night Raffa and I got together. I was twenty-seven, living in a shit-hole in Paris, going out all the time. I knew he was married, and I couldn't believe he was seducing me. I look back and see how I took my first step down the primrose path. It was a baby step, and the instant I inched closer, I stepped back. I was intrigued and terrified to let anything happen. I'd always felt judgmental of people who have affairs. And Raffa was so obviously narcissistic, and a druggie. All wrong. I'd never done anything like it before. But I knew no one else in the world quite like him. And he pursued me with such determination. It made me uncomfortable, but I also loved it: he was so totally besotted, and as deranged and reckless as our relationship was, I guess I miss that feeling of aliveness. Infatuation. I really should know better. What's wrong with me?"

"What happened with Raffa was severely traumatic. He was complex and dangerous and exciting in some ways. But there was physical and emotional abuse too. Be kind to yourself. Your language is so harsh—grotesque, disastrous—maybe you're trying to talk yourself out of your feelings, which won't work anyway, but also, it's understandable to have moments of missing what you had," I say. "And he was abusive and dangerous."

I feel jittery in this moment, needing to reiterate his abuse. I don't want to glamorize him or collude with her reminiscent enthrallment of him. I do not want to be understanding. But nor do I want to shut down whatever she's going through.

"But why would I miss him? Do I? I'm not even sure I miss him. It's more that I'm thinking about him and that whole period of my life again."

"I'm curious about where you are now. You've just recalled being pursued with passionate intensity, and the danger; that can all feel enlivening. And you have a young baby now, and a husband. That life in Paris was so starkly different. It doesn't mean you need to do anything or be with him. But you can acknowledge the longing. What do you think has brought this on now?"

"No clue. I thought I'd recovered and moved on. I like my life. I don't get it." Her voice softens. "I've worked so hard to get what I want: a baby, a husband, fulfilling work, a healthy, happy life. And I have these things. I actually have these things! You've helped me get what I want and turn my life around. And I'm so glad, but there's a part of me that struggles to enjoy what I have."

"Of course," I say. "This happens. We seek, we desire, we want so much, and then when we get what we think we've wanted . . . well, enjoyment, contentment, can elude us."

"You say 'we': Does that mean you get where I'm coming from?" she asks. "Please tell me you sometimes miss darkness? Have you been through darkness?"

I have been through darkness myself. Hypervigilant, like many trauma and abuse survivors, Alice notices everything, even when it's concealed. She's unflinchingly astute. She's someone who has kept secrets most of her life, and it's almost impossible to keep secrets from her.

"Sure, I get where you're coming from," I answer. "I've been through darkness. Not the same darkness as yours, but darkness, yes. I think sometimes you stigmatize yourself and think you're utterly alone in your struggles when you're not. Of course, you're original, but you're also not alone."

"I do feel alone. I don't know anyone else who has been in a fucked-up relationship like the one I had with Raffa. I feel unique—not in a good way."

"You *are* unique," I say. "But not because of this. I'm sorry you feel lonely."

She looks miffed by what I've said, and I wonder if part of her attachment to her trauma is that it makes her feel interesting. It can be so thickly knotted with self-esteem issues when you believe that your abuse makes you special. I hold my thoughts to see where she goes.

"Making organic soap seems almost on-the-nose symbolic for how clean I've become," she says. "I think part of my thinking about Raffa is my craving some filth. I come from filth. I *am* filth. I don't know if it's my raging ego that misses Raffa, or my low self-esteem . . ."

"Maybe it's both. . . . Let's look at the different sides." I can be direct and even tough with her at times because of the robustness of our alliance.

"Probably. My **sufferiority** is fierce. I can't decide if I'm better than everyone or completely inadequate. And I'm hurting. Or I want to be hurting. Special in some way. I just don't quite trust the cleanliness of my life. The organic soap, the baby outfits, the chubby, sober, clean-living me—is this it?"

"You're really struggling to trust the cleanliness, the health. And maybe your traumatic past, and the pain, has made you feel special in some kind of way, as complicated as that may be. How does filth feel for you?"

"Better than cleanliness. Not just because it's more exciting, but it feels somehow truer. More familiar. And right. But I do feel like a freak for admitting this. I have wanted to be safe and secure, and now I'm struggling."

"See if you can stop chiding yourself for a minute so we can understand better. What you're saying makes sense. You're not a freak. The filth may feel familiar. There's a French term: *nostalgie de la boue*—'missing the mud,' maybe even the depravity."

"Of course the French get this. I love that. The depravity—that's it. I didn't realize it was something I could possibly miss when I left it behind. Charlotte, as much as you helped me extricate myself from Raffa, you didn't warn me sufficiently."

"Warn you about what?"

"We talked about abuse, and making healthy choices, and how I might look back with compassion for my vulnerability and woundedness. I thought I'd be proud for having left him. You didn't warn me . . . you just applauded my healthy, brave choices and supported me, but you never told me I'd grieve for the terrible times too. You didn't tell me I'd feel this way, all these years later."

Had I warned Alice, would she have suffered less?

Before getting pregnant, Alice was lithe, toned, and stylish in a bohemian, slightly chaotic way. She'd wear long, flowy dresses with no bra. Though provocative, she also had a kind of natural sultriness. She remembers being precocious and hypersexual as a teenager and young woman, and felt, as many young women do, that being sexually desired was her best value. Now she's heavier and softer than before. Her fuller features give her a wholesome air of health.

I realize that, in the time we've worked together, we've both gone through numerous phases. She's a little older than I am, though it feels like we're close in age. We were in our twenties when we began her therapy, and unmarried. We both got engaged at similar moments, married, had babies. We've taken breaks away from the therapy, but we've always come back together. Over the course of our work, we've each developed and grown.

We have traveled together in a forward motion for a long while. Our alliance feels solid and lasting. But suddenly I'm struck by all that has changed. Seeing her face in the light, I detect soft, downy fuzz and fine lines I don't remember seeing before. I glimpse wiry hairs on her head and wonder if she's going gray. I have the extremely obvious but startling thought: *We have both gotten so much older.*

"Simon feels so safe," she says, opening her eyes.

"How is that for you?" I ask.

She tugs on the sleeve of her jumper impatiently. "Come on. My life now, in some ways, is all I ever wanted. I keep saying that, but it's true. Supposedly. Given everything I went through, dealing with my childhood, the agonizing insecurity and all the stuff with Raffa, and then the drama with Simon, his commitment struggles, his recovery, begging him to move in with me, finally getting him to grow up. Now he's actually good to me. He's caring. We have a decent home. He loves me as I am. He's a good father. He even does the dishes! We have worked so hard to get here, and here we are."

Here we are, all these years into therapy. Alice has had what psychotherapists call "flights into health," where she feels magically, ecstatically cured, and maybe this is a flight into sickness. She's suddenly feeling distressed and symptomatic and pulled back into something she thought she had moved on from. The ebbs and flows of letting go and holding on, changing and staying the same. I urge Alice to go further, to reevaluate her experiences and not feel tied to one fixed meaning.

"I need to be braver with myself and admit that I hate certain things I love. Simon being domestic—I love that, but it turns me off. I tell him to be vulnerable and open with me, but sometimes I find it really weak and annoying when he's emotional. This whole modern-man thing—it's also kind of unsexy to me."

"That's honest," I say.

"And motherhood is hard, as much as I adore Sophie," she says. Totally reasonable assessment. "My role in life right now isn't that fun, maybe. It's fulfilling, and grounded, but it's just so full of obligations and responsibilities. Sex feels like a chore with Simon, and we've only done it twice since Sophie was born. Is that normal?"

"It can be. It really depends on how you both feel about it. Sometimes it just takes time. Would you like to have more sex with him?"

"I don't feel attracted to him, or attractive. I doubt he fancies me, given my body these days and the fact that I'm still breastfeeding. God, we've changed. We used to go to festivals and stay up for days. We used to argue over his incessant wish to have kinky sex and take mushrooms. I was always so annoyed with him for being a man-child, but now that he's sober, now that he's actually a grown-up, he's so sensible! I miss wanting to tame him."

"That's understandable," I say. "Even though of course you'd be frustrated if he were behaving recklessly or refusing to be a responsible adult."

"True. But I've genuinely deceived myself, thinking I only want health and safety. And I do want these things. . . . I was a hot mess when I first came to you. When I was having my affair with Raffa, he used to hit me and enjoy causing pain. Do you remember?" she asks.

"Of course I remember," I say. I sound defensive—and I am. I have a very good memory for details in general and would never forget something like that. I realize she's adamant about remembering, preserving, holding on to the details from the past. My retentiveness is the storage facility for her former self.

"I've worked so hard to sort through some of my issues, so why am I returning to them so obsessively now?"

"First of all, you've been extremely busy and pressured doing and getting and reaching various milestones. You had so much action, so much happening, you may have pushed away thinking about Raffa while you were doing, doing, doing. And now that you're having just the tiniest moment of settling. For as long as I've known you, you've had a crisis, a conflict, an obstacle to a milestone you want to reach, and it's been about the next thing. Now you have a lot in place, and you're preoccupied by Raffa at this moment—interesting timing."

"Something in me needs to revisit it, since I'm not going to relive it, I suppose. I guess I need to work through something here. And have space to let it breathe again . . . *La douleur exquise* . . . Am I allowed? I feel I should be over this. It's been so long," she says. "I shouldn't want to even talk about him still."

"Ah, the **Shouldn't Shrew** is back in town. She's very naggy and loud today," I say.

"Oh my gosh, yes, Shouldn't Shrew is back! She just rocks up and is the worst houseguest ever. Brings nothing and judges me for everything. She's just following me around, wagging her finger at me." Alice lets out a little laugh.

Shouldn't Shrew is a character Alice and I named a few years ago; she comes from a few different sources and experiences in Alice's past.

"Let's just wave tootles to her for now and tell her she can do her own thing for the day. Shouldn't Shrew doesn't offer you guidance; she just tells you what you're doing wrong." Alice believes Shouldn't Shrew and gets bullied by her at times, and I enjoy stepping in and standing up to her. I'm undaunted by her and offer Alice another perspective.

Alice waves her hand. I wave too.

"Ah, that actually feels good," Alice says. "What a relief. . . . Okay . . . there's no pressure to be over things."

"No pressure. You can go wherever you want."

Alice spends the rest of the session revisiting this earlier time in her life. She goes back to certain memories and descriptions of this dark but also intoxicating relationship. She describes the sexual enthrallment, the terror, the excitement, the loneliness.

"This pandemic is such a fucker. Do you think it's making me obsess more?"

"The rules, the loss of liberties, the loss of adventure, excitement, fun—it piles up for you. I think of acedia, the Greek concept of tor-por and boredom. It really applies to this period. Not just its being a pandemic, but you may be missing a kind of youthful potential, all the more so because of the fact of motherhood, and the pandemic, on top of your unique factors."

"Point taken," she says. "You keep telling me I'm unique but also normal. Not sure what that's about."

"Maybe I want to remind you that you are indeed exceptional but you're also human," I say.

"Exceptional . . . what a concept! With Raffa, there was constant uncertainty about whether I was exceptional or worthless. Back to the sufferiority."

"The back-and-forth—am I this or am I that?—was part of what hooked you," I say.

"Yes—I'm still hooked, still deciding who I am in all of this. At least I can go back to this earlier time with you. In the rest of my life, I'm meant to live in the present or forward motion. Here I can travel back, without judgment. I'm sorry for complaining about therapy. You know how much I value this space, and you."

"You can value therapy and also find it hard. Make space for the different feelings; stop pressuring yourself to pick only one feeling for things," I say.

When she leaves, I picture what she returns to: a cluttered, beau-tiful but cramped space, a needy one-year-old she adores and resents, a husband she cringes about and also depends on. I picture what happens to her sense of self when she walks through the door, where she goes, who she becomes, what she holds on to and what she loses.

The following week, Alice looks breezy in every sense, insistent on a kind of lightness.

"I stopped breastfeeding," she says, almost boastfully. "And guess what?"

"Tell me."

"I smoked a joint for the first time in how many years?" she says with a look of excited mischief.

"How was it? Did you stop breastfeeding abruptly or has this been gradual?"

"Abrupt," she says. "I went from breastfeeding several times a day to just stopping. That's it."

"That can have hormonal effects, of course. It's a big change," I say.

"I feel fine. And a little bit like a schoolgirl, reporting this to you, but smoking a joint was . . . it was so much fun, and then it became . . . consuming. I was so out of the game, I had to find a new dealer, which wasn't easy, but a friend hooked me up. The whole thing was so planned, and I told Simon he had to grant me this joint without any judgment. So I went to our garden to smoke, and Simon and Sophie were inside, watching *Peppa Pig* together. I could see them curled up from where I sat. As I smoked, I fell into a kind of daydream, and everything felt so vivid and interest-ing and . . . within reach in some way. It was the best feeling—the feeling of youth returning to me, listening to Lou Reed with Raffa, getting stoned on my balcony every night when I lived in Paris. My observations mattered again, a little bit the way they do here, with you, but nowhere else. Anyway, as I sat there, feeling totally self-enchanted"—she laughs at herself—"I pinched my fingers to-gether and squinted at my beautiful little family. My darling hub and beloved baby girl. There they were, tucked into a tiny pinch. They almost didn't seem real. And then my pinch got smaller and smaller, until I squeezed my fingers together and couldn't see them at all. I imagined they'd simply disappeared. Poof! Gone! Vanished! No responsibilities. No accountability. No adulthood. All gone. I felt . . . so liberated. And young again. A return of vast potential. Slutty dresses, high heels, cocktails and cigarettes and lip gloss. It felt glorious. But here's the catch: I didn't miss being able to make good choices for myself. I missed the bad choices. The danger. I wanted to get rid of my husband and child and just be back in some kind of weird scenario with Raffa where he was objectifying me, grabbing my ass, spanking me so hard it hurt, calling me a slut. I missed fucking up. And being fucked up. I didn't miss the good stuff. I was nostalgic for the bad stuff. So, following our discussion last week, I'm still here, wanting darkness."

"Let's continue to think about it—the desire for darkness and degradation. It seems to titillate and enliven you, even just thinking about it. Also, Alice, it's all about you."

"What does that mean?" She looks possibly offended.

"Maybe you miss it being all about you. The time period with Raffa, as you've said, was scary and exhilarating. You made dangerous choices, but the consequences were for you and you only. You've talked about how you didn't care about his wife, so she wasn't on your mind. You were the protagonist of your life story, and for all the adventures and misadventures, it was entirely your story. Maybe there's something about that fact, the centrality of your role, that's luring you back now."

"I guess it's true that I'm no longer the main character in my story. I need to self-sacrifice as a mother. I need to serve. So many duties, so much work. Other people and their needs. And for all I do, I don't always feel visible. Most of what I do all day, and even in the night, is barely noticed. And, yeah, I'm missing the space to self-destruct when I could be entirely selfish in my suffering, and pain inflicted was on myself. You know what would happen if I had a breakdown now?"

"What would happen?"

"Probably nothing. Firstly, who would notice? If I banged my head against the wall, Simon would tell me to stop making so much noise. I have too much to lose. I can't afford the freedom of fully breaking down. I miss my vulnerability, when being hurt mattered more than keeping a baby safe. I don't know if I miss

Raffa or if I miss Simon when we were reckless." A loud siren goes by, and we pause.

"Let's go back to what you said a moment ago: missing your vulnerability, when being hurt mattered more than keeping a baby safe. That's powerful. I wonder if you miss yourself most of all."

"I don't know. I'll have to think about it. Why do you keep saying that?"

"You seem wistful for how you used to be, and perhaps you're protesting the change you feel in yourself, in your body, in your new role as a mother, by attaching yourself to pain from the past. It's a way of connecting and holding on to strands of your former self."

"That resonates. I do miss her—young Alice. I miss me." She pauses and looks down at her feet. "Where did she go? I actually feel really sad. Am I just officially old, and that's it?" she asks.

"You're getting older like everyone else, but you're not old. Do you feel old?"

"I feel desperately old, and suddenly just so separated from my beloved youth. An image comes to mind. Young me is standing across the river, waving at me, fading, like an immigrant being deported permanently. The point of no return. I'll never get to be her or see her or experience her ever again."

She pauses.

"Oh my God, Charlotte. I actually feel quite sad."

I too feel sad and overcome by the image. "That's quite a heartbreaking scene. I can imagine the sorrow if life worked that way. But it doesn't necessarily have to take such a stark direction. You can let go of some aspects of your youth and hold on to other bits."

I feel I may be trying to persuade myself of something here. I'm attempting to lift her a little too forcefully.

"Stop talking me out of this. You're the one who said I need to retell the story of my time with Raffa. He was committed to not developing or growing up. I resented that and judged that, but I also admire it about him. I guess he's my sacred monster."

"Your 'sacred monster.' Wow."

"Can I repeat some of the trauma we've gone over, the awfulness of the affair, even if you've heard it all before?"

"Of course."

She recalls various times of degradation and objectification, all with a mixture of horror and awe. "I am adamant about telling the story entirely—getting it right and solving it too, so I can be done with it and explain it all. I've gone over the night we got involved in my head a million times. I'm always trying to figure out the secret of that evening, the little hidden mystery that can explain everything that happened in my life after. I look for the meaning as though there is one, and I hope to find out why everything turned out the way it did, even though there will never be an adequate explanation. All the moments that followed were full of rubbish and treasure mixed together."

"You're telling the story in your voice, and you're finding your way. You don't need to cover or explain everything. You'll discover what you need."

"I'll keep fumbling along, then. . . . Maybe there's something about returning to the young part of me . . . I was so precocious growing up. Where does precociousness go? Maybe I have to be immature at some point, having been too mature when I was young.

"I'm repeating myself terribly, the way Raffa used to, actually, in his habits, his films, and his life. He would play the same songs over and over again, to the point of madness at times. And he'd tell the same stories. The repetition—it's part of what's bothering me, but it's also holding me hostage in some way. I thought I'd processed all of this. I don't know why I feel so undone again. I feel like I'm a different age even talking about these things. It's as if I'm right back there, in some really immature part of myself."

"And again, I wonder if a part of you longs for that—to be less mature, younger. You've just said how tragically old you feel. How do you feel when you think of the Alice you were with Raffa?"

"So young and beautiful. And now I look down at my drooping breasts, at my body, and I see a different story. I don't recognize myself. When did this happen? That time with Raffa, that time in my life—it held so much for me."

"Tell me what it held," I say.

"I felt omnipotent, even if I wasn't. There was endless potential. I was full of the promise of life, even when things felt awful. Possibilities were everywhere, and choice after choice could be made, and I got to make terrible ones a lot of the time. At least I had them to make."

"And now? Do you feel you don't have choices?"

"Not the way I did. I've made so many significant ones, albeit good ones. Now I get to choose what type of yogurts to get from Ocado. That's where I am these days—so stuck, dutiful, and dull. I was powerful in my twenties, even if it was only a kind of transient sexual appeal. I was pretty helpless, really, but I'm still in awe of what it must have been like to be me back then. Or be with me. I picture my body and my face. Oh my God, did I realize how beautiful I was?"

"I don't know, did you? You tell me."

"I knew I was appealing at moments. I felt the world stop when I walked into certain rooms. I felt my effect on some men. But I also struggled to admit how incredible I was. I was pretty, intelligent, fun, but I could never say that I knew these things were true, especially not all at once. I remember sometimes pretending to be more critical and doubting of myself than I was. It became easier for people to tell me how lovable and beautiful I was when they found out I was broken, abused—the ones I told, either about Raffa or my father. That's when people praised me. It's easy to feel sincerely regretful that a beaten woman despises herself. That's when you want to tell her she's beautiful. And she matters deeply. When she's about to kill herself. But when a young woman feels beautiful simply because she's pretty and enjoys the way she looks, she's somehow unbearable. It's much easier to root for the victim than to root for the woman who likes being exactly who she is. We are so easily threatened."

"You have such an interesting mind," I say. "And this illustrates some of your pursuit of trouble and sorrow, and your ambivalence about whether or not you're allowed to really like yourself."

"Yes, trouble and sorrow felt better than just letting myself be content and normal, maybe. My life was chaotic, but it's charming when I remember it now—I once had Raffa over for dinner in my dump of a studio flat, and we had to use toilet paper as napkins. There was a permanent smell of dead mice. It all feels romantic now. As you say, I was the protagonist of my life story, so however bad or tragic or wonderful it was, I starred."

"And now?"

"I'm no longer the protagonist. I serve constantly. And I have no space for myself. When I reach for my razor to shave my legs, I find Simon's face bristles in it. When I grab my toothbrush, I feel its wetness and realize someone else has used it. When I chug a half-empty water bottle I've opened earlier, I taste Sophie's backwash. My sense of privacy, of escape, of possible spontaneity, has got smaller and smaller. There's no room for secret drawers or hideaway shelves. I no longer have space for secrets. I think what I miss is having something that was mine and mine only, even if it was my trauma."

Between sessions, I have a moment of hesitating whether I should cross a busy road or wait for the light to change. I walk a few feet into the road. Stop, start, stop. A car nearly hits me. Had I committed to quickly cross the road a few seconds earlier or waited on the sidewalk for the light to change, either decision would have been just fine. But the hesitancy, the halting indecision, is what's unsafe. Though second-guessing postures as cautious, not committing to yes or no, even in these small, everyday ways, can put us in dangerous and vulnerable situations.

The following week, Alice reports that she's still incessantly haunted by her affair with Raffa. I think of a line I've long adored, that the purpose of therapy is "to turn ghosts into ancestors." I won- der if we can get there—if Alice will eventually be able to accept her time with Raffa as part of her history without feeling spooked, undone, haunted, as she says.

"I'm still constantly consumed by the vividness of who I am in my fantasy of my young self. I wake up at three a.m. feeling heart palpitations, picturing myself from this earlier time so clearly. Raffa pissing on me. He did that. He liked doing that. I don't know if I'm now fantasizing about it or just remembering it, or both."

"Tell me about how you see yourself in these moments," I say.

"I'm totally in charge of myself, and I'm so appealing. I'm de- voured sexually, desired so badly and irrationally. And I'm devouring back. Life is just full of lust and impulse and obsessional infatuation. Why am I playing these scenes over and over again, all these years later, week after week? It's crazy. It's been twelve years, but it feels so present. I can feel the warm trickle of piss coming from Raffa, spray- ing my stomach, my body. So nuts, so degrading," she says.

"Maybe a part of you also wishes these memories weren't from twelve years ago," I say.

"I miss Raffa," she says.

"Perhaps you also miss some part of yourself. Self-grief, in a way—that image of you waving farewell to your youth. You're try- ing to relocate yourself and retrieve clues from these moments, so you're digging and keeping yourself entrenched in the past."

"Yes. I'm walking around, feeling like these things are happen- ing to me now. I'm having imaginary chats with Raffa, and I can picture the daily life I had. The taste of bread he'd bring to me from the local bakery, the smell of his jacket, the corner of the room where I found out he'd slept with a prostitute. I'm mostly feeling nostalgic. Painfully, unbearably nostalgic, for all the brutality and intensity I went through. At the moment, I'm just sleepwalking my way through things. It's basically boredom. That's where I am. I want to feel more."

This gives us a way in—a thread we can connect to her current life. She wants to feel more.

We go back over the abuse Alice experienced with her father. We consider how playing out violence with Raffa may have fueled her fantasy that she could redo, undo, conquer her past with her father. How, with Raffa, she was determined to fix what was broken, to make things better.

We've spent a very long time in our work together discussing her sexual adventures and misadventures, her relationship with pain and suffering, and how some of her wish to be degraded and hurt in bed has to do with turning childhood trauma into adult triumph. Rather than feel like the powerless, victimized, vulnerable child beaten in her past, she wanted to be the grown-up in charge of herself, someone with mastery over her situation, making a conscious choice to be hurt and degraded. She felt in charge in the fantasies and role play with Raffa, when she was objectified and dominated. Her realizations and insights over time began to dampen her appetite to be degraded. At a certain point she tried to get Simon to act out certain violent scenarios, but he did not want to be sexually violent or domineering with her, and her thirst for this also faded. But it's back again.

I continue to be impressed that she knows so much about herself and is willing to face her inner world. I tell her so.

"I'm angry at therapy again," she says. "And all the security and safety you've helped me cultivate for myself. I miss the sickness. I'm no longer so perverted or self-destructive. It's just not as much fun to be healthy. And maybe therapy killed some of the joy of self-destruction too, because I'm too conscious and self-aware to act out. I can talk about it, but I know better than to really fuck up."

I understand. Who doesn't have the occasional longing for something shadowy and thrilling and possibly dangerous, even when we know better?

"I miss being objectified. As wrong as it is, as much as I approve of true female empowerment, I miss it so much, that feeling of only being wanted for my body. My beauty. Now I'm wanted for the whole of me. Fuck that."

"You miss being wanted for your body, and you've said recently how you dislike your body now. I feel these things are connected."

"They probably are. I'm so unseduced by myself."

"That's it, right there: unseduced by yourself. This really is about you, not Raffa," I say.

"I miss having a body that was worthy of objectification. I'm angry and enthralled by Raffa's infatuation with me. He was in awe of me physically. Everything about him, and us together, was wrong. So deeply and catastrophically wrong. I know that and understand all the ways it was terrible and traumatic. And here I am. All grown up. With a baby and a husband who loves me. Just to say for the millionth time, I should know better. But I miss being objectified and chased and hunted and devoured by the bad guy."

The most resounding yearning for her is the "unrestrained urge," as she puts it.

"The fact that Raffa couldn't help himself—I loved that bit. It was all so wrong."

"What does 'wrong' evoke in you?" I ask.

"Honestly? It makes me horny," she says. "I love that he simply couldn't resist me. With Raffa, every boundary was transgressed. That's hot, even if it's deeply wrong."

We talk about how her sexual fantasies are at odds with other areas of life; we normalize the political incorrectness of her sexual cravings. She can give herself permission to want certain things ideologically and still have conflicting libidinal urges.

"I think I pretended to stop wanting rough sex. But I still fantasize about being slapped around in bed. I also want to have equal rights, and I'm appalled by violence, and I would never want these things for my daughter," Alice says.

"I really do understand," I tell her.

I find myself saying this a great deal. Too much, I'm sure, and especially with Alice. Sometimes it's what I can offer her—deep and real understanding, acknowledging the complexities and shades of gray.

Over the following several weeks, our work moves to other topics, somewhat thematically connected, largely to do with her realization that, now that she's leaving behind her youth, she glorifies what she had. She's come to accept that happiness and misery aren't states of permanence, and contentment has always been incredibly hard for her.

She returns to the subject of Raffa one winter afternoon. "I never told him about my real feelings. Not entirely. I didn't even understand my feelings, all the conflicting ones, so I couldn't explain them. I was confused. I get it now. So I've written him a letter. Can you read it, please, before I send it to him?"

"Of course, Alice, I'll gladly read it. Are you sure you want to send the letter to Raffa? Reengaging with him concerns me."

"I want to do this. I'm not even conflicted about whether I should or shouldn't send it to him. I am sending it. I need to tell him what he's meant to me. Read it, please."

"Okay."

Dear Raffa,

I've loved you and hated you for so long. I may never fully get over you, even though I've moved on. Even though I left you. Besides making me feel sick when one mutual friend mentioned that she bumped into you once, I know nothing about you now, but I imagine you're the same, only older. I sometimes wonder if you still get erections. Or take drugs. And how many affairs you've had. If you're still with your poor wife. I wish you misery sometimes, and happiness at more generous moments. You messed me up incredibly, but I can't quite regret what we had together either. Thank you for making life better and worse.

You once took me to see the painting The Embarkation for Cythera *at the Louvre. I have no idea if you even remember this moment, maybe you did this with all your girlfriends . . . maybe you have early senility from the chronic drugs, or you're psychotic . . . your memory can't be that crisp . . . Anyway, we gazed at the painting and you said it's impossible to know if the amorous couples are coming from the island of love or arriving. We don't even know if it's dusk or dawn, what season it is, and Watteau never answered these questions. The mesmerizing ambiguity is so powerful, and I've come to accept that I will always have mixed feelings about you. You are both awful and wonderful. You're my sacred monster. That's as resolved as I can be. Please don't write back. I want this to be where the story ends.*

With love and hate,
Alice

When I finish reading the letter, my heart is racing. My father has taken me to look at this painting many times, starting when I was a teenager living in Paris. It's a work of art that obsessed me, and I loved my father's showing me the multiple possibilities of meaning when we look at the image. "Accept not knowing," he'd say.

My father has never been abusive, and he's an incredibly devoted and loving father. I feel the need to say this because I'm staggered that Alice's sacred monster took her to see this work of art and said something similar. I'm struck by the tender and generous side of Raffa. Monsters can be lovable.

I really need to work hard at this moment to separate my intensely personal associations with this work of art and Alice's life story. Therapists sometimes do better when we work with something that's unfamiliar. When I hear about something I cannot relate to, I'm attuned, modest, curious, and do my best to learn. I know what I don't know. With Alice, I'm a little too familiar with some of what she's describing—not just with this painting but also with many other details of her life experiences.

I keep insisting on our differences, primarily in her childhood and her parents, just drastically different from my own. I get the sacred monster thing. Some of her struggles are familiar to me, and I have to be on my guard. However well intended, over-relating can be minimizing, impatient, mis-attuned, imposing, and unproductive. When we think we know what someone is experiencing, we shut down learning and discovering. This happens all the time in friendships, in families, and sometimes in therapy. We assume we know what's there, and we fail to see things in new ways.

Identifying with Alice seeing this particular painting jolts me out of over-relating. It's a vivid reminder that this is her story, not mine. I can't assume I know what's best for her. She wants and needs to confront Raffa, and this is her way.

"Alice, that's a beautiful letter," I say. "I'm moved by what you've said, and you've said it powerfully."

"I've chosen to write this and send it to Raffa, and I love it. Thank you. I feel like I've processed something. And maybe sending him a letter is a little bit dangerous, but that's a risk I'm willing to take."

And then she says something quite spectacular: "Change is hard. Growing pains are called growing pains for a reason. It hurts to grow. So how do we keep growing once the pain stops?"

PARADOX AND YOU

We are all contradictory in certain ways. Acknowledging our paradoxes and recognizing our mixed feelings can help us make sense of how we relate to ourselves and others. We can even, with a dose of humor at times, admit the ways we might be hypocritical. It's an enormous relief to be unvarnished with ourselves—and a few trusted others, perhaps—about our uncensored secret sides.

Sometimes the paradox shows up with success: many of us think we crave success but also struggle when it's within reach. This ambivalence comes up in therapy often. Abraham Maslow called this the Jonah complex. "We fear our highest possibilities," he wrote in *The Farther Reaches of Human Nature*. There's thrill in the "godlike possibilities we see in ourselves in such peak moments. And yet we simultaneously shiver with weakness, awe, and fear before these very same possibilities. So often, we run away from the responsibilities dictated, or rather suggested by nature, by fate, even sometimes by accident, just as Jonah tried in vain to run away from his fate."

And finally, this part is especially encouraging: "Conscious awareness, insight, and 'working through' is the answer here. This is the best path I know to the acceptance of our highest powers, and whatever elements of greatness or goodness or wisdom or talent we may have concealed or evaded."

We may be playing a torturous game with ourselves where we try to get what we want, but we also self-sabotage. Most of us do this at some point, in our love lives or professionally, where we pursue something important to us and block ourselves too. In therapy, I often refer to this as driving with the handbrake on.

The ambivalence about success is a big one, as it touches on issues of self-esteem and self-worth profoundly, and familiar stories of struggle feel more comfortable to us than trusting success. We need to consider what it would take to succeed, including allowing for failure and hurt along the way.

Consider turning ghosts into ancestors. Ghosts can distract you from allowing for success. Think of a time when you've made a healthy decision on the outside—behaviorally—but inside you have what psychotherapists call a trauma bond, where you feel a powerful urge to return to the source of harm, the relationship that hinders you, such as the toxic boss who traumatized you. This wounded part of you may push forward on the one hand while looking back with deep nostalgia and ambivalence about the abuser, as in Alice's story. It can be helpful to name these dark desires and beliefs and to consider what you would say to the ghost.

Don't turn a trip into a fall. When it comes to the Jonah complex, part of what happens, for many of us, is that when we feel we've lost our way, we give up quickly. Holding on to a sense of success even when things don't go our way is part of resilience, that much-hyped concept.

Jonah's story ends well. He spends time in the whale's belly, and when the whale spits him out, he finds a new, more enlightened path.

Chapter Twelve

CONTROL

We all have control issues, throughout our lives, whether it's about food, drugs, money, our bodies, rules, other people, how we are viewed, our relationship with time. There's always something we wish we could control, or control better. Babies can form attachments to the oddest objects. In the oral stage, they learn about things by taking them in, literally; they'll put anything in their mouths, no matter how absurd, dangerous, or illogical. And then when we come between babies and whatever they've got hold of, there's separation fury. Loss and control are closely linked. This is true throughout life. Toddlers, children, adolescents, and adults all want control in different ways. Though we regress and act infantile occasionally, we spend our lives trying not to be as helpless as a baby.

The child's discovery of time is the discovery of endings. Each day ends, birthdays come and go, the school year ends, the party is over, it's time to go to sleep. We wish we could bring things to a quick end, or we beg for extensions. "How much longer? Are we there yet?" asks the restless child, and at another moment begs, "Please, can I stay up a little longer?" And there's always the wish for more, for delaying the inevitable: "Just one more time, one more story?" At the same time, children learn to enjoy expecting the next event, a fun occasion, a holiday, a plan to look forward to. Tolerating waiting is part of discovering delayed gratification. But this is a challenge at all stages of life.

The desire for control is about safety and mastery. We like to think that we can oversee what happens, and we want the security of a sense of certainty. We may react intensely when we feel helpless or controlled by others. "I'll go to my room because I want to, not because you told me to!" shouts the defiant child who finally accepts punishment but on her own terms. "You're so controlling!" yells the angry adolescent when parents set an early curfew. The workplace micromanager can make an office feel toxic. The controlling partner can make every encounter a stifling negotiation. We might gladly surrender control in select areas of life, especially when we choose trusty guides and partners in life. What a joy to let go and mean the words "Entirely up to you." But we want to decide when and how we give up control.

We struggle to control time. Some love planning and others avoid it. It could be a lunch date with a friend next week or a marital plan to grow old together. Plans give us a sense of what comes next, and we feel we can shape and influence our environment. We may look forward to a plan or we may resent and resist it. Knowing what's ahead can feel invigorating or predictable. The tension between our wish for safety and our thirst for excitement hovers over the issue of control. Do we stick with the stable day job that feels steady and financially secure but dull, or take a risk and strike out on our own? Can we tolerate the tempestuous and sultry dalliance that's sexually thrilling but emotionally insecure?

We feel a degree of control when we take charge of our schedule, make our plans, and feel on top of all the details. Occasionally, we fantasize that we are timeless and immortal. But the limitation of scheduling threatens this illusion in countless ways. We can't be in two places at once. We can't accomplish everything.

We can't do everything. We might avoid making plans because we're determined to guard our time or wait for an opportunity. When we're stuck, conflicted, scared, socially anxious, making any kind of time commitments can feel daunting, but indecision about plans can also be hugely frustrating. One person is liberated by a plan that feels restrictive to someone close. When our prayers seem to be answered and we know each step of our path ahead, we may soon discover that too much control and predictability feels utterly limiting. There's a saying: "We make plans and God laughs." Unexpected events derail what we envisaged. There's always a degree of uncertainty in life.

We fight age and struggle with time passing not just for ourselves but for everything and everyone around us. No matter how in charge we think we are, we are constantly dealing with the threat of loss that surrounds us. We lose loved ones, we lose our youth, we lose items, we lose time. We must let go of so much, and it can feel unbearable. In the words of Marie Bonaparte, "In all human hearts there is a horror of time." We know we are mortal, but it's another thing to accept this fact, and time reminds us. The fleetingness of life threatens our sense of control. It's a great and valuable challenge to figure out a way to get comfortable with this discomfort. Time gets us all in the end.

We can choose to pause, but it's hard to do in practice. We know we're burnt-out, anxious, sleep-deprived, and everyone tells us to live in the moment, be mindful and calm, but we live in a frenzied world that brims full of chatter and distraction. We look at screens too much and forget to be present.

Therapy can be a space where we crave, and sometimes find, what T. S. Eliot called "the still point of the turning world." We stop and consider where we are, how we've got here, where we want to go. Reworking the past can help us live our lives more fully. In a session, it's perfectly normal and helpful to recall and reexperience moments from years earlier with vividness and strong feelings.

We often return to earlier times and see things in new ways. Those memories then become rich sources of meaning and discovery in the present.

Freud argues that the passage of time is part of what makes life rich and plentiful. "Limitation in the possibility of an enjoyment raises the value of an enjoyment," he wrote. Think of holidays, parties, beluga caviar, short and sweet romances, special occasions, limited-edition items, French handbags with years-long waiting lists: we might cherish what's rare and scarce, and if we have too much, too often, it may start to feel like diminishing returns. But for many of us the anxiety of finitude can make it almost impossible to enjoy the moment.

I became acutely aware of time in my work with George, a young man who came to me in a panicked, agonized state. Penelope, his beloved thirty-five-year-old wife and the mother of their two young children, was dying of a rare form of heart failure. Though she was young, the end of her life was on the near horizon. His planned future was being stolen from him. He dreaded and tried to prepare himself for the horrific loss. Psychotherapists call this **anticipatory grief**. Time was running out. Time was robbing him. Time was inescapable.

In our relationship together, we began to fight the ticking clock, but it was anxiety making, fantastical, impossible. Time snatches things in the most ruthless way. Even if it isn't personal, it feels persecutory. We tried to deny time too, and that didn't work. When we understood and accepted the constraints of time, George let go of some of his illusions and discovered a kind of creative richness that helped him cope with his pain. He discovered trust and ease within himself. He began to accept the deep unacceptability of loss.

GEORGE'S TIME

It's one of those thick gray winter mornings in London when the sky feels close and unforgiving. On my walk to work, I feel menaced by the cold, heavy air, as though it's out to get me. I'm grumpy and sleep-deprived. My baby kept me up most of the night, though I wasn't really sleeping anyway. I'm agitated by the size of my perpetual to-do list. But inside my consulting room, seated across from George, between us there's light and life. It's our third session, and from our moment of meeting he has a tender, fierce familiarity.

"It's excruciating, Charlotte," George says. His voice is mellifluous. I always take him seriously, whether he's discussing a sandwich or a philosophical concept. He has the faintest hint of a Greek accent, but he's lived in the UK since he was a teenager, and he uses English with more eloquence than most native speakers. He's tall and slender, with a forceful, animated face like an El Greco portrait.

I look at him and tilt my head. I only realize I have done this because he tilts his head in response, and I catch his gaze. I don't need to ask him what's excruciating. I know he'll tell me. He uses words with acrobatic agility, but we communicate nonverbally as much as with language. He's a pianist, and his musicality comes through in his gestures: the way he folds and unfolds his hands, drums his fingers, taps, strokes upwards, draws expansive circles as he speaks. Right now his hands are tightly gripped together. He's holding on by his fingernails.

"The doctors started using the word 'palliative' for Penelope."

Oh God. He's been dreading and predicting this moment. We consider how it is for him to hear this word. He tells me about its etymology: it comes from the Latin word for cloak. Now the word "palliative" is interesting. How does he feel?

"I just have to make the most of each moment I have left with Penelope," he says. "I wasted so much time. We dated for most of our twenties, and I delayed proposing for so long. I avoided fully committing. We put off having babies for years. 'What's the rush?' I'd say. She was ready ages before I was. And now this is happening.

Oh my God. How is this happening?" He hitches a breath. "It was difficult for me to get here today, for me to take the time."

Everything feels rushed in George's present life, including therapy. He struggles to get here, and he struggles to leave.

"I'm glad you're giving yourself this space."

"It's the only place where I can be myself. You give me permission. Outside of here, I'm hassled in every direction. I'm full of feelings I cannot show."

I feel privileged to see his inner world. I ask about holding back everywhere else.

"I don't want to burden Penelope with my grief. It's not fair to do that to her," he says. But it comes at a cost. Hiding his feelings distances them, and the gap grows bigger each day. "I'm pulling away in some ways, but I'm also reaching for her and failing to hold on."

His breathing sounds shallow and choppy. He describes the dilemma: "I look at her and know she'll be gone soon. I cannot bear it and I don't want her to see my despair. I try to just take in what I can."

Therapy is his sustenance, he says. "Thank goodness I'll always have this." In our initial session, we agreed our work would be open-ended. Was this my way of trying to give him something timeless? Exceptionalism is already a feature of our dynamic. I'd planned on saying no to any new work. George and I had agreed I would assess him and refer him on. It somehow felt important to work with him. Justifiable clinically, not working with him would have also been justified clinically. I made the choice, and I think it was simply because we worked well together. In other parts of my life, I've resented feeling preoccupied and overscheduled, but I'm able to find utter availability within me to hold space for George.

"I constantly conceal my feelings—not just from Penelope, but everywhere else. I hide my devastation from the girls. Our relatives are too fragile. I need to keep it together at work. And Penelope's doctors are for her, not me. Some of my friends ask me how I am, but I can't get into it, so I say the same stock line again and again: 'You know, making the most of our time.' But I can't open up."

"What do you think would happen?"

"A giant flood. That's what would happen. If I started to let it out, I'd collapse—no, I would *drown* in my tears. I have to stay afloat."

"What an image." Even though he says he's open with me, I take his emotional flood warning seriously.

"My friends ask at all the wrong moments anyway, when there are constant disruptions, people nearby. It's too rushed. You know how it is with small kids, truncated conversations. There just isn't enough time. For anything. I'm falling short at work too. And we have so many bills, and the girls have all these clashing playgroups, nursery schedules. I cannot keep up with it all." The tempo has sped up, and I see a sheen of sweat on his forehead.

"You're carrying so much, George. The sheer pressure. Allow yourself to pause. At least for a moment—here." This is my way of trying to get him to slow down without saying the words.

"Pausing. Hmm, that's hard for me."

"I get it," I say. It's hard for me too. "What about in music? How do you feel about pauses there?"

"In music . . . wow, that's interesting. In music, the rests help me hear what I'm playing. Silence is full of meaning. People listen when you pause. I'm quite good at timing silences and pausing there. But in my current situation, I can't. I glanced at the sky on the way here, and the clouds looked giddy. I suddenly couldn't bear to think that Penelope and I won't get to enjoy looking at the sky together for much longer. I almost turned back to tell her to look up at the clouds."

"And?"

"I phoned her. I was already rushing to get here. But anyway, she was half-asleep and I think the call annoyed her, instructing her to go to the window and look at the clouds. She told me all she could see was a gray sky. I'm getting so much wrong. Maybe I shouldn't have left her to come here. We're running out of time, and I should be with her constantly while she's still alive."

The same sky I had found oppressive, he found giddy. Perspective! I was grumpy and ungrateful in my sense of the sky today. His elation sounds pressured and elegiac, and he's drenched in guilt.

"I'm completely out of tune. I'm everywhere and nowhere. I feel so out of control," he says. "And I can't let go." He looks at me with a kind of desperation. "How can I get through this? What if I don't? I have no choice. The girls need me. But what if I can't survive?"

"As you said at the start of the session, it's excruciating. You might feel like you can't get through this, of course. You're in such a challenging situation, and you're already surviving, even if it feels unbearable. Well done," I say.

I tell him in as soft and gentle a voice as possible that our time is up.

"What? Already? No." He's disbelieving.

"I'll see you next week at the same time," I say.

"Quickly, can you tell me again what you said about my anxiety and explain how I should cope with my situation?" he asks.

I cannot possibly answer these questions quickly and we need to stop! This is more than what's called the "doorknob moment" when a client drops a bombshell on the way out. This is simply a plea to have more. I don't want to shut him down, undo the meaningful discussion we've had with a hasty recap or glib slapdash takeaway tips. He's put me on the spot and he's stalling and pulling me over the line. What do I do? I can't go on; I'll go on.

"We'll pick this up next week. I don't want to do you a disservice by giving you something hurried when we're out of time."

"Just a minute longer?"

"I'm so sorry, George, I know there's so much, but we really have to stop," I say.

I have a session scheduled right after George, and I know this client will arrive promptly. I'm desperately thirsty and my water glass is empty.

"Okay. Please, Charlotte, can you email me telling me something I can do between our sessions? I'm sorry. I know we're over time. I'm sorry. Thank you so much."

I'm practically shooing him out the door at this point. I probably won't have time to run to the kitchen and get water before my next session. "I'll email you," I say hurriedly as I'm walking him to the door. He opens his phone to check his calendar for our next appointment, which we've already confirmed. He asks another question. A tense-sounding "Yes, yes, yes, okay" from me. More minutes vanish before he's fully left. My next client arrives. I hold my thirst for another fifty minutes.

That evening I spend a disproportionate amount of time composing a thoughtful email to George with ideas for between-session self-care. He thanks me profusely. He stays in my mind, and perhaps his bid for bonus minutes and help is his way of holding on to me. Though I'm giving him my all, it's not enough.

His charisma and mannerisms evoke feelings of élan mixed with deep sorrow in me. I think of his descriptions of Penelope as she was before: a cellist, fiery, striking, bold, secretly shy. And their two young daughters, three and five. Will the three-year-old have any memories of her mother? What's the five-year-old's sense of what's happening? I ache when I think of Penelope. Her illness is a reminder of the absurd fragility of life. It seems ludicrous that medicine cannot save her. This torturous situation is happening for no good reason, and I feel George's agony. It's dismal, unacceptable, desperately unfair, and yet he's brimming with life. Why is it that reminders of death can be oddly life enhancing?

Very quickly, our relationship seems to form and blossom into something lively, dynamic, and full. It feels as though we go further and deeper in a handful of sessions than some of my work with other clients over a period of years.

I wonder if George has always been this way or if some of the vitality I feel from him is his response to impending loss—his surging life force. There's a kind of exuberance in his sadness, and the deep love he has for Penelope makes her illness more astonishing. I feel he needs to honor her and that's a big part of our work. He tells me about her salty laugh, her droll anecdotes, her love of sea bass, her quirky fondness of Marvin Gaye. He pushes me to see the beauty and pain of existence, to notice little details I too easily overlook. When the demands of motherhood or marriage vex me, I think of George and I stop myself from taking things for granted, from being a spoiled brat, even internally. My work with him urges me to value what I have and feel a heightened consciousness about ordinary everyday moments.

With all of life's uncertainties, I want therapy to be a reliable trusty space he can count on each week where he can fully encounter himself. By giving him a safe, caring relationship in which he can express himself freely, I encourage George to discover parts of himself he strenuously avoids or denies elsewhere. George begins to revise some of his world beliefs. He feels that time has passed and his power and freedom have faded. He's almost unbearably nostalgic but also regretful describing his former self and the life he imagined he and Penelope would have. George is in a state of mourning for the loss of the healthy wife he fell in love with. In mourning the decline of his wife, he is also mourning his past self; her sense of him as a vibrant, masculine protector is fading as her illness advances.

His circumstances have torn him in every direction; he's needed by his family, pressured financially, required to hold things together, and internally there's a kind of fragmentation in his sense of self. And he's a perfectionist in his expectation that, somehow, he can get this right.

He's able to express with me feelings he hides from others, allowing him to explore what it means to be him and understand how he's split off troubling parts of himself. He felt he saved Penelope when they first fell in love. George saved her from her dysfunctional family, and he saved his sense of self rescuing her. He still thinks he can rescue her. He still thinks he can save her. How, he doesn't know, but he cannot let go of his determination. We explore the origins of his identity as the strong male, the fantasy that he can provide, protect, and rescue. His father, an academic, encouraged him to be scholarly and work hard. His mother died when he was eight, and his father seemed detached and consumed by work. George resented him for not caring enough. And he blamed himself for his mother's death, an emotional wound that scarred him deeply. Penelope's illness has reopened this wound.

In adult mourning, we revisit early experiences of loss. We return to his loss of his mother. George was marked as a gifted pianist from the time he was four, when his mother organized lessons for him, and they had a grand piano in their living room where he practiced daily. "I was a bit of a king baby," he recalls. "Her only son. And she loved classical music, going to concerts. I remember the sight of her dressed up, wearing elegant jewelery and smelling of fur and perfume. And when I played the piano for her, she made me feel like I could master anything." A few years later, she got sick. He believed that if he played the piano well, he could help keep her alive.

He continued his piano lessons and practiced assiduously, and his mother continued to get sicker. He bargained, negotiated, and tried to play better and learn more. He struggled to learn "Träumerei" by Schumann, a solo piano piece, and when he finally did, he played it for her, and she seemed unmoved by his performance. And then she died.

George remembers thinking if only he'd played with more expression, he'd have engaged his mother. He was mechanical in his performance; he didn't modulate. Even as he tells me now that it's as though he believes that an enlivening performance would have given his mother more life. He still shudders when he hears "Traümerei."

"Looking back, it was only when I met Penelope that I felt fully capable again," he says. "I was finally the man I'd always wanted to be: strong, powerful, noble, competent. She liked everything about me. She even liked the smell of my sweaty armpits after sex. And my hands. She fell in love with my piano playing. *Sehnsucht*, nostalgic romantic classical music, was her favorite. She liked what I composed too. She'd throw her head back and close her eyes, drinking it all in. It was as good as sex, those moments."

He misses that too. "We were so sexual, so physical. Greedy for kisses, and so giving. She wanted me all the time. I felt so large. Just so large. That's the feeling I had: I was huge. And then seeing her become a mother, and grow our babies—I loved her more the bigger she got. I didn't find her sexual when she was pregnant, but I was in awe." He's astonished to remember how recently she grew life as her life comes to a close.

"We may never have sex again," he says.

She's already so weak, and neither of them want to. Their relationship has shifted into something closer to parent and child in its dynamic, which has desexualized things further.

"What I long for is when it was just us, madly in love, prechildren. I miss how she saw me and how I saw her. How we felt about ourselves and discovered ourselves from being together. She's dependent on me but she's distant, and even though I try to do everything for her, I'm also letting her down," he says.

I ask him if he feels let down by her too. A hard thing to admit when anticipating loss, and he's relieved by the invitation to express his feelings of abandonment by her. "She's leaving me. She's leaving me to raise our girls. Alone. And alone with grieving her too. I wonder if I can do any of it on my own, going forward. Can I keep the goodness, or will it die with her death?"

We contemplate her emotional legacy, and a pang of horror sets in. "She's still here! How can I be packing her up like this? But I also can't count on her. I don't know where to position myself."

He begins to cry, and he wipes his face on his sleeve. "I cannot figure out how to think of Penelope. Is she here or is she already gone? I cannot save her. All I can do is savor her," he repeatedly tells me.

I realize at this moment that he's desperately resolved not to be like his remote, unsentimental, withdrawn father. He isn't his father. But it's also impossible for him to get this situation precisely right. I tell him that. He cannot control this.

His life is filled with pain, and there's so much more pain to come. He is fulfilling to work with, for me—almost suspiciously so. Psychotherapists can fall into the trap of the "perfect client." George brings a certain musicality into our work together. I feel it in the back of my neck: small shivers. I get lost in the rhythms, enchanted. He's bright and accomplished, and he willingly investigates his statements, rummaging for hidden notes. Emotionally expressive, he describes sorrow but he's also able to laugh—not in a defensive way, but in a way that feels life-affirming, a counterbalance to his bitterness and despair. George's humor breaks into his thoughts and gives his remarks a generous dimension.

Just observing him, listening to him, I feel as if our work together is important, as if I'm doing something terrific and life changing with him. Our connection is clearly a kind of mutual idealization. He tells me he feels "hugged" by my words. The closeness between us feels exciting and anxious. The anxiety I feel is about scarcity: I'm mirroring his anxiety. In our work in these therapy hours, I'm giving him something important, to be sure, but it's not nearly enough.

I interrupt my enchantment whenever I call time at the end of our sessions. "We will have to stop there," I hear myself say each week, minutes past the end.

"No!" He boos and theatrically punches the air. "How are we at the end already?" It feels as though he's moved the sun and the stars to get here, and I'm ejecting him when he's just begun. It's a mini rejection, my sending him away. It's hard for him to find the time for himself each week, but our fifty minutes per session feels inadequate. It's a microcosm of the horrific and real time deficit he feels with Penelope.

My supervisor helps me grasp how our relationship is marked by nervousness that George needs to engage and control the sessions to hold on to me. His charismatic mannerisms, his seductive use of language, his need to be outstanding, suggest an underlying fear that I'll cease to be available for him if he doesn't give everything. And I'm my absolute best with him too. We are both perfectionists in our relationship, which is rooted in a sense of glory and fear of inadequacy. George is living a familiar pattern here, applying the work ethos instilled in him by his father that he must give it his all to have anything. His hard work didn't save his mother—isn't saving Penelope—but he's still reenacting this belief. And in some ways too he's the little boy playing Schumann for his mother. And in my response to him, I'm a little too enraptured, longing to support him and nurture him. I want to counteract his experience that his mother was unmoved by him. I'm deeply moved!

We are both afraid of wasting time. For months, this urgency permeates our work. There's a kind of terror that time is running out or has already vanished. The fleetingness of life gives me a rushing, almost panicked wish to remember every moment with George.

The notes I write about our sessions have a hyperkinetic intensity. I jot down his descriptions of Penelope eating grilled calamari, the births of their two girls, the songs they dance to, their shared adoration of lemon with all seafood. I want to preserve and honor his story of Penelope, and our time together, our work, feels significant, even monumental, in a way that isn't ordinary. My notes are full of granular details, as though it's all exceptional. There's a grandiosity in my thinking that all these moments have supreme importance and so I must document them exquisitely.

George tells me he recognizes me by the sound of my shoes when he's in the waiting area. "I hear you coming down the hallway. Tick tock, tick tock." I wonder if he connects my footsteps with the sounds of time passing: Is it his sense of time passing with each step? Does he feel that the walk to our therapy room takes time out of our session? And then there are the obvious and even ludicrous ways time comes into our work, when he's bothered by a literal loud ticking clock, a replacement for the usual digital one, which he can't stand.

"I don't mind metronomes as long as I'm the one composing or giving a lesson," he says, "but that clock, the sound of the tick—it's like a soldier shouting at me to march on. Go! Go! Go!"

He asks if we can make it go away, and I agree—giving some drama to the moment—so I take the batteries out of the clock, right there, during the session! This provides temporary relief. But even without the noise of time passing, we're still restrained, and I'm required to be the responsible grown-up and keep track of time. I glance at my wristwatch and feel a pang of guilt when he catches me looking. Why does it feel rude for me to track the time, like yawning in someone's face, when it's part of my role, my way of maintaining authority over the therapy space?

"I'm so sorry but we must stop," I say to George. I feel as if I am always stopping, ending. Always apologetic for the fact of time passing.

When the usual digital clock is back in the therapy room the following week, he expresses relief that the loud ticker is gone. I ask if he wants me to position the clock so we can both see it. "God no," he says. "I just want to forget about it. One of the nice things about being here is that I get to be the child and I don't need to keep track of time."

He's right, in a way. My asking him if he wants to see the clock during therapy might be my attempt to share the burden of calling time at the end of our therapy hours; understandably he doesn't want this responsibility. As our work continues, George is conflicted about whether he wants time to pass or not, a manifestation of his **chronophobia**. There's still no hope that Penelope will recover, and he finds himself fast-forwarding to her death and beyond, and then he feels bad for wishing time away. But he's also guilt-ridden if he fails to appreciate a fleeting moment. He's caught in a kind of liminal space—a zone that's like a waiting room. He spends so much time in waiting rooms, both literally and psychologically, caught somewhere between life and death.

There is so much waiting as time runs out. He waits for her test results, for scans, for treatments, for phone calls and documents and files and prescription orders, and it feels endless, tedious, out of control, and yet time with his wife is far too brief, devastatingly cut short by her illness. It's brutal to wait for a loved one to die. When there's no hope for recovery, it's completely natural to look forward to the person's death while dreading it.

George feels isolated, in part because Penelope still doesn't show despair, and so he feels he can't either. "Maybe she's in denial," he says, "but she seems optimistic that she may live a lot longer. I don't think she's given up hope. And I feel I can't show her that I have. So I have to perform fake hope."

"There's no hope that she'll be cured or live much longer?" I ask.

"No, and that's not because I'm being gloomy. It's because there's no cure and she's growing sicker, and this is reality. But I feel bad for knowing this, for not believing in a miracle cure, for just waiting for her to die. And I feel especially bad when I'm impatient and think, *Hurry up.* I don't want her to die, but I also sometimes do—not because I want her to be dead, but because I know it's coming so I'm just waiting for the end. Isn't that terrible? I can't believe I'm saying this, feeling this."

His ambivalence about waiting for her death is completely understandable, and I say this. He feels responsible, though it would be **magical thinking** to believe that his attitude will decide whether time rushes forward, stays still, or turns back.

We talk about the magical thinking that made him believe playing the piano could determine his mother's fate. "No matter how well you played the piano, your mother still would have died. And by the way, you might have played 'Träumerei' brilliantly," I say. "The fact that you learned Schumann for her, it's so touching."

I ask him about his perfectionism and his sense of his mother's response to his playing. "Have you ever considered that she might have been too ill to take in the music—that maybe it was too much? Or maybe she was deeply moved with feelings of losing you, hearing you play that Schumann piece. Schumann's solo piano pieces evoke the full force of feeling. It's a powerfully wistful scene. Hearing her child play this music, knowing she was dying, maybe she couldn't tell you what that was like for her. You've assumed her response was just about how well you played, and it might have been about so much else."

I think of a classical musician I know who once described Schumann as a joy to listen to and "a pain in the arse to play," and I'm suddenly aware of the pressure George put on himself to learn this challenging piece for his mother when he was only eight. And here is this gargantuan pressure on him now to master an impossible situation.

George has limited memories of his mother, but his last memory of her is when he visited her in hospital. He didn't know he would never see her again. "Take in each moment," she said to him. He remembers the force of these words. And he remembers leaving her bedside before he felt ready. A relative told him it was time for lunch; they had to go.

"I dislike that auntie still," he says. "She took me away from her. I had to go to lunch instead of spending more time with my mother."

"Oh, George," I say. "I'm so sorry she took you away at that moment. I wish you'd got to stay longer, but it still would have been too brief, your time with your mother. It was inevitably going to be too brief—not because of how you spent those moments, but because she died so young."

"That's true. She died so young, and I was so young. And now it's happening again, a variation on a theme." He lets out an impassioned whimper but quickly recovers his determined composure. " 'Take in each moment.' What a message."

"And? How do you feel about that message now?" I ask.

"What do you mean? I think it's brilliant. She was so right. Appreciating life. She helped me so much."

I feel I need to tread delicately here. Deathbed messages can be tricky and pressuring if they're taken as instructions for how to live. We lean in so attentively and absorb the words of dying people, assuming there's profound wisdom in them and we have no choice but to obey and take it to heart.

There can be incredible, crystalline insights from dying people. But whatever the intention (and sometimes we don't know: a dying person might feel wretched, furious, terrified, inconsolable, desperate, medicated, foggy, delirious), deathbed remarks can mess us up, and especially because of our wish for closure and resolution, we can elevate these end-of-life moments. We wish for the finale to have beauty and everlasting meaning. But we need some distance to consider and reconsider how to make use of these final remarks.

"Take in each moment" is a beautiful idea. But if taken literally, it's an impossibly tall order. Some moments matter more than others. We can select and prioritize, but we can't hold on to everything.

I suggest that the way George's relatives didn't and still don't talk about his mother's death has left him alone with the memories, alone to metabolize her deathbed remark to him, alone with the grief. Yes, he says, he felt alone until he met Penelope, and now he feels alone again, except with me.

He begins to consider telling her that he feels he wasted time in his twenties and it's part of his guilt now. Survivor's guilt for Penelope being sick and guilt for disobeying his mother's message to take in each moment.

"I've squandered so much time. I've done so much wrong. I let my mother down. And I let Penelope down. I want to make up for it now. I want to hold on to each moment. I can't sleep. I just stare at Penelope, trying to memorize her face. What if I forget her eyes, the bridge of her nose, how her skin feels, smells? Will I remember the sound of her voice? I've missed so much already. I took the piss for so many years, messing around, sometimes getting drunk, taking her for granted, forgetting that life is fleeting. I will regret not appreciating her every moment. I know I'll look back and hate that I didn't take in every moment."

Ferociously concentrated on remembering and capturing past experiences and each moment now, it's as if the story of Penelope and his sense of self will disintegrate without the cohesive thread of vivid memory. He describes the scent of combed cashmere, apples, firewood, dry autumn air. Of all the senses, smell is deeply evocative. An associative scent makes us time travelers. I love hearing these stories and join him in cherishing these details, but it's the agonizing reproach and guilt that I feel we must tackle.

"You're so romantic in your endeavor, and in some ways it's beautiful and heartfelt, but it's simply too much pressure. You are adamant in your intentions to appreciate all that you have, but no matter what, you cannot stockpile the sensations of every minute," I say. "And you weren't unusual for spending time in your twenties assuming there was no urgency to rush into marriage and parenthood. You had no idea that this was ahead. But you cannot make up for lost time by trying to control time now."

I realize I've colluded with his fantasy of taking in each moment, caressing details as though we can memorialize it all. He believes that celebrating these memories can stop the flow of time. Of course, no one can savor every moment of life. We never hold on hard enough to stop time. No matter how precious, we miss stuff. We forget to notice. We get distracted. Or we notice and we still lose. George taking Penelope for granted in the past is not why she's dying now. In his state of anticipatory loss, the pressure to appreciate is so extreme, he struggles to accept the past, he chides himself for imagining life ahead, and he has difficulty trusting that he can simply have ordinary experiences.

The details he brings me, I cherish and try to preserve automatically, as though I'm the custodian, the archivist, the historian of his life. And I'm rather undiscerning. In the words of Charles Rycroft, the British psychoanalyst and cultural essayist, psychotherapy serves as the "assistant autobiographer." But the autobiography is never complete.

I love memories he's shared with me and may always hold on to them—his time with Penelope in a modest boat in Greece, the smell of their sun-baked skin, sun cream, salt, the wooden boat—but I too need to let go of some of the moments of George's life and allow myself to discern and select the salient details rather than trying to catch and hold it all.

"Memory hoarding won't stop her from dying. You can't outsmart loss." I feel harsh when I say this, as though I'm pouring icy water on his head.

He puts his head in his hands. "I'm losing her. Even though I can't let go, she's still going. I need to accept this." He cannot control what's happening by freezing time. He can't change the past by ruminating over squandered moments. He begins to look at his fight with the clock. He begins to let himself accept the horrendousness of what's slipping away.

"In music, there's something called tempo rubato. You can speed up or slow down; there's rhythmic and expressive freedom. I love it. Timing is everything in music. You control time but you also obey it. Art in motion." George lights up when he talks about music, his life's work. "I guess it's paradoxical in this way, but I've missed that lesson. I've fantasized about traveling in time. If only I could. I'd return to the euphoria of falling in love with Penelope when we were healthy, young, and so physically loving. And maybe I would go back even further, to early childhood, when there was a seemingly endless supply of my mother's love and I didn't know about time, before she got sick, before I started playing Schumann."

Feeling in love warps our sense of time. Marie Bonaparte writes, "Every lover, however wretched his condition may otherwise be, finds himself transported into fairy-land." She adds, "That is why every lover swears eternal love."

George forgot about time when he and Penelope fell in love. And that's part of the euphoria of youthful love. He didn't waste their twenties. He loved her and she loved him, and he delayed change until he came round. Completely human.

There are sessions when, instead of talking about his wife's illness, George talks about other periods, whatever comes to mind. He recalls university days, childhood summers, all in search of what it's meant to be him. Maybe he's reminding himself of his identity from other ages, looking for a coherent thread in his sense of self. In recalling the past, it's as if time leaves us alone, at least temporarily. I feel keenly attuned to him, and we engage in a kind of playful space. The chronology is up to us and together we can go anywhere we want, back in time, to his childhood, to his adolescence, to any phase of life we choose.

I'm so caught up in being attuned to him, our relationship transports us away from time, away from what's happening in his life, perhaps imagining that we can redo his childhood experiences or undo his pain. It feels as though we are the symbiotic mother and son in some of these sessions.

"You get me," he says. "You understand me better than anyone. I feel like a child in the best way. Ahhhh." He lets out a sigh of satisfaction, of contentment, and his face has a sanguine expression.

Our enraptured dynamic returns us to earlier moments in his life and we address historical emotional issues. But we must also address the present situation, the significance of his wife's illness, and what this means for his life. By acknowledging and discussing his longing to be a child, to have me take care of him, to control and navigate the clock, to escape the responsibilities of adulthood, time becomes a source of creative richness.

"There's always that distance that comes when someone's dying. I never considered that with my mother," he reflects. "She was the ultimate authority for me, and I'm beginning to realize how she grew further away, and her illness took her away, the way it's taking Penelope away. I keep trying to reach them and I can't. I just can't."

This feels like a moment of reckoning. "The more I try to control time, the more out of control I feel. I'm not responsible for death," he says. "Or time passing. You know, in one version of Greek mythology, Cronus, the god of time, devours his children."

"That's fascinating," I say. "If Cronus eats his children, he's also what made them exist in the first place. So time creates and devours. Timing is what brought you and Penelope together. You've described the happenstance of how you met. And the fortuitous timing for both of you. How you both felt saved by your relationship. Time makes so much possible even if it also eats us up."

"Yes! Time does create, even if it also destroys. It's what made us meet, made our daughters who they are. And now Penelope's dying, and I cannot protect her or save her. But I'm also saving her in some ways: her daughters will carry her legacy, and some of my memories too. She's internally with me. But I cannot hold on to everything. She's slipping away. That's reality."

I am again reminded of how babies get upset when they are separated from an object or from a person they're attached to. They cry and they plead. They learn over time that loved ones come back and separation doesn't mean permanent loss, that relationships persist despite separation and setbacks. But sometimes there's simply the fact of loss. The missing stuffed animal might not be replaceable. There will be new ones, but they'll be different. Separation can be permanent, without reunions. Loss is a painful and undeniable part of loving and living.

"I'm an absurdist," he tells me. "I don't like chaos, but neither do I think there's some inherent order and meaning in life. I believe we make meaning. It's like learning music and composing music. There isn't just one definitive song we find: there are endless variations of a tune. Countless rhythms and melodies. And unheard melodies too, which can be sweeter. I don't think Penelope got sick for any reason. But it's happened, and I do think that we insist on making meaning. And the meaning I've made—that I'm making—is that it's nice, exceptionally nice, to feel noticed, to feel heard. Therapy is a repository for the memories and the mixed notes. Thank you for listening. For really listening, and for helping me find the melodies. I listen to myself here. And there are so many notes—not just sad ones, but exuberant ones too. I can tell you about dancing with the girls, the good times mixed with the sorrow. You know, I've worried about how others see me. If I seem happy, what's wrong with me? Aren't I supposed to be permanently devastated? *How can George be happy with everything that's happening? Doesn't he love his wife?* But I've also worried that people hear my story and think I'm a sad song. *That poor man losing his wife, with two young daughters.*" He stops his soliloquy and reflects for a moment.

"Since coming here, I don't worry about other people's narratives about my situation. I know my own. I don't want pity, and my life isn't a one-note tune, but I can't control how others view me if they don't really know me. I know you've felt sad for me, but you don't think I'm tragic, even if you feel this story has tragic elements. You listen to the range. I can't spare my daughters the heartbreak of losing their mother, which I hate. But I feel soothed by the range of experiences. I've wasted moments, I've cherished others. I'm observing it here, listening to how it comes together, and you're listening to me. This keeps me going. I know you're not my mother, or my wife, or any kind of replacement, but this is where I feel alive right now."

Without doing huge amounts of interpreting or challenging, I have helped keep George going simply by listening to him, by seeing him, and by helping him listen to and see himself. Sometimes my role is quite simple. Our connection cannot compensate for loss. The time limit of our sessions is the reality principle of our boundaries and limits, the difference between a mother who is on tap through the night and a scheduled session that is available only at the agreed time. I want him to live life more fully, not engage in therapy fully and live life partially. But for now, therapy reminds him that he is alive and textured.

Ultimately, I cannot protect George from the pain of experiencing loss. Penelope dies before her thirty-sixth birthday. George's graceful mind is in full force, and though he continues to miss her mightily and in new ways, I help him feel less alone in his struggle—or rather, our psychotherapeutic relationship allows me, paradoxically, to join him in his experience of aloneness. He somehow survives. He makes it to the other side of a tragic and profoundly painful experience while giving himself the gift of remaining open to life and experience. He lets time flow and carry him along in its tide.

CONTROL AND YOU

A friend of mine told this joke at his wife's birthday party: For psychotherapists, if you're late, you're hostile; if you're early, you're anxious; if you're on time, you're obsessional. His wife is Laura Sandelson, a colleague and dear friend. She's incredibly punctual. What made the joke funny was how poised and conscious and healthy she is about time. She's reliable but also discerning about how she spends her days and her years. In the small ways and the big ways, she's worked out how to deal with time well. There's a sense of mastery and comfort that comes with a healthy relationship with time. She's considerate to others, and her reliability is a lovable and trusty trait, but she knows how to prioritize. She doesn't give her time

away to please people at the expense of her contentment. Time is a
boundary for all mortals. Learning to make solid choices within the
givens helps us come closer to living the lives we want. It's a forever
calibration and requires ongoing fine-tuning.

No human being is immune to the passing of time and loss.
Even when we stop to smell the roses, nothing lasts forever. We
all struggle with this, eventually. There is invariably a link between
control and time. This plays out in myriad ways, such as when we
lose a loved one, even when we lose a photograph or a beloved item,
or we lose a job and with it our sense of self. We are incessantly
dealing with loss and issues around control. We might compulsively
try to overachieve, hoping to mark the passing of time with accomplishments. We plan anxiously, ambitiously. We might also avoid
and procrastinate. We struggle to let go. On a small scale, our frustration tolerance is tested every day, when we wait in queues, get put
on hold, deal with customer service, tell someone to hurry up. Even
the pace of walking with another human being is very much about
timing. It's a challenge to match the speed of others, to keep up with
a brisk walker or slow down for someone walking in high heels, a
meandering child, a slow-moving relative.

Control issues around time sneak into relationship squabbles;
one is always rushing, and the other is often dilly-dallying. One
is habitually late, and the other is anxiously prompt. One watches
too much TV and the other one struggles to pause. Couples and
friends also fight over whose time is more valuable, a sore point in
the division of labor. We feel the tension between time and control
in bigger ways when we are enraged by a spouse and lament over the
time we've committed to the relationship: *He's taken years of my life!
I've promised him all the years to come!* And how we choose to spend
our time emotionally shapes relationships too.

At moments of what is only ordinary, transient despair, the loss
of control over our time can be overwhelming. When we have a
deadline and our children are screaming at us and need us and the

house is a mess and we are rushing to get dinner on the table, we feel restricted and thwarted. When we want to help a friend but we're under pressure at work and time is against us, we feel trapped. When we want to spend time doing the things we love and we have endless administrative tasks, we feel helpless. No goal large or small will ever feel as if it is within reach at these moments. For others, our day job is so brutal and stressful, we don't have enough mental space to properly think about our dreams and desires. And for so many people, secret ambitions to focus on something like painting or getting involved with a charitable project are forever left unreached, because there is "no time" for that.

Time robs us, left and right. We see it when the mirror shows us something that doesn't match our inner picture of our faces. The ticking clock robs the young too, who have illusions of invincibility and endlessly infinite stretches of time lying ahead. The biological clock torments relationships with the pressure to procreate sooner rather than later. Although men have more time to procreate, the sense that there's no rush can be a pernicious illusion. The fantasy of endless time can keep people from committing, from choosing, from living fully, from valuing life as it's happening because of the belief that one day life will become something else. Life is happening right now. And life will end.

Time also heals, of course. It can be our friend as well as our foe. It can soften horrible feuds. It can allow for wisdom, perspective, forgiveness, understanding. In medicine, any number of treatments depend on the "titration of time."

And wisdom comes with life experience. One of the reasons I decided to be a psychotherapist was my wish for a lifelong profession. I've had the privilege of meeting eminent legends in their eighties and nineties: Otto Kernberg, Albert Ellis, Jerome Bruner, Irvin Yalom. I once held the door open for Betty Joseph when she arrived at the Institute of Psychoanalysis in London to give a lecture. She was in her eighties at the time and wore high heels. She walked slowly but with pep and force. "I can get the door all by myself, you know, but thank you," she said. I was embarrassed by her remark, but I love it now. She was bold and determined. She had the vast wisdom of her long life, but her mind remained open. She talked about bulimia and social media. This is the way to grow old if I'm lucky enough to get to. Age is respected in psychotherapy. I remember feeling self-conscious about being so young when I started my training. Youth wasn't seen as an advantage. Sometimes the passage of time can have its benefits. We never have total control, but—given whatever time is available—we have choices.

AFTERWORD

Understanding what we want and what we don't want gives us clarity about our choices. We can select and prioritize from an assortment of desires. We can live our lives with more ease and joy.

It's difficult and essential to ask ourselves what we want and to keep asking. Live the questions.

We're often frightened by our inner lives. We're scared that we'll drown in the depths of our emotions. We dread the intense pressure of our conflictual longings. We're ashamed of our secrets, and we're proud of our fantasy versions of life and of ourselves. Caught in the grip of sufferiority, we can avoid addressing what matters deeply to us. We might be incredible and life might just happen to us, or we might be disastrous and hopeless. When we get into the sufferior zone, we can stay trapped with our unlived lives . . .

Our secret wants aren't nearly as dangerous as our gatekeeping. When we face ourselves and pay attention honestly and intimately, we come alive. We make our own choices. We let go of dusty resentments and make space for fresh experience and discovery. The world is full of getting and spending and laying waste. We can sleepwalk our way through life if we're disconnected from our real internal world. Allow yourself to participate fully in your life. Look at the life you're living. Don't wait for your imaginary unlived life to happen. Insist on living this life as fully as possible.

We're unreasonably frightened of feeling responsible for our lives, but that's where we have power and efficacy and authorship. It's where we have freedom, even if the freedom feels oppressive. It is up to us to live our own lives. This one, astonishing, precious life. Pointing at obstacles, blaming others, leaves us with ashes. Life isn't what we signed up for, but we can always do something, even if it's looking up at the sky, noticing a detail, expressing love.

Pride and shame are troublemaking twins we can't fully shake off. But take note of the ways they intimidate us. Consider the ways we all conceal and perform desires. We have gargantuan depths, however far we choose to look. Whether other people understand their inner worlds or not, you can have a sense of the vicissitudes of being human. Trust your own authority about your own experiences in these ways. Be curious. If you can acknowledge difficult feelings, you're already able to survive them. Pay attention to what it's like to be you, but also look outside of yourself. If you find yourself obsessing over the stuff you want, step back and distill the bigger desires. You can still want stuff. But think about what it's really about when you long for something. Look at what's underneath.

There's so much that doesn't go our way and isn't within our control, but it's an incredible discovery to realize that when we change our approach and attention, we can make our own choices. When we really strive for what we want, it's usually challenging and full of surprises. It requires perseverance. What we deeply want is often thrilling and scary. And there's always more. There's more to understand, more to learn, and so many more longings. The session ends, the book ends, and it's worth looking back at all we have, all we've been through, and all we've experienced. It can be years later that a moment in therapy makes sense or feels significant in a new way. The best thing therapy can do is give encouragement. Have deep curiosity about the human experience.

The artist Georges Rouault wrote: "An artist is like a galley slave, rowing toward a distant shore that he will never reach." We all have a distant shore we'll never reach. But we can get so much richness from life while accepting that we are always rowing. Stretch yourself to consider the stories of desire. Learning never ends, and the particulars of life experiences are remarkable. Keep asking yourself what you want, and while you see the distant shore, notice and appreciate where you are, where you've come from, and all that it means to be you.

GLOSSARY

This glossary is a compilation of terms, definitions, and discussions of concepts and expressions. I've borrowed ideas from art, philosophy, literature, neologisms I've coined. In therapeutic relationships, the language and metaphors that emerge can be profound, playful, sometimes joyous. There are times therapy terms help, when ordinary language falls short and familiar words are simply not enough to convey the deepest feelings and experiences. At other moments too, in the course of work with a client, a private language develops, a dialect of encoded meanings that enhances the collaborative process immeasurably.

Anticipatory grief: Mourning something before its death. In this state, we anxiously try to prepare ourselves for the inevitable loss we see coming, and it's the mind's way of trying to get ahead of the grief, trying to control what's uncontrollable. We're still often shocked and surprised by death when it happens. Anticipatory grief looks ahead but doesn't get ahead of what's to come.

Anticipatory grief can be an mindset for some—maudlin and sad about the end of a weekend before it's Sunday—preparing for nostalgia and separation. Getting ready for life's sorrows can impede fresh experience, and, as noted, looking ahead may not get us ahead.

However, it's extremely helpful as a provocative reminder of limits and loss and regret. Awareness of mortality can help us live, and anticipating loss reminds us of what we have.

Aphanisis: Loss of sexual desire. The term comes from the disappearance of a star. It can feel punishing and rejecting to others. It happens for so many reasons. The loss of any desire can feel like failure, some form of death, but it's survivable.

Askhole: Someone who asks for help and then ignores or dismisses it. We can all be askholes on occasion, and it's useful to name it and tame it. You might say, *I'm going to be an askhole and tell you about my dilemma, and I say that I want your opinion, but don't expect me to actually go with your recommendation.* Askhole conversations can be draining and unfulfilling for participants caught off guard. **Unaskedholes** offer unwanted advice, telling us what to do even though we never sought their opinion.

These issues come into therapy in helpful ways, enabling people to deal with askholeness in themselves or others by recognizing when advice is needed and when it's actually best to make our own choices. Therapy is a testing space for working through dilemmas and finding insights, not an advice service. The concept speaks to our reluctance and our ambivalence about getting help and trusting authority.

Bootleg desires: A symbolic concept of what happens to the downstairs desires we push away: the secret longings that are out of clear sight but not out of our mind. Bootleg desires operate covertly. We've illegalized them because they're at odds with most of our life choices. Some of these outlawed desires ended up on the banned list because we had other pressing demands at that time. Rediscovering old pursuits, having fresh experience, widening the parameters— these set up an open mindset for the twists and turns of desires, what's available and what's out of reach, the social and cultural messages of what's acceptable and what's banned. Some of our banished desires go underground and start operating covertly.

We struggle to voice our desires if they're taboo, which is also part of why we store them. We can also be afraid to voice our longings because we don't want to discover their unattainability. Why bother to admit we want freedom when it feels impossible? So instead there's an agitation, a kind of discontent, that plays out.

Candor as a mask: Honesty is wonderful but it doesn't mean it's the whole story. Being open and authentic can be misleading in its bold, unvarnished presentation. It's hiding in plain sight. It may be true, the candor, but it can throw people off the scent for hidden struggles.

Cherophobia: An aversion to happiness. We can feel suspicious of joie de vivre. It can be oddly challenging to trust that things are joyful and going well. There can be a guilt for feeling joy, a doubt that creeps in as though misery must follow or is somehow closer to the truth. One client, discussing the word, described the image of cherubs shooting arrows into anything that seemed positive.

Chronophobia: The fear of time. Some of us want time to speed up or slow down, or we find ourselves dwelling in our unlived life, in response to a core moment we struggle to recover from or an imaginary situation we hope will happen one day. Therapy helps us gather our thoughts about age and identity and review how we spend our days so we can prioritize what matters to each one of us.

Comparanoia: The paranoid feature has to do with the intense distorted perspective that magnifies contrasts. When we're preoccupied by comparisons, we tend to exaggerate and minimize. When we're comparanoid, we're preoccupied by angsty comparisons and contrasts with how we imagine other people's lives. We construct stories about how others view us, what others have that we're missing. We demand ongoing evidence of our position and status, and the plot fixates over pursuing confirmation of our enoughness through others. The shifting sands of judgments are mercurial and can distract us from thinking clearly about our values and priorities and intentions. Constant comparisons about who has more rob us.

Compersion: The opposite of *Schadenfreude*, or perhaps its saintly twin, compersion is the exuberant sense of joy for what others have, the pleasure in seeing others flourish and thrive. What a rosy glow we get when we enjoy witnessing others succeed! A relational equivalent to gratitude, compersion is a heartening awareness of how beautiful life is—and especially when sharing it with people we care about.

Complisults: We often give mixed messages. We communicate with each other in all sorts of peculiar ways. We make digs while seeming to be friendly. We deliver criticism that has a surprisingly flattering aspect. Complisults require unpacking because very often we're caught off guard at the moment we receive a complisult. The intention of the complisulter can be ambiguous and is sometimes disavowed by affect even as the words are spoken. Unlike backhanded compliments, complisults are often a genuine mix of praise and criticism. It's up to us to figure out what to make of it.

Congruence: Alignment between your values and your priorities. Not every desire you have will sit comfortably with your values, of course, and not every choice you make will be harmonious with your context and purpose, but congruence is a state of balance and ongoing fine-tuning to calibrate what matters to you at different times in your life.

Conversation vacation: This is a term for what can happen when your mind drifts off while you're with other people. You might appear to be present, but you're daydreaming or thinking about something else even as you nod as if agreeing with something being said. Where do you go on these mini breaks? Are you protesting by checking out? Rebelling? Conversation vacations seem like an interesting defense mechanism for making situations more bearable, perhaps a way of creating a compromise space for the conflict between should and want. If you sense that your therapist is momentarily absent on a conversation vacation, say something, address whatever is going on. Your therapist may deny that it's happening but will stay better focused. There's a chance your therapist will admit to going off somewhere while you're speaking, and this could also be useful to reflect on, for what this says about whatever is going on in the therapist's counter-transference in your relationship. Talk about it.

Curtain of rejection: The risk of rejection keeps many of us from approaching what we want in life. The threat of making mistakes, of humiliation, of rejection, is too painful to risk. Therapy can be a testing ground for peeking behind the curtain and understanding it from the inside out.

Defamiliarization: Defamiliarization is a perspective shifter. When we get stuck, and we all do, we've often narrowed our perspective. Narrowness stops us from seeing what we're looking at and stops us from listening to what we hear. A sense of estrangement and alienation from what we have seen countless times without really looking. A literary device that can add to the suspense of a drama, this technique helps in resuscitating our capacity for wonder. It's particularly helpful for adjusting our perspective when we're emotionally gridlocked with someone overly familiar to us. What we think we know well, we struggle to understand. Defamiliarization injects air and separateness into our viewpoint, inviting us to be reintroduced. Practice this with a friend or partner, or your mirrored reflection.

Set aside ten minutes to be deliberately unknowing and present. You're encountering something fresh and astonishing. Concentrate and discover where your curiosity takes you.

Decisive moments: A wonderful concept from the photographer Henri Cartier-Bresson, decisive moments crackle with autonomy and authority. Celebrations of our existence and self-authorship, these instances are the antidote to feeling stuck and immobilized.

Decisive moments are occasions of conscious, intentional choice. They're not the moments when everything gets magically better or instantly improved. They're marked by our decision to show up for ourselves and help form the plotlines of our life stories.

We can't hoard every detail. We lose and let go and miss so much of what happens, but it's what we do with what happens to us. A decisive moment can come when you choose to have therapy, stop drinking, have a realization about a relationship, a friendship, a life decision. These moments can also come when you pause and take note of an accomplishment, a feeling, a thought, a realization. Why do they matter? Simply because we make a point of insisting that they do. When we make a decision for ourselves, even if it's internal and private, we can have an ecstatic sense of agency and empowerment. Like photographs that capture a particular fleeting perspective and wisp of life, decisive moments make occasions out of what could otherwise be ordinary and insignificant. They're vivid and specific. They preserve spots of time that could easily be overlooked or forgotten. Sometimes they just come our way; other times we seek them out.

Desire: Wanting or wishing for something to happen. Desire and destiny are almost the same words etymologically. Desire derives from the Latin *desiderare*, "to long or wish for," which itself derives from *de sidere*, "from the stars." Artists, philosophers, and poets are often vividly acquainted with the power of desire. They depict it so emotively, so fervently. This approach to desire offers a great strategy for contemplating how we can go about living more fully. Our big desires from life are the stars we can gaze at without fully reaching. Would we even want these things in absolutes? Some fantasies are better as fantasies, and we can find earthly joy and satisfaction and meaning along the way.

Ego strength: I use the term (borrowed from Freud) to refer to cultivated resilience, stamina in our sense of self. Ego strength is part of our emotional competence and capacity to grow and learn from challenges. Our ego strength enriches our lives with meaning and helps us develop culturally, socially, and emotionally in our understanding of self in relation to others. Ego strength is one way we can treat sufferiority (see below) and can lead to resolution by assimilating the grandiose bits with the acceptance of limitations and flaws, integrating and adjusting and finding the shades of gray. A strong enough ego faces contradictory messages, learns from mistakes, communicates with clarity.

Choosing to practice self-respect helps establish ego strength. Whereas self-esteem usually involves judgment and can be mercurial, self-respect can develop out of principle. It's not based on the approval of others. As Joan Didion describes it, "to free us from the expectations of others, to give us back to ourselves."

When we have self-respect and ego strength, we have capacity to give to others but not to the point of people-pleasing. There's dignity and rationality in a sturdy ego. It's not grandiose, swaggering fantasies of superiority. Nor is it denying and selfless.

Discouraging the existence of ego (and blaming ego for any problems in the world—"too much ego" or "ego is bad") works against vulnerable people, shaming them for thinking too much of themselves, for thinking they matter. The pressure to deny ego sets up a false spin and feeds power dynamics in insidious ways. If you're ever given an ego-shaming speech—and the ego in discussion might not be yours, but a general lecture about the nobility—do take note of why this person feels this way. Unlike narcissism and megalomania, ego is about accuracy and safety. It's self-respecting enough to keep people-pleasing in check. Sheeple pass on the message from higher up and might believe in the scentless virtues of sans-ego living. But why be so self-denying? *"Ego" means self.*

Enoughness: A subjective sense of what's good enough. A state of adequacy, sufficiency. The concept applies to our sense of self, our expectations of others, the limits and edges of what we give, what we take in. Those afflicted with sufferiority struggle to trust enoughness. Sufferior people can even play the part of the hell-bent detective on a frenzied quest to prove and confirm enoughness. The Enoughness Detective looks in the wrong places and piles up stacks of unreliable material, calling it "evidence." Feedback and consumer culture constantly promote the idea of "moreness": we can fill ourselves excessively—with data and information and food, through materialism, social media, and compulsive reassurance seeking—without feeling fulfilled. The Enoughness Detective follows every fake lead and wastes time with unreliable witnesses. The case will never be solved, because psychological enoughness can't be codified and measured in these ways. To some degree, achievement and accomplishment will influence our measurements of how well we're doing. But if we serve and please others to prove our own enoughness, we find ourselves desperately scrambling in emotional quicksand. We set ourselves up when we try to outsource verification of our enoughness to the opinions of others. Our hunger for positive reinforcement gets desperate, and the more we snack, the less nourished we feel. We wait for messages like junkies, and our highs feel shorter. Diminishing returns make us all the more determined to prove ourselves. Our rejection sensitivity can induce a paranoid state of threat and insecurity, along with old imprints of our sense of enoughness and embedded attitudes about our role and value. Satisfaction and joy with what we have and who we are comes from self-respect, from trusting our own authority, accepting mistakes and limitations.

Femasculating: The disempowerment of women, comparable to "emasculating." It's astonishing that there was no such word until now.

Found objects *(objets trouvés)*: Another term borrowed from art. Found objects are details and items not normally considered the usual material that becomes art. In the therapeutic relationship, we assemble these found objects and bring things together in unlikely ways, and it can be reparative and creative. It allows for assimilation and acceptance, and experiences that felt entirely rubbish can turn out to contain treasure. The process involves a kind of narrative collage where the therapist and client assemble and glue pieces together. It's also about *décollage*, which means ungluing, cutting away. We don't need to hold on to every detail. We can destroy and scrap and clear space in a valuable way. *Décollage* is particularly helpful for holding space for trauma and allowing us to select the details we want and not feel we must hoard every moment. Over time, the therapist and client can connect different moments, joining and adjusting and attaching different pieces together. Sometimes found objects are painful events that over time become sources of humor. And it might be that you retrace a source of pain and discover a character from your past who seemed both banal but also threatening once upon a time. And now that person can become part of the story of what it means to be you, in a way where you have authority and can reshape and reframe what you make of certain details.

Frenemyship: A relationship full of ambivalence, often going both ways, and usually unacknowledged rivalries that play out at different times. There can be real love and tenderness in frenemies, but often there's an underlying fantasy of marking glory that's full of edifying conditionals. *If only* the other person could be a certain way, or *one day* that person will realize and appreciate certain things. . . . Judgmentalism and righteousness can overtake empathy.

Haecceity: It means "thisness." I remember the moment at university when a philosophy lecturer explained its brilliance: "It's the essence!" he exclaimed. "It's what makes each and every one of you exactly who you are, and no one else. Do not forget this. Please! It's extraordinary, the fact that we are all inimitable. A brilliant word." His passion was enough to wake up any sleepy student. The medieval philosophical concept of essence is translated from Aristotle's Greek *to ti esti* (τὸ τί ἐστι) or "the what [it] is." I simply pass on the message: every life is inimitable and unique.

Humblebrag: This familiar term is psychologically illuminating for demonstrating our awkwardness around ego issues. We wish, on the one hand, to show off, but we're sheepish about admitting it. Humblebragging usually comes in the form of a faux complaint that smuggles in a boast. It's hard to baldly show off or downright admit what's actually wrong. Humblebragging is a symptom of how we've been fed mixed messages socially. Most of us crave recognition or affirmation, and we don't feel that we're allowed to boast or even call attention to something we want people to know. So rather than show off, we smuggle in self-praise in a way that we hope will covertly alert people to our wonderfulness. It's not so covert, and it usually backfires, but it's insecurity badly expressed.

Identity crisis versus identity stagnation: Erik Erikson's concept of development emphasizes the expansion that can come with identity crises, particularly during adolescence. Though often painful and disturbing, an identity crisis makes space for growth and change. We can experience identity crises post-adolescence and well into old

age. As uncomfortable as an identity crisis may be, it can push fresh
discoveries and learning throughout life. When we're unaware and
automated, we can sink into identity foreclosure, going through the
motions, playing narrow roles without active participation or purpose. Identity stagnation can become a life of quiet desperation.
Disconnected from our innermost selves, we can look the other way
and stay in flight. The tug of a crisis sends out alerts and confronts
us with fault lines. We can embrace the terror of change and uncertainty in our stories of identity, or we can cling to the worn-out,
static script. Allow yourself to update!

"If only . . ." and "One day . . ." fantasies: "If only . . ." fantasies tilt
backwards and are full of yearnings for the other, imaginary versions
of life. "If only . . ." scenarios may be about the past, but they can
haunt our approach to the present and future.

"One day . . ." fantasies gaze at the vague horizon of the future
and are full of intention and sometimes miracles.

"If only . . ." stories and "One day . . ." stories are both really
about putting responsibility anywhere but the present self. And actually, taking responsibility for your life right now and seeing what's
possible are quite worthwhile.

Insight as a defense: I came up with this term because I finally allowed myself to see that I was doing this. Some of us like to think
and feel, and make links, and this can be a wonderful excuse not to
change. We can be psychologically minded, receptive to feedback
and interpretations, and expressive. We come up with all sorts of
realizations. We are aware of certain patterns and habits and problems. But nothing shifts. This is insight as a defense. We may believe
that understanding ourselves is enough. Sometimes we need to do
more than understand if we keep making missteps.

In therapy, you're the one talking about what's going on in your
life, and your therapist sees you in the session but cannot be expected

to know or sort out how you may be immobilized and hiding behind your insight. It's fascinating to think about and work through.

Intermittent reinforcement: We struggle with uncertainty and scarcity but we also get addicted to playing against the house and occasionally winning small jackpots. This hooks us into unhealthy romantic entanglements most of all. We feel tortured by our continued interest in this flaky person. Hot and cold, we never feel fully safe in our footing in these dynamics. A familiar and tricky dynamic. Look for the exit sign and get support in place!

La douleur exquise: The enthrallment of pain. We sometimes delight in suffering and struggling, emotionally and physically. Pain can be pleasurable.

Lesbian rule: This is a concept from Aristotle's *Ethics*. It's a pliable kind of measuring form from the island of Lesbos that masons used to fit to irregular curves. Aristotle argues that we cannot simply apply rules and theories without paying attention to the contingencies and details of a situation. The Lesbian rule is about flexibility and adjusting to particulars. I think this can apply to therapy too. We cannot insist on straight lines only. Each therapeutic relationship has its idiosyncrasies, and while the boundaries and framework contain and guide the process, I try to meet each individual in an open, unassuming way, embracing the uncertainty of conversation, making space for discovery and fresh experience. I learned about the Lesbian rule at university when I studied philosophy, and bringing it into my therapeutic approach feels essential, because it captures the importance of creativity in how I approach human beings. I appreciate guidelines and principles and structural underpinnings. But therapy should be a space where we can wander, play, and cocreate something personal. It cannot be manualized or scripted. It has to allow for surprise and twists and turns. That's part of the creative force of therapy.

Adjusting to the curves is a beautiful and practical approach to living. The Lesbian rule is also useful as a guide for thinking about our wants. Rather than demand absolutes, the Lesbian Rule guides us to adjust, compromise, and think flexibly in situations.

Limerence: Obsessive, infatuated state of attachment. The term was coined by the psychologist Dorothy Tennov. Characteristics can include rumination, giddiness, absorption, euphoria, fantasy, and intense attraction to another person. It's often what happens in the early stage of falling in love. "The air tastes fresh, the birds are singing, and oh, the sheer wonder of life!" is how it feels one minute, but there's also that splash of insecurity, and it's so intoxicating that, for some, it's like smoking crack, with highly addictive components. Anyone experiencing limerence should be sent a memo saying: "Enjoy, but warning: Do not make any major life-altering decisions based on how you feel at this moment." And I'm sorry to say that this won't last forever. You may protest, and many do, and insist that this is a permanent state. It's not. It might turn into love. It might fizzle. Whatever happens, limerence is either (a) incomplete, (b) temporary, or (c) both. The only way limerence can last is if it remains mostly at fantasy level, and real-life closeness is scarce or nonexistent, which makes it (a).

Magical thinking: Believing that thoughts and feelings will determine outside events. Children often feel that they've caused things to happen, and residues of beliefs and superstitions can creep into adult mindsets easily. Radical acceptance of circumstances helps us deal with whatever happens to us and see what we're responsible for and what's outside our control. As adults, catching our embedded magical beliefs helps us reorient our expectations. We can revisit situations we've blamed ourselves for and feel giddy unburdening ourselves. What a relief that our inner worlds did not actually call the shots. Spotting illusions of power can help us feel comfortable with our innermost thoughts.

Matrescence: Identity challenges of motherhood. The term comes from anthropologists. Postpartum depression and anxiety is only one example of how the adjustment to motherhood can be a struggle.

The process of becoming a mother can mean giving birth to a new identity as well as a new baby. *Oh,* you think, *but I also want to hold on to a bit of the pre-motherhood me, the fun-loving, adventurous bit. And the professional me, that's important too, and will be, so I must keep that part too. Or not. I want to do motherhood fully and properly and wholeheartedly. Wait, I forgot to even mention my partner!* Oh, so many selves, and a crying baby. And for all the different selves, you might feel that none of these versions fully fit. And you might be going through this and find yourself flourishing. Or raging. Whether it's the best of times, the worst of times, both, or neither, it's a major deal, as big and seismic a change as going through puberty, if not bigger. "Adolescence" is an everyday term—an obvious, known thing. Why is "matrescence" not?

Mesmerizing ambiguity: We love and hate someone, something, maybe ourselves, and it's all we can think about. And we love and hate that we keep fixating. Our minds try to work out and categorize what something is, and when our contradictory feelings refuse to stay neatly in just one box, we can continue to obsess. Obsessing can be a procrastinating, stalling tactic, and a self-punishing way of avoiding real-life participation. Tolerating the mixed messages can also feel rewarding and fulfilling. Characteristics may overlap with intermittent reinforcement, but the ambiguity is more aesthetic than addictive.

Musturbation: Coined by Albert Ellis. Musturbating is when we demand that something *must* be a certain way when it simply is not. I attended Ellis's weekly live talks in New York in 2005. He was in his eighties and his ornery, confrontational style was quite something to witness. Brave volunteers would go onto the stage and reveal their issues and he would shout interventions at them. I remember one young woman who seemed quite vulnerable. "You're in denial and you're musturbating all over yourself!" he barked at her. On another occasion he said, "Masturbation is procrastination: you're only screwing yourself!" and he had the entire audience join him to sing these words. He felt that musturbation, like masturbation, locks people in their own worlds, away from experience and reality and relationships.

Nostalgie de la boue: A desire for depravity and degradation. It means "mud nostalgia" in French and was coined by the dramatist Émile Augier. A duck placed on a lake with swans longs to be back in his pond and eventually returns. Many of us miss the mud in different ways, whether it's the mud of darkness and horror or the mud of returning to something more earthy and natural.

Pyrrhic victory: Anything that's a Pyrrhic win is already too expensive. It means winning the battle but losing the war. Or losing the battle and still losing the war. Engaging in certain battles is diminishing for all sides. Pyrrhic victories can be compulsively negative and taxing. We get drawn in without full clarity about what we want from them or what progress would look like. Acknowledging the conflicting longings helps clarify and reroute the direction of travel.

If you find yourself locked into a Pyrrhic duel, consider the costs . . . pivot . . . and shift to a Pyrrhic duet, where you can step into a new rhythm.

Reactance: This describes our dislike of being told what to do. When we feel coerced into a choice, we veer off the opposite way, sometimes to our own detriment. Reactance speaks to our rebellious side, our wish for freedom. Ask yourself what your ego wants and consider what would help you face this part of yourself.

Role suction: Pulled into a social role in a group. The role can be based on needs and fantasies, and sometimes gets projected by the group and felt by the individual. Ego strength is valuable for remaining connected to the self that isn't represented by the group. Role suction happens constantly and it's useful to be aware of how easily we get distorted and reshaped in human encounters. Recast yourself.

Rumpelstiltskin burnout: Rumpelstiltskin is profoundly misunderstood. He is unboundaried and vague about what he wants. He's a people-pleaser and rescuer, offering his skills and services to the talentless princess, spinning straw into gold. But he's mortally frustrated by his unmet needs. In a tragic story of workplace burnout and obscure agendas, Rumpelstiltskin negotiates only at desperate moments of emotional flooding and blistering resentment, and after he's offered his services. His temper works against him. He's vilified and gets no credit for his hard work. Finally, when he does admit what he wants, he falls apart. Expressing the feelings he's pushed away undo him, and he splits into two.

  Rumpelstiltskin is a cautionary story about expecting people to give you what you want when you haven't even understood what it is you want. If you spin straw into gold, do not expect people to be sufficiently appreciative afterward. Advocate for yourself.

Schadenfreude: Malicious glee at another person's suffering. We all have this occasionally—when we learn about someone's struggle or failure, or find out about people's sorrows—and honesty, at least with yourself, is a healthy approach.

Sehnsucht: A popular German word loosely translated as "life longing." *Sehnsucht* is intense, passionate, wistful, and it's often for something unattainable and deeply romantic. It's also a romantic type of classical music. C. S. Lewis loved the concept and defined it as "inconsolable longing"; he flipped the usual "wishful thinking" to suggest that *Sehnsucht* is about "thoughtful wishing." Freud wrote about *Sehnsucht*: "I believe now that I was never free from a longing for the beautiful woods near our home, in which . . . I used to run off from my father, almost before I had learnt to walk." Aged sixty-six, Freud felt that his "strange, secret longings" were "perhaps . . . for a life of quite another kind."

Sehnsucht is a helpful concept for thinking about the intense nostalgia some people experience at various stages of life. The pining is for something that's irretrievable, often irreproachable, and there's incredible force and sway in longing for something romanticized from childhood. *Sehnsucht* speaks to the idea of an optimal life, and many of us, even if we don't specifically pine for some part of our childhood, have moments of realization and moments of desiring an alternative utopian life.

Sheeple: Sleepwalking people who conform and follow whatever group they're in, without consideration or consciousness.

Shouldn't Shrew: This is the name given by one of my clients to a particular inner voice, but it applies to many of us. Names can help us locate and manage pesky and persistent ways of speaking to ourselves. The Shouldn't Shrew shows up uninvited, judges everything, does nothing to help, and scolds perpetually. A bit of a downer, dour and suspicious of enthusiasm or optimism, eyes rolling at any hint of joy. It's as if Shouldn't Shrew needs to take the wind out of your sails. Shouldn't Shrew comes in ostensibly to keep you out of trouble but also to make sure you're not getting carried away and thinking too much of yourself. Shouldn't Shrew appears to stop you from certain missteps but also from enjoying being you. At this point you might think this is your inner critic. Sure, they're all related, but what marks Shouldn't Shrew is the specific disapproval of joy and pleasure and the censorship of thoughts and feelings. Shouldn't

Shrew gives no suggestions for what might actually work, or guidance, except to encourage your paralyzing shame and hesitance to be
yourself, even in your own mind.

Shouldn't Shrew was inspired during one of my sessions by
Karen Horney's term "Tyranny of the Should," a brilliant concept
she coined in the 1940s. The denial of ego is a real problem. We
should be perfect and outstanding but we should also hold back
from enjoying what we've done or admitting anything that might
reveal an ego. I think a healthy ego is valuable and essential for
understanding and getting what we want, and ego strength is something worth cultivating. It means you have a healthy recognition of
your worth, understand your strengths and areas for development,
and can advocate for yourself.

Sufferiority: A combination of superiority and inferiority, with an
extra *f* to convey the suffering it causes. The term describes a sense
of pride and exceptionalism that is mixed with feelings of shame and
inadequacy. It is inspired by countless cases I've seen in my work
and by my own experiences, and is also based on a discussion I had
with the journalist Arielle Tchiprout. We shared and empathized
and emphatically agreed that it would help to have a concise term or
word capturing this state of mind. Many of us are in search of glory
and feel dreadful and frustrated when life falls short—or we fall
short. (Oh, that's the worst!) We have secret yearnings and fantasies
for the lives we want and sufferiority can interfere. Very often it feels
like an either/or rather than a both/and perspective. Either you're
better than the rest or you're no good at all. It's difficult to consider
that you might actually have certain strengths that distinguish you
in some ways and you're deeply flawed in other ways. Adler's superiority complex and inferiority complex offer valuable groundwork
for thinking about these issues, but with a notable, central distinc-
tion: sufferiority is often secret. The grandiose beliefs have often
been displaced or sacrificed by humble obligations. Part of the grid-

lock and conflict comes from never admitting, or even considering, what might be possible and desired. So the dread of overestimations are usually unsubstantiated. Fresh experiences and real possibilities are ways forward to explore what it means to be you and what you want from your life. You don't need to decide if you're incredible or dreadful. You're probably both and lots that's in between. We all are. You do need to decide to ask yourself what you really want.

Sufferiority can be a form of procrastinating and avoiding responsibility for what's possible now. You can't let go of your fantasies of glory, the promises of life, but you haven't yet made use of them. You blame and regret, fixate and obsess, and look for causes in the past. If only this one moment were different, life would now be glorious. It can also be a sense of falling short of other people's expectations, particularly if loved ones have overburdened us with big dreams. In the negative spirals of sufferiority, self-involvement (but not self-awareness) is unpleasant: you feel like nothing and yet you're all you can think about. This can be an extreme diminishment of the ego, and the cautionary tales of ego can keep you quiet and frozen. You might judge others when you're not imagining the snubs and attacks on you. It's torturous perfectionism getting in the way of discovering your own desires and seeing what's possible. Catch your sufferiority.

Tempo rubato: Robbed time. Refers to the art of flexible time in how we express and play music.

Transference: The feelings we bring to our experience of a therapist.

Trauma bonding: This describes our peculiar attachment to deeply hurtful relationships. It's our odd loyalty to the sacred monsters who have eroded our sense of self. Even when we know on some level that we're in an unhealthy dynamic, we can feel attracted to what's bad for us. Clinging to the potential of turning things around is wishful thinking. Trauma bonds keep us waiting for miracles. We can liberate ourselves from the grip by opening our eyes.

Unlived life: There's the life you live. You also have the unlived life, where you store fantasies of all you could have been and might still be. You can never live out all of life's possibilities, but the unlived life holds stacks of charming alternatives: failed junctures, under-developed talents, half-baked adventures, roads almost taken. Past and future bend the rules of time in the unlived life. Full of fantasy and embroidered scenarios, you play out ideal scenes without the burden of proof. Adam Phillips captures the appeal: "In our unlived lives we are always more satisfied, far less frustrated versions of ourselves." But believing in the betterness of your unlived life sets you up for resenting the life you're living.

Consider the desires you've stored in your unlived life at the expense of living.

Unpotentiated: The power and promise of possibilities. Childhood is a time where we imagine so many choices and possibilities. When we make choices, we give up endless alternatives. But if we avoid choosing, we miss out on the marrow of life, waiting for meaning to show up.

Vaginismus: Vaginismus is when the body suddenly tenses in reaction to the pressure of vaginal penetration.

Emotional vaginismus is a powerful metaphor for thinking about the idiosyncrasies of how we relate to our innermost selves and other people. Sometimes we close ourselves off. At other moments we feel unexpectedly shut out. Metaphorically, we all experience emotional vaginismus at times, not letting others into our inner world or being shut out by others.

FURTHER EXPLORATION

EPIGRAPH

Winnicott, D. W., *The Maturational Process and the Facilitating Environment: Studies in the Theory of Emotional Development* (Routledge, 1990).

INTRODUCTION

Bergis, Luke, *Wanting* (Swift Press, 2021).

1. TO LOVE AND BE LOVED

Shaw, George Bernard, *The Complete Prefaces, Volume 2: 1914–1929* (Allen Lane, 1995).

Tennyson, Alfred, *In Memoriam A. H. H.*, https://www.online-literature.com/tennyson/718/.

Yalom, Irvin D., *Staring at the Sun* (Piatkus, 2020).

Lunn, Natasha, *Conversations on Love* (Viking, 2021).

Miller, Arthur, *The Ride Down Mt. Morgan* (Methuen Drama, 1991).

2. DESIRE

Tolstoy, Leo, *Anna Karenina* (Penguin Classics, 2003).

Williams, Tennessee, *Spring Storm* (New Directions Publishing Corporation, 2000).

Lehmiller, Justin, https://www.sexandpsychology.com/blog/2020/7/17/how-we-see-ourselves-in-our-sexual-fantasies-and-what-it-means/.

Dutka, Elaine, "For Hines, 'Noise/Funk' Redefines Tap" (Los Angeles (CA) *Times*, 12 March 1998).

Twain, Mark, *The Complete Works of Mark Twain: All 13 Novels, Short Stories, Poetry and Essays* (General Press, 2016).

Torres, C. M. W., *Holding on to Broken Glass: Understanding and Surviving Pathological Alienation* (America Star Books, 2016).

Wise, R. A., McDevitt, R. A., "Drive and Reinforcement Circuitry in the Brain: Origins, Neurotransmitters, and Projection Fields," *Neuropsychopharmacology* (2018 Mar); 43(4):680–689. doi: 10.1038/npp.2017.228. Epub 2017 Oct 6. PMID: 28984293; PMCID: PMC5809792.

3. UNDERSTANDING

Jung, Carl, *Flying Saucers* (Routledge, 2002).

Miller, Alice, *The Drama of the Gifted Child* (Basic Books, 2008).

Wright, Frank Lloyd, https://franklloydwright.org/redsquare/. And to find out about the erasure of women who worked on his projects: https://www.architectmagazine.com/design/culture/the-women-in-frank-lloyd-wrights-studio_o.

Williams, Tennessee, *Camino Real* (New Directions, 2010).

4. POWER

Rückert, Friedrich, "The Two Coins" (rendition of the third of the *Maqamat* by al-Hariri of Basra), quoted in Freud, Sigmund, *Beyond the Pleasure Principle* (Penguin Modern Classics, 2003).

Wilde, Oscar, *Lady Windermere's Fan* (Methuen Drama, 2002).

Russell, Bertrand, *Power: A New Social Analysis* (Routledge, 2004).

Keltner, Dacher, *The Power Paradox: How We Gain and Lose In-*

fluence (Penguin, 2017) and https://greatergood.berkeley.edu
/article/item/power_paradox.

Solnit, Rebecca, *Whose Story Is This?* (Granta, 2019).

5. ATTENTION

Plath, James, ed., *Conversations with John Updike* (University Press
of Mississippi, 1994).

Aesop, *The Complete Fables* (Penguin Classics, 1998).

Winnicott, D. W., *The Maturational Processes and the Facilitating
Environment: Studies in the Theory of Emotional Development*
(Routledge, 1990).

Sontag, Susan, Vassar speech, 2003.

6. FREEDOM

Perel, Esther, https://www.estherperel.com/blog/letters-from
-esther-2-security-and-freedom.

Next Visions Podcast, Season 2, Episode 1, "Belonging and Rein-
vention," with Charlotte Fox Weber and Erwin James, https://
medium.com/next-level-german-engineering/next-visions
-podcast-season-two-406043d6b36e.

Sartre, Jean-Paul, *Critique of Dialectical Reason: Volume 1* (Verso,
2004).

Fromm, Erich, *The Fear of Freedom* (Routledge, 2001).

Koch, Christof, *Consciousness: Confessions of a Romantic Reductionist*
(The MIT Press, 2017).

Rich, Adrienne, *Arts of the Possible: Essays and Conversations* (W. W.
Norton & Company, 2001).

7. TO CREATE

Pound, Ezra, https://www.theparisreview.org/authors/3793/ezra
-pound.

Auden, W. H., *The Age of Anxiety* (Princeton University Press, 2011).

O'Brien, Edna, https://www.nytimes.com/1984/11/18/books/a

-conversation-with-edna-obrien-the-body-contains-the-life
/-story.html.

Richardson, John, *A Life of Picasso* (assorted volumes).

Horney, Karen, "Dedication," *American Journal of Psychoanalysis* (1942), 35, 99–100.

Murdoch, Iris, *Existentialists and Mystics: Writings on Philosophy and Literature* (Penguin, 1999).

Luca, Maria, *Integrative Theory and Practice in Psychological Therapies* (Open University Press, 2019).

Mead, Margaret, "Work, Leisure, and Creativity," *Daedelus* (Winter, 1960).

8. TO BELONG

Maslow, Abraham, "A Theory of Human Motivation," *Psychological Review* (1943).

Markovic, Desa, https://www.academia.edu/16869802/Psychosexual _therapy_in_sexualised_culture_a_systemic_perspective.

Uwannah, Victoria, https://examinedlife.co.uk/our_team/vicki -uwannah/.

Mead, Margaret and Baldwin, James, *A Rap on Race* (Michael Joseph, 1971).

Tallis, Frank, *The Act of Living* (Basic Books, 2020).

9. TO WIN

Colby, Kenneth Mark, "On the Disagreement Between Freud and Adler," *American Imago*, Vol 8, No 3 (1951).

Adler, Alfred, *Superiority and Social Interest* (W. W. Norton & Co, 1979).

Rosenberg, Marshall, *Nonviolent Communication* (Puddle Dancer Press, 2015).

Angel, Katherine, *Tomorrow Sex Will Be Good Again* (Verso, 2021).

Chaplin, Charlie, quoted in conversation with the screenwriter Walter Bernstein (New York, 2010).

de Beauvoir, Simone, *All Men are Mortal* (W. & W. Norton & Company, 1992).

Mewshaw, Michael, *Sympathy For the Devil: Four Decades of Friendship with Gore Vidal* (Farrar, Straus and Giroux, 2015).

10. TO CONNECT

Angelou, Maya, *I Know Why the Caged Bird Sings* (Virago, 1984).

Fox Weber, Nicholas, *The Bauhaus Group: Six Masters of Modernism* (Yale University Press, 2011).

11. WHAT WE SHOULDN'T WANT
(AND WHAT WE SHOULD)

Bennetts, Leslie, *The Feminine Mistake: Are We Giving up Too Much?* (Hachette Books, 2008).

Motz, Anna, *If Love Could Kill: The Myth and Truth of Female Violence* (W&N, 2023).

Dimitri, Francesco, *The Book of Hidden Things* (Titan Books, 2018).

Angel, Katherine, *Tomorrow Sex Will Be Good Again* (Verso, 2021).

Maslow, Abraham, *The Farther Reaches of Human Nature* (Penguin, 1994).

12. CONTROL

Bonaparte, Marie, "Time and the Unconscious," *International Journal of Psycho-Analysis* (1940); v.21, p. 427–42.

Bertin, Celia, *Marie Bonaparte: A Life* (Harcourt, 1982).

Eliot, T. S., *Collected Poems, 1909–1962* (Faber Paper Covered Editions, 2002) and https://www.themarginalian.org/2015/11/18/t-s-eliot-reads-burnt-norton/.

Rycroft, Charles, *A Critical Dictionary of Psychoanalysis, Second Edition* (Penguin, 1995).

Lowenthal, David, The Past is a Foreign Country—Revisited (Cambridge University Press, 2015).

AFTERWORD

Fox Weber, Nicholas, *Leland Bell* (Hudson Hills Press, 1988).

GLOSSARY

Didion, Joan, https://www.vogue.com/article/joan-didion-self
-respect-essay-1961.

Philips, Adam, *Missing Out: In Praise of the Unlived Life* (Farrar,
Straus and Giroux, 2013).

ACKNOWLEDGMENTS

So many people have supported and encouraged me throughout this process. Adam Gauntlett: you are brilliant and you've changed my life. Ella Gordon, Alex Clarke, Trish Todd: you are fantastic editors and wonderful people. Thank you, Serena Arthur, Elise Jackson, Jessica Farrugia, Sean deLone, and everyone at Wildfire and Atria. You've made this come alive in magical ways. My wonderful husband, Robbie Smith: you've been endlessly patient and supportive in giving me space to write and freak out and feel exhilarated. Thank you for being an incredible father to our children while I've been absent for chunks of time. I couldn't have written this book and been a mother without you. You encourage me and accept all my sides. Wilder: you are sensitive and dazzlingly astute with your insights. Beau: you are affectionate, bold, and hilarious. I love you both inestimably. You've tolerated my incomplete presence throughout this time period.

My parents taught me how to love words and people. Thank you to my exceptional mother, Katharine Weber: your crispness and brightness is astounding. And my beloved father, Nicholas Fox Weber: I cherish our deep closeness, and your exuberance and passion for life inspires me. You both continue to allow me to be a child at times, which is such a luxury, and you've also helped me individuate and grow up (a work in progress). Thanks for the encouragement, Lucy Swift Weber and partner Charles Lemonides, Nancy Weber, Daphne Astor, Ann Smith, Dave Smith, Beth-Ann Smith, and my whole extended family.

Leslie Bennetts, my fairy godmother: you have given me support, space, a feeling of deep rapport, compassion, humor, and wisdom at countless moments. You've helped me grow. The world needs women like you. You want women to succeed. JP Flintoff: deepest thanks for helping me think through countless issues and for your unwavering encouragement. Philip Wood: you're so deeply intelligent and kind and perceptive. Thank you for your clinical guidance and your profound thoughtfulness. Laura Sandelson: you're the essence of a true friend in myriad ways, offering insight, fun, nurture, and deep loyalty and affection. Daniel Sandelson: you've saved me at critical moments and you're rational, brilliant, and deeply understanding. You're life-enhancing, beloved friends.

Emmett de Monterey: you make quarter birthdays and Tuesdays a celebration. Violetta and Kostas, Emma and Paul Irwin, Joanna Green, Jack Guinness, Lauren Evans, Arielle Tchiprout, Natasha Lunn, Cate Sevilla, Charlotte Sinclair, Anna Motz, Paola Filotico, Francesco Dimitri, Morgwn Rimmel, Caleb Crain, Frank Tallis, Nick Pollitt, Vicki Uwannah, Kate Dryburgh, Anil Kosar, Katie Brock, Flora King, Mathilde Langseth Hughes, Deja Lewis Chamberlain, George Gibson, Heather Thornton, Kristina McLean, Tonya Meli, John Macdonald, Jemima Murray, Lizzie Dolin. Thank you, all!

Kelly Hearn, co-founder of Examined Life and friend, you're such an empowering woman. Thanks to everyone at the School of Life and Alain de Botton, and my wonderful teachers, Maria Luca, Desa Markovic, Karen Rowe: you've all been formative.

Everyone at the Josef and Anni Albers Foundation and Le Korsa, I value my connection with you. Thank you, Maya Jacobs, Kristine, all the helpful and supportive mothers and friends, and the people I have met and learned from along the way. And the people who come to me for therapy. I feel privileged to do my work.

ABOUT THE AUTHOR

Charlotte Fox Weber grew up in Connecticut and Paris and went to the University of Bristol, where she studied English and philosophy. She did her psychotherapy training at the Tavistock and Portman NHS Foundation Trust, the Institute of Psychoanalysis, WPF (Westminster Pastoral Foundation), and Regent's University London. She is registered and accredited by the UK Council for Psychotherapy (UKCP), and she is a registered member of the British Association for Counselling and Psychotherapy (BACP).

Charlotte founded the School of Life Psychotherapy in 2015 and now works in private practice and cofounded Examined Life. She is also a trustee on the board of the Josef and Anni Albers Foundation.

Tell Me What You Want is her first book.